A BIBLIOGRAPHY OF DOMESDAY BOOK

A BIBLIOGRAPHY OF DOMESDAY BOOK

David Bates

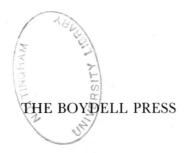

THE BOYDELL PRESS

© David Bates 1985

First published 1986
for the Royal Historical Society

by The Boydell Press
an imprint of Boydell & Brewer Ltd
PO Box 9, Woodbridge, Suffolk IP12 3DF and
51 Washington Street, Dover, New Hampshire 03820, USA

British Library Cataloguing in Publication Data

Bates, David
  A bibliography of Domesday book.
  1. Domesday book – Bibliography
  2. Real property – England – Bibliography
  3. Great Britain – History – Medieval
  period, 1066–1485 – Sources – Bibliography
  I. Title
  016.3333'22'0942   Z2021.D6
  ISBN 0 85115 433 6

Library of Congress Cataloging in Publication Data

Bates, David, 1945–
  A bibliography of Domesday book.

  1. Domesday book – Bibliography
  2. Great Britain – History – Norman period,
  1066–1154 – Bibliography.
  3. Great Britain – History – Anglo-Saxon period,
  449–1066 – Bibliography.
  I. Title.
  Z2017.B37   1986   [DA190.D7]
  016.3333'22'0942 84–19482
  ISBN 0 85115 433 6

Printed in Great Britain by
St Edmundsbury Press, Bury St Edmunds, Suffolk

CONTENTS

For Jonathan and Rachel

PREFACE

The aim is to include in this Bibliography all items which have contributed to our understanding of Domesday Book. Since this unique record has provided material for a significant proportion of all serious scholarship on English history from the Anglo-Saxon settlements until the early Norman period, and since it has had a continuous history as a working document from 1086 until the twentieth century, decisions about what to include and what to leave out have often been delicate ones. I have tried to follow a policy of placing in the Bibliography only items which try to make a positive contribution to the elucidation of the Domesday Book text. Such must include identifications of place-names and persons, interpretations of terminology and statistics, and assessments of how the record was made and of its administrative and legal significance. They also take in discussions of the topography and geography which lie behind the Domesday Book entries. Studies of this kind, which began to be made in the 1930s, are invaluable as an external test of Domesday Book's accuracy and can sometimes indicate omissions. They also illustrate the significance of the arrangement and content of the entries. I have excluded work which merely uses Domesday Book without seeking to elucidate it.

The intention has been to make the Bibliography comprehensive from 1886 to the present and selective before 1886. Critical comment has been kept to a minimum, being used only for the purposes of explaining titles which are not self-explanatory, indicating a relationship between items, and on occasions providing some assessment of a particular study's worth. The contents have been confined to published work and theses, in consequence, excluded. The latter can without difficulty be located through P. M. Jacobs, *History theses, 1901–70: historical research for higher degrees in the universities of the United Kingdom* (University of London: Institute of Historical Research, 1976), J. M. Horn, *History theses, 1971–80: historical research for higher degrees in the universities of the United Kingdom* (University of London: Institute of Historical Research, 1984) and the annual lists published by the Institute of Historical Research.

This Bibliography has inevitably been compiled in awareness of the gathering momentum of the preparations for the nine-hundredth anniversary in 1986. The publications of the next few years, the appearance of a facsimile edition and the use of the computer are likely to bring about major advances in the interpretation of the record. The tone of the present work has, nonetheless, remained as far as possible bibliographical and retrospective. Just occasionally I have mentioned important work in progress, but have done so in the knowledge that much more is being done. It is hoped that this Bibliography will have brought together the achievements of two centuries and more. The material included peters out towards the end of 1984. Once the dust of 1986 has settled, there may be a case for a supplementary bibliography to complete the basis required for the future. The usefulness of such a publication was stressed after the 1886 commemoration by none other than John Horace Round (*The Athenaeum*, no. 3249, 1 Feb. 1890, 148), but fruitlessly and for different reasons from those advanced here.

Many technical difficulties have been encountered in trying to organise the material into accessible form. The division into General and Local Sections is the only logical one and the reasons why many items have been placed in one or the other are self-evident. On occasions, however, they may not be and sometimes a good case could be made for placing a work elsewhere. I have usually placed studies dealing with the whole or most of Exon Domesday Book and Little Domesday Book in the General Section in spite of the fact that, strictly speaking, they deal with only a small number of counties. It goes profoundly against the grain to think of, for example, Stenton's studies of the Danelaw, Douglas' essay on the social structure of East Anglia, or Finn's books on Exon Domesday Book and East Anglia as local studies on the same plane as an article identifying a single place-name. On the other hand, there are many publications which identify the holdings of a single landholder in several counties or which analyse an estate stretching through several counties. These, unless they have a wider significance for our understanding of Domesday Book, have been placed in the relevant parts of the Local Section. An attempt has been made to prevent items being 'lost' through the means of making each county section self-contained by drawing attention in a short introduction to relevant items listed elsewhere and through prefacing the General Section with references to major works which are likely to contain material for all or most counties. The counties used are the pre-1974 ones. These are still recognizable and are the units used by the vast majority of the studies listed below.

In a work which has stretched its author's knowledge of British geography and of local periodical literature beyond breaking-point, many obligations have been incurred. Some have suffered from the impetuosity and inexperience of an author who is not by nature a bibliographer. To the former, I am profoundly grateful. To the latter, I apologise. My greatest debt is to Mrs Kathleen Thompson who assisted with the early collection of material, read the entire text, patiently corrected errors and inconsistencies of presentation and gave me the benefit of her considerable knowledge of Domesday Book. Professor J.C. Holt has overseen the project on behalf of the Royal Historical Society and has provided firm advice and a clear direction. Dr Elizabeth Hallam has been a valuable source of counsel and encouragement throughout. Dr Christopher Lewis has read several sections of the typescript and has given assistance well beyond the call of duty. Others who have read parts of the work while it was being prepared or have given good advice are Miss P. Brown, Mr Peter Boyden, Dr Paul Courtney, Dr David Crook, Miss Barbara Dodwell, Dr Diana Greenway, Dr T. P. Hudson, Mr Brian Ll. James, Mr John Kenyon, Dr Edmund King, Dr Clive Knowles, Professor Henry Loyn, Dr Phillip Morgan, Mr A. E. B. Owen, Mrs D. M. Owen, Dr Alexander Rumble, Mr Ian Soulsby, Dr F. R. Thorn, Mrs C. Thorn, and Dr Ann Williams. All have done something to save me from making mistakes. I alone am responsible for the errors which remain.

Research has been undertaken mainly in the libraries of University College, Cardiff, the Public Record Office, the British Library, the Institute of Historical Research and the National Museum of Wales. All the librarians who have tolerated my rapid perusal of large numbers of books and journals are warmly thanked. Travelling has been supported by grants from the Wolfson Foundation and the British Academy.

The final debt to mention is to my family. My wife Helen has given consistent encouragement and support. What I owe her is beyond words. My children Jonathan and Rachel have often turned into enthusiastic supporters of the project. My spirits have been uplifted when one or the other has announced that 'Daddy is working on Domesday Book'. It seems to me that something so substantial as William I's Great Survey has more significance for a young child than most subjects that an academic historian can work on. This gives me a reason to dedicate the book to them, although there are many better ones which could be mentioned. May 1986 and beyond be happy times for them and for all others whose lives have been touched by Domesday Book.

ABBREVIATIONS

AASRP	*Associated Architectural Societies Reports and Papers*
AgHR	*Agricultural History Review*
AHR	*American Historical Review*
Ant.	Antiquarian
Arch.	Archaeological
Arch. Camb.	*Archaeologia Cambrensis*
Arch. Cant.	*Archaeologia Cantiana*
Archit.	Architectural
Assoc.	Association
Battle	*Proceedings of the Battle Conference on Anglo-Norman Studies* (from vol. 5, *Anglo-Norman Studies*)
BBAOJ	*Berks., Bucks. and Oxon. Archaeological Journal*
Berks.AJ	*Berkshire Archaeological Journal*
BIHR	*Bulletin of the Institute of Historical Research*
BJRL	*Bulletin of the John Rylands Library*
Brit.	British
CHS	*Collections for a History of Staffordshire*
DB	Domesday Book
DCNQ	*Devon and Cornwall Notes and Queries*
DMon	Domesday Monachorum of Christ Church, Canterbury
EcHR	*Economic History Review*
EHR	*English Historical Review*
EPNS	English Place-Name Society
Geog.	Geographical
ICC	Inquisitio Comitatus Cantabrigiensis
IE	Inquisitio Eliensis
JBAA	*Journal of the British Archaeological Association*
JCNW	*Journal of the Architectural, Archaeological and Historic Society of the county and city of Chester and North Wales*
JDANHS	*Journal of the Derbyshire Archaeological and Natural History Society*
Jour.	Journal
JRIC	*Journal of the Royal Institution of Cornwall*
MA	*Medieval Archaeology*
MC	*Montgomeryshire Collections*
NA	*Norfolk Archaeology*
N&Q	*Notes and Queries*
NH	*Northern History*
ns	new series
NSJFS	*North Staffordshire Journal of Field Studies*

PBedsHRS	*Proceedings of the Bedfordshire Historical Record Society*
PCAS	*Proceedings of the Cambridge Antiquarian Society*
PDNHAS	*Proceedings of the Dorset Natural History and Archaeological Society*
PHFCAS	*Proceedings of the Hampshire Field Club and Archaeological Society*
PSIANH	*Proceedings of the Suffolk Institute of Archaeology and Natural History*
Proc.	Proceedings
Pubs.	Publications
RB	*Records of Buckinghamshire*
Rev.	Review
RPLAAS	*Reports and Papers of the Lincolnshire Architectural and Archaeological Society*
RTDA	*Reports and Transactions of the Devonshire Association*
SANHSP	*Somerset Archaeological and Natural History Society Proceedings*
ser.	series
Soc.	Society
SurreyAC	*Surrey Archaeological Collections*
SussexAC	*Sussex Archaeological Collections*
TBAS	*Transactions of the Birmingham Archaeological Society*
TBGAS	*Transactions of the Bristol and Gloucestershire Archaeological Society*
TCWAAS	*Transactions of the Cumberland and Westmorland Antiquarian and Archaeological Society*
TEAS	*Transactions of the Essex Archaeological Society*
TEHAS	*Transactions of the East Hertfordshire Archaeological Society*
THSLC	*Transactions of the Historic Society of Lancashire and Cheshire*
TLAAS	*Transactions of the Leicestershire Architectural and Archaeological Society*
TLAHS	*Transactions of the Leicestershire Archaeological and Historical Society*
TLCAS	*Transactions of the Lancashire and Cheshire Antiquarian Society*
TLMAS	*Transactions of the London and Middlesex Archaeological Society*
TLSSAHS	*Transactions of the Lichfield and South Staffordshire Archaeological and Historical Society*
TNSFC	*Transactions of the North Staffordshire Field Club*
Trans.	Transactions
TRHS	*Transactions of the Royal Historical Society*
TRS	*Transactions of the Radnorshire Society*
TSAS	*Transactions of the Shropshire Archaeological Society*
TTS	*Transactions of the Thoroton Society*
TWNFC	*Transactions of the Woolhope Naturalists Field Club*
VCH	Victoria Histories of the Counties of England
WANHM	*Wiltshire Archaeological and Natural History Magazine*
YAJ	*Yorkshire Archaeological Journal*

GENERAL STUDIES

Editions of DB

Domesday Book has been edited in full only once. Subsequent editions
and translations, notably the photozincographic facsimile, the VCH
and the Phillimore, have been published county by county and are
listed in the relevant place.

1 *Domesday Book; seu liber censualis Willelmi primi regis Angliae inter archivos
regni in domo capitulari Westmonasterii asservatus. Jubente Rege Augustissimo Georgio
Tertio praelo mandatus*, 2 vols (London: printed by J. Nichols, 1783). This
edition of the two volumes of Great and Little Domesday, remarkable
for its exactitude, was the work of Abraham Farley. For the few
corrections needed, see the volumes of the Phillimore edition. See also
4614. The circumstances of DB's publication have been admirably
described in **469**.

2 *Domesday Book: seu libri censualis, vocati Domesday Book, indices. Accessit
dissertatio generalis de ratione huiusce libri* (London: printed by Command,
1816). Customarily described as vol. 3 of **1**, this index and introduction
were the work of Sir Henry Ellis. The index of persons was superseded by Ellis' own work (**109**), but the index of place-names in DB
form is still valuable, having not been fully superseded by **420**.

Editions of DB 'satellites'

This section contains the editions of texts identified as having been
related to an earlier and now lost stage of the DB Inquest proceedings,
as well as the Herefordshire DB of the twelfth century. Translations of
'satellites' are not included here, but are placed in the appropriate
county section. Because the study of the 'satellites' is so intimately
bound up with the making of DB, the introductions to the various
texts often contain important discussions of that subject. Equally all
work on the making of DB, and most especially the writings of V. H.
Galbraith and Sally P. J. Harvey, is indispensable to the interpretation
of the 'satellites' (**303, 364, 410, 426, 449**). For a full commentary on
the DB-related texts from Evesham and Worcester see the Phillimore
editions of Gloucestershire and Worcestershire DB (**2141, 4523**).
There is an important tabular comparison of DB and Exon in **396**.

11 *Libri censualis, vocati Domesday Book, additamenta ex. codic. antiquiss. Exon Domesday; Inquisitio Eliensis; Liber Winton; Boldon Book* (London: printed by Command, 1816). Customarily described as vol. 4 of **1**, this edition of the 'satellites' Exon DB and IE, along with Liber Winton and Boldon Book, was the work of Sir Henry Ellis. The edition of IE, like **12**, was based on what is now regarded as an inferior ms., Trinity College, Cambridge, ms. O.2.1. There are several county editions of Exon and the Geld Inquest (**1508, 1704, 1916, 4431**). For Liber Winton, see now, F. Barlow, 'The Winton Domesday', in F. Barlow, M. Biddle *et al*, *Winchester in the early middle ages* (Oxford: Clarendon Press, 1977), 1–68.

12 HAMILTON, N. E. S. A., *Inquisitio comitatus Cantabrigiensis ... subjicitur Inquisitio Eliensis* (London: printed for the Royal Society of Literature of the United Kingdom, 1876). Used Trinity College, Cambridge ms. O.2.1, rather than the better ms., Trinity College, Cambridge ms. O.2.41, but did provide variant readings. For a translation, **1316**.

13 HUNT, W. (ed.), *Two chartularies of the priory of St Peter at Bath*, Somerset Rec. Soc., 7 (1893). For two 'satellites'. See **306, 410**.

14 BALLARD, A. (ed.), *An eleventh-century inquisition of St Augustine's, Canterbury*, Records of the social and economic history of England and Wales, 4 (London: OUP for the British Academy, 1920). See **349, 350** for references to other St Augustine's 'satellites' not published here.

15 DOUGLAS, D. C., 'Some early surveys from the abbey of Abingdon', *EHR*, 44 (1929), 618–25.

16 FOWLER, G. H., 'An early Cambridgeshire feodary', *EHR*, 46 (1931), 442–3.

17 DOUGLAS, D. C., *Feudal documents from the abbey of Bury St Edmunds*, Records of the social and economic history of England and Wales, 8 (London: OUP for the British Academy, 1932). For criticisms of the evaluation of these texts, **360, 364**.

18 DOUGLAS, D. C., *The Domesday monachorum of Christ Church, Canterbury* (London: OUP for the Royal Historical Society, 1944). This edition omitted a list of estates which was not part of the ms. on which the edition was based, but which later copies show to have belonged with it. This was later published in **21**. For criticisms of this edition, see review by R. Lennard, *EHR*, 61 (1946), 253–60. See also **410**. There is a mediocre translation, **2625**.

19 GALBRAITH, V. H. & TAIT, J., *Herefordshire Domesday, circa 1160–1170*, Pipe Roll Soc., 63 (ns, 25) (London: printed for the Pipe Roll Soc., 1950). For a transcript of the Herefordshire folios made in Henry II's reign. The introduction is important, if occasionally misguided.

20 SAWYER, P.H., 'Evesham A, a Domesday text', *Worcester Historical Society, Miscellany*, 1 (Worcester: printed for the Worcestershire Historical Soc., 1960), 3–36. The introduction is valuable.

21 HOYT, R.S., 'A pre-Domesday Kentish assessment list', in P.M. Barnes & C.F. Slade (eds), *A medieval miscellany for Doris Mary Stenton*, Pipe Roll Soc., ns, 36 (1962), 189–202. Additional to **18**, with a valuable commentary.

22 SAWYER, P.H. (ed.), *Textus Roffensis*, Early English manuscripts in facsimile, 11 (Copenhagen: Rosenkilde & Bagger, 1962). See fos 209–10.

General Works

Many among the items listed below contain material for most of the counties surveyed. Especially important in this respect are **109, 115, 153, 194, 200, 222, 226, 228, 236, 238, 240, 260, 265, 278, 280, 282, 283, 286, 290, 292, 295, 297, 298, 323, 330, 333, 338, 360, 362, 363, 364, 409, 420, 432, 454, 466**.

101 BRADY, R., *An introduction to the old English history* (London: T. Newcomb for S. Lowndes, 1684). The Appendix contains a list of tenants-in-chief and annotated translations of specimen entries. The Glossary contains attempts to explain DB terms. A notable work.

102 BRADY, R., *A complete history of England from the first entrance of the Romans under the conduct of Julius Caesar unto the end of the reign of king Henry III* (London: T. Newcomb for S. Lowndes, 1685).

103 GALE, R., *Registrum honoris de Richmond, exhibens terrarum et villarum quae quondam fuerunt Edwini comitis infra Richmondshire descriptionem, ex Libro Domesday* (London: R. Gosling, 1722). See the appendices by A. Agarde explaining DB's terms. There is a summary of earl Alan's DB holdings. Agarde's contribution is important.

104 WEBB, P.C., *A short account of Danegeld: with some further particulars relating to William the Conqueror's survey* (London: printed for the Society of the Antiquaries, 1756). Notable for announcing the discovery of ICC.

105 WEBB, P.C., *Account of Domesday Book with a view to promote its being printed* (London: printed for the Society of the Antiquaries, 1756).

106 DENNE, S., 'Doubts and conjectures concerning the reason commonly assigned for inserting or omitting the words *ecclesia* and *presbyter* in Domesday Book', *Archaeologia*, 8 (1787), 218–38. Demonstrated that DB does not provide a full record of churches through the use of maps and other types of record. See further **159, 247**.

107 KELHAM, R., *Domesday Book illustrated* (London: Nichols, 1788). Some discussion of the text, lists of tenants with notes and a selection of 'difficult' passages translated.

108 HEYWOOD, S., *A dissertation upon the distinctions in society and ranks of the people under the Anglo-Saxon governments* (London: W. Clarke, 1818). Made extensive use of DB.

109 ELLIS, H., *A general introduction to Domesday Book*, 2 vols (London: printed for the Commissioners of the Public Records, 1833. Reprinted, London: Frederick Muller, 1971). One of the major works of DB scholarship. Contains a substantial introduction which is still of interest and an abstract of population. Also indices of tenants-in-chief in 1086, of landholders TRE and TRW before the Survey, and of under-tenants in 1086. Dated, but still indispensable.

110 PHILLIPPS, T., *Index to the genealogies of tenants in capite, with the counties in which they had possessions, in the year 1086, in Domesday Book* (no indication of place of publication or publisher: 1838–42).

111 LÉCHAUDÉ D'ANISY, A. L. & SAINTE-MARIE, H.-J.-J.-R., marquis de, *Recherches sur le Domesday ou Liber censualis d'Angleterre* (Caen: Lesaulnier, 1842). The purpose of this work was to describe the Norman origins and the later histories of the Anglo-Norman and French families mentioned in DB. Only one volume containing the letter 'A' was ever published.

112 MORGAN, J. F., *England under the Norman occupation* (London: Williams & Norgate, 1858. Reprinted, London: Replika Press, 1931). An attempt to elucidate the structure of the rural society of DB. Full of material.

113 ANON, 'Domesday Book', *Leisure Hour*, 15 (1866), 766–8.

114 PEARSON, C. H., *History of England during the early and middle ages*, 2 vols (London: Bell & Daldy, 1867). Appendices contain a discussion of the hide and, more important, calculations of values of royal, ecclesiastical and baronial lands by county.

115 FREEMAN, E. A., *The history of the Norman Conquest of England, its causes and its results*, 6 vols (OUP: 1867–79; 2nd edn, vols 1–4, 1870–6; 3rd edn, vols 1–2, 1877). See vol. 5 for Freeman's discussion of DB. The appendices to vol. 4 contain much important material on TRE landholders and on the DB evidence for the transfer of lands from English to Normans. The appendices to vol. 5 contain discussions of many important problems: 'Notes on time in Domesday', 'Unjustly seizures of land', 'The use of the words *Franci* and *Angli* in Domesday', 'The *antecessores* of Domesday', 'Leases and sales in Domesday', 'The use of the word *vis* in Domesday', 'The king's writ and seal', 'Notices of outlawry in Domesday', 'Notices of wives and daughters in Domesday', 'Grants of alms in Domesday', 'Castles and destruction in towns', 'The king's reeves', 'Notes on commendation in Domesday', and 'Classes in Domesday'. Freeman is always worth consulting, even if much of his work has been superseded.

116 PEARSON, C. H., *Historical maps of England during the first thirteen centuries* (London: Bell & Daldy, 1870). An early and very simple attempt to map some DB information.

117 BOULT, J., 'The hide of the land', *THSLC*, 24 (1871–2), 1–24.

118 ALLEN, W. F., 'The rural population of England, as classified in Domesday Book', *Trans. Wisconsin Academy of sciences, arts and letters*, 1, (1872), 167–77. Reprinted in W. F. Allen, *Essays and monographs* (Boston: G. H. Ellis, 1890), 319–30.

119 ALLEN, W. F., 'The origin of the freeholders', *Trans. Wisconsin Academy of sciences, arts and letters*, 4 (1876–7), 19–24. Reprinted in W. F. Allen, *Essays and monographs* (Boston: G. H. Ellis, 1890), 312–18.

120 ALLEN, W. F., 'The English cottagers of the middle ages', *Trans. Wisconsin Academy of sciences, arts and letters*, 5 (1877–81), 1–11. Reprinted in W. F. Allen, *Essays and monographs* (Boston: G. H. Ellis, 1890), 300–11.

121 EYTON, R. W., 'Notes on Domesday', *TSAS*, 1, (1878), 99–118. A statement of Eyton's opinions on DB.

122 WINTERS, W., 'Historical notes on Domesday Book', *Reliquary*, 21 (1880–1), 209–14.

123 CLARK, G. T., 'Of the castles of England at the Conquest and under the Conqueror', *Arch. Camb.*, 4th ser., 12 (1881), 1–16. Points out that DB is incomplete as a record of castles.

124 MAITLAND, F. W., 'The criminal liability of the hundred', *Law magazine and review*, 4th ser., 7 (1881–2), 367–80. Reprinted in H. A. L. Fisher (ed.), *The collected papers of Frederic William Maitland*, 3 vols (Cambridge UP, 1911), 1, 230–46.

125 EYTON, R. M., 'The ms. collections of the late Rev R. W. Eyton', *N&Q*, 6th ser., 6 (1882), 82–3. Reprinted as 'The manuscripts left by Mr Eyton', *TSAS*, 10 (1887), 7–9. Note that Eyton's papers apparently included an analysis of Odo of Bayeux's DB fief.

126 ELLIS, A. S., 'The carucate', *N&Q*, 6th ser., 6 (1882), 41–2.

127 ROUND, J. H., 'The carucate', *N&Q*, 6th ser., 6 (1882) 189–91. A reply to **126**.

128 BOULT, J., 'The carucate', *N&Q*, 6th ser., 6 (1882), 191–2. A reply to **126**.

129 ELLIS, A.S., 'The carucate', *N&Q*, 6th ser., 6 (1882), 229–30. Cf. **127, 128**.

130 ROUND, J.H., 'Archaic land tenure in Domesday', *The Antiquary*, 5 (1882), 104–6. For communal rights of DB burgesses.

131 SEEBOHM, F., *The English village community* (London: Longman, 1883; 2nd edn, 1883; 3rd edn, 1884; 4th edn, 1915. Reprinted, Cambridge UP, 1926). A famous book which argued that serfdom and inequality had their origins in Roman times. See chapter 4 for a general treatment of the DB evidence.

132 BOND, E.A., *et al* (eds), *The Palaeographical Society: facsimiles of manuscripts and inscriptions* (London: William Clowes, 1884–94). For facsimiles of fos 103, 313 of Exon. The short commentary is of importance because it made the suggestion that a fair copy was made of Exon.

133 BEDDOE, J., *The races of Great Britain: a contribution to the anthropology of western Europe* (Bristol & London: J.W. Arrowsmith & Trubner & Co., 1885). Reissued with an introduction by D.E. Allen (London: Hutchinson, 1971). A classic early work of anthropology which *inter alia* tried to use the personal names of DB to estimate the racial composition of Britain's population. See for the survival of the English as under-tenants.

134 BIRCH, W. de G., 'The Domesday Book', *JBAA*, 41 (1885), 241–61. A description of the DB mss.

135 ANON, 'The Domesday commemoration', *The Athenaeum*, no. 3078 (23 Oct. 1886), 535; no. 3079 (30 Oct. 1886), 566–7; no. 3080 (6 Nov. 1886), 602–3; no. 3081 (13 Nov. 1886), 635. Contributions by I. Taylor, J.H. Round, H. Barkly.

136 ROUND, J.H., 'The early custody of Domesday', *The Academy*, no. 758 (13 Nov. 1886), 328. A comment on **162**.

137 TAYLOR, I., 'The Domesday plough', *The Athenaeum*, no. 3082 (20 Nov. 1886), 671–2.

138 HALL, H., 'The early custody of Domesday Book', *The Athenaeum*, no. 3083 (27 Nov. 1886), 706–7.

139 ANON, 'Domesday Book, part 1', *Walford's Antiquarian*, 11 (1887), 3–10.

140 BIRCH, W. de G., *Domesday Book* (London: SPCK, 1887; 2nd edn, 1908). A 'popular account'. Not very reliable. See **146, 147**.

141 LE SCHONIX, R., 'On the Domesday Book', *Reliquary*, ns. 1 (1887), 43–7.

142 PELL, O.C., 'On the Domesday geldable hide, what it probably was and what it certainly was not; with an explanation of the Domesday terms *terra ad carucam, carucata*, and *virgata* from information contained in certain mss. of the 13th century, including the Hundred Rolls', *PCAS*, 6, no.1 (1887), 65–176. A similar version of this paper appeared in **156**. Pell's work is generally dismissed as worthless. See **169–172, 174–177**.

143 PELL, O.C., 'Upon *libere tenentes, virgatae*, and *carucae* in Domesday, and in certain ancient mss. containing surveys of sixty manors in the counties of Hertford, Essex, Norfolk, Suffolk, Huntingdon and Cambridge; and upon Ware, what it probably meant or implied, and the prevalent use of the word both here and on the Continent in ancient times', *PCAS*, 6, no.1 (1887), 17–40. See **142** for comment.

144 ROUND, J.H., 'The early custody of Domesday Book', *The Antiquary*, 15 (1887), 246–9; 16 (1887), 8–12.

145 HALL, H., 'The early custody of Domesday Book', *The Antiquary*, 16 (1887), 162–4.

146 ROUND, J.H., 'Domesday Book', *The Athenaeum*, no.3132 (5 Nov. 1887), 605; no.3135 (26 Nov. 1887), 710. Critical of **140**. See Birch, W. de G. in *The Athenaeum*, no.3134 (19 Nov. 1887), 675.

147 ROUND, J.H., 'Ingulfus redivivus', *The Academy*, no.809 (5 Nov. 1887), 304; no.811 (19 Nov. 1887), 338; no.813 (3 Dec. 1887), 371–2. Critical of **140**.

148 ROUND, J.H., 'The *virgata*', *EHR*, 2 (1887), 329–32. Also comments on the Battle abbey surveys, see **4119, 4120, 4121, 4157**.

149 WALKER, B., 'On the *Inquisitio Comitatus Cantabrigiensis*', *PCAS*, 6, no.1 (1887), 45–64. Provides a tabulation of comparative hidation in ICC and DB of the holdings of bordars and cottars.

150 MOORE, S., 'On the study of Domesday Book', in P.E. Dove (ed.), *Domesday studies: being the papers read at the meetings of the Domesday commemoration 1886*, 2 vols (London: Longmans, 1888–91), 1, 1–36. A survey of ordinary quality. See **168** for some specific criticism.

151 CLARKE, H., 'On the Turkish survey of Hungary, and its relation to Domesday Book', in P.E. Dove (ed.), *Domesday studies*, 1, 37–46.

152 TAYLOR, I., 'Wapentakes and hundreds', in P.E.Dove (ed.), *Domesday studies*, 1, 67–76.

153 ROUND, J.H., 'Danegeld and the finance of Domesday', in P.E.Dove (ed.), *Domesday studies*, 1, 77–142. A paper of central importance for the subject.

154 TAYLOR, I., 'The ploughland and the plough', in P.E.Dove (ed.), *Domesday studies*, 1, 143–88.

155 ROUND, J.H., 'Notes on Domesday measures of land', in P.E.Dove (ed.), *Domesday studies*, 1, 189–225. Critical of the work of Eyton (**1904, 3602, 3705, 3806**) and to a lesser extent of Seebohm (**131**) and Taylor (**154**). An important paper for the carucate, sulung and ploughland.

156 PELL, O.C., 'A new view of the geldable unit of assessment of Domesday, embracing the divisions of the *libra* or pound of silver and the weights and measures of uncoined metal, flour, cloth etc., as made by the Angli, Mercians, Danes, Normans and Celts, and their connection with the true understanding of the words *hide, carucate, virgata, villanus, anglicus numerus*, etc.', in P.E.Dove (ed.), *Domesday studies*, 1, 227–385. See **142** for comments on Pell's work.

157 CLARKE, H., 'Note on the order of Domesday Book', in P.E. Dove (ed.), *Domesday studies*, 2, 387–97. A muddled and unconvincing contribution.

158 PARKER, J., 'The Church in Domesday with especial reference to episcopal endowments', in P.E.Dove (ed.), *Domesday studies*, 2, 399–432.

159 REID, H.J., 'Parish churches omitted in the Survey. The presbyter', in P.E.Dove (ed.), *Domesday studies*, 2, 433–46.

160 SAWYER, F.E., 'The scope of local elucidation of the Domesday survey', in P.E.Dove (ed.), *Domesday studies*, 2, 447–57. Extremely general. Deals mainly with Sussex.

161 BIRCH, W. de G., 'The materials for the re-editing of the Domesday Book, and suggestions for the formation of a Domesday Book Society', in P.E.Dove (ed.), *Domesday studies*, 2, 485–515.

162 HALL, H., 'The official custody of Domesday Book', in P.E. Dove (ed.), *Domesday studies*, 2, 517–37. See **136, 138, 144, 145**.

163 ROUND, J.H., 'An early reference to Domesday', in P.E.Dove (ed.), *Domesday studies*, 2, 539–59. For land disputes in DB discussed in the context of other contemporary records.

164 PELL, O.C., 'Summary of a new view of the geldable unit of assessment of Domesday', in P.E.Dove (ed.), *Domesday studies*, 2, 561–621. See **142, 156**.

165 ANON, 'Domesday commemoration 1886. Notes on the manuscripts etc. exhibited at H.M. Public Record Office', in P.E.Dove (ed.), *Domesday studies*, 2, 623–47.

166 ANON, 'Domesday commemoration 1886. Notes on the manuscripts and printed books exhibited at the British Museum', in P.E. Dove (ed.), *Domesday studies*, 2, 651–62.

167 WHEATLEY, H.B., 'Domesday bibliography', in P.E.Dove (ed.), *Domesday studies*, 2, 663–95. Incomplete.

168 TANCOCK, O.W., 'The Domesday Book in the reign of Edward III', *The Athenaeum*, no.3167 (7 July 1888), 34–5. Critical of **150**.

169 ROUND, J.H., 'Domesday measures of land', *Arch. Rev.*, 1 (1888), 285–95. Cf. **156, 170**.

170 PELL, O.C., 'Domesday measures of land', *Arch. Rev.*, 2 (1888–9), 350–60. Cf. **169**.

171 ROUND, J.H., 'Domesday measures of land', *Arch. Rev.*, 4 (1889), 130–40. Cf. **170**.

172 MAITLAND, F.W., 'Domesday measures of land', *Arch. Rev.*, 4 (1889), 391–2. Cf. **156**.

173 MAITLAND, F.W., 'The surnames of English villages', *Arch. Rev.*, 4 (1889), 233–40. Reprinted in H.A.L.Fisher (ed.), *The collected papers of Frederic William Maitland*, 3 vols (Cambridge UP, 1911), 2, 84–95. On the absence of village surnames in DB and its significance.

174 PELL, O.C., 'Domesday measures of land and modern criticism', *Arch. Rev.*, 4 (1889), 241–58. Cf. **169, 171, 172**.

175 STEVENSON, W.H., 'The long hundred and its use in England', *Arch. Rev.*, 4 (1889), 313–27. Cf. **156, 170, 174**.

176 ROUND, J.H., 'Domesday measures of land', *Arch. Rev.*, 4 (1889), 391. Cf. **174**.

177 PELL, O.C., 'The long hundred', *Arch. Rev.*, 4 (1889), 460–2. Cf. **175**.

178 REID, H.J., 'The Domesday commemoration', *The Athenaeum*, no.3210 (4 May 1889), 568–9; no.3213 (25 May 1889), 663. For a reply see P.E.Dove, *The Athenaeum*, no.3211 (11 May 1889), 599.

179   ROUND, J. H., 'Churchscot in Domesday', *EHR*, 5, (1890), 101.

180   ROUND, J. H., 'Gafol', *EHR*, 5 (1890), 523–4. Cf. **181**.

181   STEVENSON, W. H., review of **150–167, 4004, 4604**. Cf. **180**.

182   HALL, H., *The antiquities and curiosities of the Exchequer* (London: Elliot Stock, 1891). For custody of DB.

183   MAITLAND, F. W., 'Frankalmoign in the twelfth and thirteenth centuries', *Law Quarterly Review*, 7 (1891), 354–63. Reprinted in H. A. L. Fisher (ed.), *The collected papers of Frederic William Maitland*, 3 vols (Cambridge UP, 1911), 2, 205–22. For *elemosina* in DB.

184   ROUND, J. H., 'The introduction of knight service into England', *EHR*, 6 (1891), 417–43, 625–45; 7 (1892), 11–24. Reprinted in J. H. Round, *Feudal England* (London: Swan Sonnenschein, 1895; 2nd edn, London: Allen & Unwin, 1964), 225–314 (1st edn) and 182–245 (2nd edn). These famous essays established once and for all that the *milites* of DB were the men who contributed to a lord's feudal quota. Round also discussed the problem of DB assessments and the Worcester relief of 1095.

185   VINOGRADOFF, P., *Villainage in England* (Oxford: Clarendon Press, 1892). Mainly used later legal records, but with some reference to DB peasants and to ancient demesne. See **189**.

186   ROUND, J. H., '*Carucata terra*', *EHR*, 7 (1892), 532.

187   ROUND, J. H., '*Terra ad duplum*', *EHR*, 7 (1892), 533.

188   ROUND, J. H., 'The words *solinum* and *solanda*', *EHR*, 7 (1892), 708–12. Cf. **131, 185**.

189   SEEBOHM, F., 'Villainage in England', *EHR*, 7 (1892), 444–65. Cf. **185**.

190   POLLOCK, F., 'The Devonshire Domesday', *RTDA*, 25 (1893), 286–98. Devon evidence used to discuss some general problems.

191   ROUND, J. H., 'Domesday Book', *The Athenaeum*, no. 3433 (12 Aug. 1893), 228–9. Continues **146**.

192   MAITLAND, F. W., 'The origin of uses', *Harvard Law Review*, 8 (1894–5), 127–37. Reprinted in H. A. L. Fisher (ed.), *The collected papers of Frederic William Maitland*, 3 vols (Cambridge UP, 1911), 2, 403–16. For the phrase *ad opus regis*.

193   POLLOCK, F. & MAITLAND, F. W., *The history of English law before the time of Edward I*, 2 vols (Cambridge UP, 1895; 2nd edn, 1898;

2nd edn reissued with an introduction by S. F. C. Milsom, Cambridge UP, 1968). For DB as a legal text. Important.

194 ROUND, J. H., 'Domesday Book', in J. H. Round, *Feudal England* (London: Swan Sonnenschein, 1895; 2nd edn, London: Allen & Unwin, 1964), 3–146 (1st edn) and 17–123 (2nd edn). Round's great essay on DB. The use of 'satellite' texts employed here is the foundation of all modern study of the making of DB. The most serious weakness is that Round made no use of Exon (see **303, 364**). The essay contains much of local and institutional significance and is of central importance to the subject.

195 ROUND, J. H., 'The hundred and the geld', *EHR*, 10 (1895), 732. An addition to **194**.

196 BARING, F. H., 'Domesday Book and the Burton cartulary', *EHR*, 11 (1896), 98–102. The earliest suggestion that the Burton abbey surveys indicate considerable omissions of population in DB. See **225, 251, 391, 405, 3825**.

197 POLLOCK, F., 'A brief survey of Domesday', *EHR*, 11 (1896), 209–30.

198 WHALE, T. W. & REICHEL, O. J., 'Analysis of Exon Domesday', *RTDA*, 28 (1896), 391–463; 34 (1902), 289–324.

199 BARING, F. H., 'Domesday and some thirteenth-century surveys', *EHR*, 12 (1897), 285–90. An attempt to ascertain the size of peasant holdings.

200 MAITLAND, F. W., *Domesday Book and beyond* (Cambridge UP, 1897). Reissued, with a useful critical introduction by E. Miller (London: Collins, 1960). Reissued with an introduction by B. Lyon (New York: Norton paperbacks, 1966). Maitland's stated purpose was to use DB ('the knowable') as a means to understand early English society. The book consists of three long essays on 'Domesday Book', 'England before the Conquest' and 'The Hide'. This is one of the classics of English historical scholarship. Much has dated or been modified, but the book remains of central importance for DB studies. An indispensable companion is J. Tait's review in *EHR*, 12 (1897), 768–77, which dealt exclusively with Maitland's views on the DB manor and the origins of the borough.

201 BARING, F. H., 'The Conqueror's footprints in Domesday', *EHR*, 13 (1898), 17–25. Reprinted with 'some additions and alterations' in **237**, 207–16. An important article which used falls in manorial values to suggest the movement of William's army in 1066. Not all the detailed arguments have been accepted. See also **392, 393**.

202 TAYLOR, C.S., 'The origin of the Mercian shires', *TBGAS*, 21 (1898), 32–57. Reprinted in condensed form in H.P.R.Finberg (ed.), *Gloucestershire studies* (Leicester UP, 1957), 17–51. Used DB hidage statistics.

203 BARING, F.H., 'The hidation of some southern counties', *EHR*, 14 (1899), 290–9.

204 BENNETT, R. & ELTON, J., *History of corn-milling*, 2 (London & Liverpool: Simpkin, Marshall & Co. and Edward Howell, 1899). See chapter 9 for a seemingly complete list of DB mills.

205 HALL, A., *Index of counties in Domesday Book* (London: R.Gordon, 1899). Of singularly slight value.

206 BATESON, M., 'The laws of Breteuil', *EHR*, 15 (1900), 73–8, 302–18, 496–523, 745–7; 16 (1901), 92–110, 332–45. For DB boroughs.

207 CORBETT, W.J., 'The Tribal Hidage', *TRHS*, ns. 14 (1900), 187–230. For tables of hides and hundreds in all hidated counties.

208 INMAN, A.H., *Domesday and feudal statistics* (London: Elliot Stock, 1900). An eccentric and confusing work. DB statistics are expressed in terms of county comparisons.

209 ROUND, J.H., 'The *Breviates* of Domesday', *The Athenaeum*, no.3803 (15 Sept. 1900), 346–7. See further **262, 19, 417, 4523**.

210 ROUND, J.H., 'The Domesday manor', *EHR*, 15 (1900), 293–302. For *manerium*, the vill and geld collection. Cf. **200**.

211 ANDREW, W.J., 'A numismatic history of the reign of Henry I, 1100–1135', *The Numismatic Chronicle*, 4th ser., 1 (1901), 1–515. For DB mints. For fundamental criticism, **2016**.

212 ROUND, J.H., 'The companions of the Conqueror', *Monthly Review*, 3 (June 1901), 91–111. For the tenants and sub-tenants of DB.

213 MAXWELL LYTE, H.C., 'Domesday Book', *Pall Mall Magazine*, 37 (May–Aug. 1902), 209–16. Notable for its description of a consultation of DB in connection with Edward VII's coronation.

214 ROUND, J.H., 'The castles of the Conquest', *Archaeologia*, 58 (1902), 313–40.

215 TAIT, J., 'England and Wales in 1086', in R.L.Poole (ed.), *Historical atlas of modern Europe from the decline of the Roman Empire* (Oxford: Clarendon Press, 1902), no.XVII. A notable early DB map.

216 TAIT, J., 'Large hides and small hides', *EHR*, 17 (1902), 280–2. Evidence is mainly drawn from Cambs. and Wilts. See **200, 4429**.

217 THOMPSON, E. M., *et al* (eds), *The New Palaeographical Society: facsimiles of ancient manuscripts, etc.*, 1st ser., 2, pt 2 (London: for the Society, 1903–12), plate 240. A facsimile of the first folio of the PRO *abbreviatio* of DB.

218 LIEBERMANN, F., *Die Gesetze der Angelsachsen*, 3 vols (Halle: M. Niemeyer, 1903–16). This famous edition and commentary on early English law contains numerous comments on DB material.

219 WHALE, T. W., 'Date of the Domesday survey; and use of some of its terms', *RTDA*, 35 (1903), 156–66.

220 ARMITAGE, E. S., 'The early Norman castles of England', *EHR*, 19 (1904), 209–45, 417–55. For castles of DB. This work was expanded in **243**.

221 BALLARD, A., *The Domesday boroughs* (Oxford: Clarendon Press, 1904). See critical reviews by M. Bateson, *EHR*, 20 (1905), 143–51 and O. Reichel in *DCNQ*, 4 (1906–7), 61–3. See further **229, 230**.

222 BATESON, M., *Borough customs*, 2 vols, Selden Soc., vols 18, 21 (London: Bernard Quaritch, 1904, 1906). Invaluable for the systematic collation of DB with later charters and custumals.

223 ROUND, J. H., 'The officers of Edward the Confessor', *EHR*, 19 (1904), 90–2. Identifies some sub-tenants.

224 PRYCE, T. D. & ARMITAGE, E. S., 'The alleged Norman origin of castles in England', *EHR*, 20 (1905), 703–18. A criticism of **220** and a reply.

225 ROUND, J. H., 'The Burton abbey surveys', *EHR*, 20 (1905), 275–89. Reprinted in *CHS*, ns, 9 (1906), 271–89. See **196, 251, 391, 405, 3825**.

226 VINOGRADOFF, P., *The growth of the manor* (London: Swan Sonnenschein, 1905; 2nd edn, London: Allen, 1911; 2nd edn, repr., New York: Kelley, 1968). An important book.

227 WHALE, T. W., 'History of the Exon Domesday', *RTDA*, 37 (1905), 246–83.

228 BALLARD, A., *The Domesday inquest* (London: Methuen, 1906; 2nd edn, 1923). A sound survey reviewing current opinions.

229 BALLARD, A., 'The burgesses of Domesday', *EHR*, 21 (1906), 699–709. A reply to M. Bateson's review, see **221**. See also **230**.

230 BATESON, M., 'The burgesses of Domesday and the Malmesbury wall', *EHR*, 21 (1906), 709–22. Cf. **221, 229**.

231 GUILLOREAU, L., 'Les possessiones des abbayes mancelles et angevines en Angleterre d'après le Domesday Book', *Revue historique et archéologique du Maine*, 60 (1906), 5–23.

232 STUBBS, W., 'The Domesday and later surveys', in A. Hassall (ed.), *Lectures on early English history by William Stubbs* (London: Longmans, 1906), 184–93.

233 STEVENSON, W. H., 'A contemporary description of the Domesday survey', *EHR*, 22 (1907), 72–84. For the account by Robert Losinga, bishop of Hereford.

234 ROUND, J. H., 'The Domesday *ora*', *EHR*, 23 (1908), 283–5. See **399**.

235 STENTON, F. M., *William the Conqueror and the rule of the Normans* (London: Putnam, 1908; repr., 1911). Contains a good general account.

236 VINOGRADOFF, P., *English society in the eleventh century* (Oxford: Clarendon Press, 1908). Vinogradoff's major work on DB. See review by J. Tait, *EHR*, 24 (1909), 333–6. The appendices contain valuable statistical surveys.

237 BARING, F. H., *Domesday tables for the counties of Surrey, Berkshire, Middlesex, Hertford, Buckingham and Bedford and the New Forest* (London: St Catherine Press, 1909).

238 ZACHRISSON, R. E., *A contribution to the study of Anglo-Norman influence on English place-names* (Lund: H. Ohlsson, 1909). Cf. **350**.

239 BJÖRKMAN, E., *Nordische personennamen in England in alt- und fruhmittelenglischer Zeit* (Halle: M. Niemeyer, 1910). Superseded by later work, **292**.

240 G.E.C. (G. E. Cockayne) *et al*, *The complete peerage of England, Scotland, Ireland, Great Britain and the United Kingdom, extant or dormant*, 13 vols (new edn, London: St Catherine Press, 1910–59). A mine of information on DB tenants.

241 STENTON, F. M., *Types of manorial structure in the northern Danelaw*, Oxford studies in social and legal history, 2 (Oxford: Clarendon Press, 1910).

242 DUPONT, E., 'Les donations anglaises par Guillaume le Conquérant aux églises et aux abbayes de France', *Revue d'histoire de l'église de France*, 2 (1911), 457–64. Simply a list of their DB holdings.

243 ARMITAGE, E. S., *The early Norman castles of the British Isles* (London: Murray, 1912). The fundamental work on the castles of DB. For doubts on the identification of a castle at Clitheroe, **2724, 404**.

244 BARING, F.H., 'The Exeter Domesday', *EHR*, 27 (1912), 309–18. An article which was vital for the development of studies of the making of DB. See further **303, 364**.

245 FARRER, W. (ed.), *Early Yorkshire charters*, 3 vols (Edinburgh: Ballantyne, Hanson & Co., 1914–16). The annotations contain much material on the landholders of DB.

246 HEMMEON, M. de W., *Burgage tenure in medieval England*, Harvard Historical Studies, 20 (Cambridge, Mass.: Harvard UP, 1914). See **248**.

247 PAGE, W., 'Some remarks on the churches of the Domesday survey', *Archaeologia*, 66 (1914–15), 61–102. For a summary and some comments, see *Pro. Soc. Antiquaries*, 2nd ser., 27 (1914–15), 54–8. See also **374, 1767**.

248 BALLARD, A., 'The laws of Breteuil', *EHR*, 30 (1915), 646–58. Cf. **246**.

249 FORSSNER, T., *Continental-Germanic personal names in England in Old and Middle English times* (Uppsala: Appelbergs Boktryckeri, 1916).

250 MORRIS, W.A., 'The office of sheriff in the Anglo-Saxon period', *EHR*, 31 (1916), 20–40. For DB references to *firma* before 1066 and for sheriffs' estates.

251 BRIDGEMAN, C.G.O., 'The Burton abbey twelfth-century surveys', *CHS* (1916), 209–300. See also **196, 225, 391, 405, 3825**.

252 DEMAREST, E.B., 'The hundred-pennies', *EHR*, 33 (1918), 62–72. See **263**.

253 MORRIS, W.A., 'The office of sheriff in the early Norman period', *EHR*, 33 (1918), 147–75. See **462**.

254 STEPHENSON, C., 'The aids of the English boroughs', *EHR*, 34 (1919), 457–75. For boroughs where geld and fyrd-service was apparently combined into a subsidy and for ship-service.

255 DEMAREST, E.B., 'The *firma unius noctis*', *EHR*, 35 (1920), 78–89. For criticism, see **263**.

256 STENTON, F.M., *Documents illustrative of the social and economic history of the Danelaw*, Records of the social and economic history of England and Wales, 5 (London: OUP for the British Academy, 1920). The introduction contains numerous insights into DB for the Danelaw counties.

257 RUTTER, J.A., 'Domesday: villeins on comital manors', *DCNQ*, 11 (1920–1), 310–15. Deals with the South-West. For a shorter version, see *N&Q*, 12th ser., 11 (1921), 65, with a reply by O.J. Reichel at p. 152 and a rejoinder by Rutter at p. 192.

258 SALZMAN, L.F., *English industries of the middle ages* (Oxford: Clarendon Press, 1923).

259 ROUND, J.H., ' "Domesday" and "Doomsday" ', *EHR*, 38 (1923), 240–3.

260 FARRER, W., *Honors and knights' fees*, 3 vols (vols 1 & 2, London: Spottiswoode, Ballantyre & Co., 1923–4; vol. 3, Manchester UP and London: Longmans, 1925). Indispensable for the holdings and identification of many DB sub-tenants.

261 MAWER, A. & STENTON, F.M. (eds), *Introduction to the survey of English place-names*, EPNS, 1, pt 1 (Cambridge UP, 1924). See especially R.E. Zachrisson on French influence on the spelling of the DB place-names, but see also **350**. And see J. Tait on DB tenants who are commemorated in place-names.

262 SEYLER, C.A., 'The early charters of Swansea and Gower', *Arch. Camb.*, 79 (1924), 59–79, 299–325. For the Breviate.

263 STEPHENSON, C., 'The *firma unius noctis* and the customs of the hundred', *EHR*, 39 (1924), 161–74. Reprinted in C. Stephenson, *Mediaeval institutions: selected essays* (Cornell UP, 1954), 139–55. Argues against Demarest, **252, 255, 2721**. See further **270**.

264 RAMSAY, J.H., *A history of the revenues of the kings of England, 1066–1399*, 2 vols (Oxford: Clarendon Press, 1925). Derivative, relying on the DB totals in **114**.

265 CORBETT, W.J., 'The development of the duchy of Normandy and the Norman Conquest of England', in J.R. Tanner *et al*, *The Cambridge Medieval History*, 5 (Cambridge UP, 1926; repr., 1929, 1943, 1948), 481–520, 885–94. See for the much-quoted calculations of the values of the estates of the greater DB landholders. See further **381, 464**.

266 DAVIES, R.T., *Documents illustrating the history of civilization in medieval England (1066–1500)* (London: Methuen, 1926), 1–18. For brief extracts from DB, statistics of population, and an attempt to enumerate the manorial holdings of the chief landholders.

267 GEORGE, R.H., 'The contribution of Flanders to the Conquest of England 1065–1086', *Revue belge de philologie et d'histoire*, 5 (1926), 81–99. For the DB holdings of Flemings.

268 STENTON, F.M., 'The free peasantry of the Northern Danelaw', *Bulletin de la société royale des lettres de Lund* (1925–6), 73–185. Reprinted (Oxford: Clarendon Press, 1969), with an index. For tables concerning the numbers of sokemen.

269 STEPHENSON, C., 'The origin of the English town', *AHR*, 32 (1926–7), 10–21. See further **282**, and the telling criticisms of Tait, **290**.

270 DEMAREST, E.B., '*Consuetudo regis* in Essex, Norfolk and Suffolk', *EHR*, 42 (1927), 161–79. A restatement of earlier arguments. Cf. **263**.

271 DOUGLAS, D.C., *The social structure of medieval East Anglia*, Oxford studies in social and legal history, 9 (Oxford: Clarendon Press, 1927).

272 MORRIS, W.A., *The medieval English sheriff to 1300* (Manchester UP, 1927; repr., 1968). For the sheriff in DB. Cf. **462**.

273 TAIT, J., 'The *firma burgi* and the commune in England', *EHR*, 42 (1927), 321–60. For the renders of the DB boroughs.

274 DOUGLAS, D.C., 'Fragments of an Anglo-Saxon survey from Bury St Edmunds', *EHR*, 43 (1928), 376–83. For leets, hundreds and geld.

275 WILLIAMS, J.F., 'Local history and the Domesday Book', *The History Teachers' Miscellany*, 7 (1929), 137–40.

276 HOUGHTON, F.T.S., 'Salt-ways', *TBAS*, 54 (1929–30), 1–17.

277 STEPHENSON, C., 'The Anglo-Saxon borough', *EHR*, 45 (1930), 177–207. See further **282**. Cf. **290**.

278 CAM, H.M., '*Manerium cum hundredo*: the hundred and the hundredal manor', *EHR*, 47 (1932), 355–76. Reprinted in H.M.Cam, *Liberties and communities in medieval England* (Cambridge UP, 1944; repr., London: Merlin Press, 1963), 64–90. An important article for manors with pertinent hundreds and manors said to receive 'third pennies'.

279 STENTON, F.M., *The first century of English feudalism 1066–1166* (Oxford: Clarendon Press, 1932; 2nd edn, 1961). This great work on the history of Anglo-Norman feudal society contains numerous insights into that society as it is recorded in DB.

280 CAM, H.M., 'Early groups of hundreds', in J.G.Edwards *et al* (eds), *Historical essays in honour of James Tait* (Manchester: printed for the subscribers, 1933), 13–26. Reprinted in H.M.Cam, *Liberties and communities in medieval England* (Cambridge UP, 1944; repr., London: Merlin Press, 1963), 91–106. Contains valuable evidence from throughout England for hundredal groupings.

281 DARLINGTON, R.R., 'Aethelwig, abbot of Evesham', *EHR*, 48 (1933), 1–22, 177–98. For Evesham's estates, for the Conqueror's devastation of the N.W. Midlands, and for printed DB related texts from Evesham cartularies. For the last, see further **20, 2141, 4523**.

282 STEPHENSON, C., *Borough and town: a study of urban origins in England* (Cambridge, Mass.: The Medieval Academy of America, 1933). A major work whose general conclusions were convincingly overturned by Tait, **290**.

283 ANDERSON, O.S., *The English hundred-names* (Lund: H.Ohlsson, 1934). For the etymologies of the English hundred names. This and **297, 298** cover all counties except Cornwall. An extremely useful work.

284 STENTON, F.M., 'Domesday tenants in chief', *Genealogists' Magazine*, 6 (1934), 238–40.

285 JEULIN, P., 'Un grand honneur anglais: aperçus sur le comté de Richmond en Angleterre, possession des ducs de Bretagne (1069/71–1398)', *Annales de Bretagne*, 42 (1935), 5–42.

286 CLAY, C.T., *Early Yorkshire charters. 4–5: Honour of Richmond. 6: The Paynel Fee. 7: The Honour of Skipton. 8: The Honour of Warenne. 9: The Stuteville Fee. 10: The Trussebut Fee. 11: The Percy Fee. 12: The Tison Fee* (Wakefield: West Yorkshire Printing Co. Ltd., for the Yorks Arch. Soc. Record Ser., 1935–65). These major contributions to the history of feudal society contain material on the landholders of Yorks. DB and their landholdings which frequently stretched through many other English counties. Of great significance for the tenants-in-chief and under-tenants of DB and for Yorkshire land-holding.

287 JOLLIFFE, J.E.A., 'A survey of fiscal tenements', *EcHR*, 1st ser., 6 (1935–6), 157–71. Cf. **307**.

288 DARBY, H.C. (ed.), *An historical geography of England before A.D. 1800* (Cambridge UP, 1936). Reissued and revised as H.C.Darby (ed.), *A new historical geography of England* (Cambridge UP, 1973).

289 MORGAN, F.W., 'Domesday woodland in south-west England', *Antiquity*, 10 (1936), 306–24.

290 TAIT, J., *The medieval English borough: studies on its origins and constitutional history* (Manchester UP, 1936; repr., 1968). The authoritative work on the constitutional history of the DB boroughs. It contains a mass of material and remains indispensable. Cf. **269, 277, 282**.

291 DOUGLAS, D.C., 'The Domesday survey', *History*, 21 (1937), 249–57. A valuable survey of an important DB scholar's views. Some notable comments on early DB scholarship.

292 FEILITZEN, O. von, *The pre-Conquest personal names of Domesday Book* (Uppsala: Almqvist & Wiksells, 1937). An indispensable guide. See **294** for criticisms and corrections. Cf. **350**, for the personal- and place-names of Exon.

293 JEULIN, P., 'La consistance du comté de Richmond en Angleterre d'après le Domesday Book', *Annales de Bretagne*, 44 (1937), 250–78. For cautionary remarks, **381**.

294 KÖKERITZ, H., 'Notes on the pre-Conquest personal names of Domesday Book', *Namn och Bygd*, 26 (1938), 25–41. Cf. **292**.

295 TENGVIK, G., *Old English bynames* (Uppsala: Almqvist & Wiksells Boktryckeri, 1938). A thorough survey.

296 ALEXANDER, A.J.P.B., 'Manorial title: a tentative explanation of its extent and limitations', *RTDA*, 71 (1939), 311–19. Unconvincing.

297 ANDERSON, O.S., *The English hundred-names: the south-western counties* (Lund & Leipzig: C.W.K.Gleerup & O.Harrassowitz, 1939). See also **283, 298**.

298 ANDERSON, O.S., *The English hundred-names: the south-eastern counties* (Lund & Leipzig: C.W.K.Gleerup & O.Harrassowitz, 1939). See also **283, 297**.

299 DODWELL, B. 'The free peasantry of East Anglia in Domesday', *Trans. Norfolk & Norwich Arch. Soc.*, 27 (1939), 145–57.

300 DOUGLAS, D.C., *English scholars 1660–1730* (London: Eyre & Spottiswoode, 1939; 2nd revised edn, 1951). For early DB scholarship and plans to publish DB. See further **469**.

301 HODGEN, M.T., 'Domesday water mills', *Antiquity*, 13 (1939), 261–79.

302 KNOWLES, Dom. D., *The monastic order in England, 943–1216* (Cambridge UP, 1940; 2nd edn, 1963). See App. VI for DB values of the estates of individual monasteries.

303 GALBRAITH, V.H., 'The making of Domesday Book', *EHR*, 57 (1942), 161–77. An article which revolutionised opinion on the way in which DB was made. Cf. **194** and see further **317, 364, 410, 426, 449**.

304 NEILSON, N., 'Early English woodland and waste', *Journal of Economic History*, 2 (1942), 54–62.

305 RICHARDSON, H.G., 'The medieval ploughteam', *History*, 26 (1942), 287–96. Against the 8-oxen ploughteam. See **311, 327**.

306 LENNARD, R., 'A neglected Domesday satellite', *EHR*, 58 (1943), 32–41. For the Bath abbey satellites. See **13, 410, 3737**.

307 LENNARD, R., 'The origin of the fiscal carucate', *EcHR*, 1st ser., 14 (1944–5), 51–63. Cf. **287**. Reasserted the view that origins were Scandinavian.

308 LE PATOUREL, J., 'Geoffrey of Montbray, bishop of Coutances, 1049–1093', *EHR*, 59 (1944), 129–61. For a brief discussion of bishop Geoffrey's DB estates.

309 STENTON, F.M., 'English families and the Norman Conquest', *TRHS*, 4th ser., 26 (1944), 1–12. Reprinted in R.W. Southern (ed.), *Essays in medieval history* (London: Macmillan, 1968), 93–105; and in F.M. Stenton, *Preparatory to Anglo-Saxon England*, ed. D.M. Stenton (Oxford: Clarendon Press, 1970), 325–44. For an evaluation of DB as a source for the survival of the English as landholders.

310 STEPHENSON, C., 'Commendation and related problems in Domesday', *EHR*, 59 (1944), 289–310. Reprinted in C. Stephenson, *Mediaeval institutions: selected essays* (Cornell UP, 1954), 156–83. Cf. **316**.

311 LENNARD, R., 'Domesday plough-teams: the south-western evidence', *EHR*, 60 (1945), 217–33. Cf. **327, 394**.

312 LENNARD, R., 'The economic position of the Domesday villani', *Economic Jour.*, 56 (1946), 244–64. Cf. **331**.

313 LENNARD, R., 'The economic position of the Domesday sokemen', *Economic Jour.*, 57 (1947), 179–95. Cf. **331**.

314 MILLER, E., 'The Ely land pleas in the reign of William I', *EHR*, 62 (1947), 438–56. For IE.

315 STEPHENSON, C., 'Notes on the composition and interpretation of Domesday Book', *Speculum*, 22 (1947), 1–15. Reprinted in C. Stephenson, *Mediaeval institutions: selected essays* (Cornell UP, 1954),

184–204. Proposes a different organisation of the seven circuits from that generally accepted. Concerned with inconsistencies of language in DB.

316 DODWELL, B., 'East Anglian commendation', *EHR*, 63 (1948), 289–306. Cf. **310**.

317 GALBRAITH, V.H., 'Domesday Book', in *Studies in the public records* (London: Nelson, 1948), 89–121. A development of his earlier theories (**303**) and important reflections on the use and study of DB.

318 RUSSELL, J.C., *British medieval population* (Albuquerque: University of New Mexico Press, 1948). Argued for a multiplier of 3.5 as against the usual 5. For severe criticism, **384**. See also **352, 405**.

319 BUCKATZCH, E.J., 'The geographical distribution of wealth in England, 1086–1843', *EcHR*, 2nd ser., 3 (1950–1), 180–202. For the relative wealth of DB counties. Cf. **444**.

320 DARBY, H.C., 'Domesday woodland', *EcHR*, 2nd ser., 3 (1950–1), 21–43.

321 FORSBERG, R., *Contribution to a dictionary of Old English place-names* (Uppsala: Almqvist & Wiksells, 1950).

322 GALBRAITH, V.H., 'The date of the geld rolls in Exon Domesday', *EHR*, 65 (1950), 1–17. Argues for a date in summer 1086 against **3705**. See further **343**. For critical comment see **323, 4429**. Corrects a printing error in **11**.

323 HOYT, R.S., *The royal demesne in English constitutional history, 1066–1272* (Cornell UP, 1950). An important work for the DB royal lands with valuable appendices on the geld exemption of manorial demesne and *terra regis* in Cambs. and Northants. See also **324, 325**. Cf. **411, 445**. On Northants., cf. **3226**.

324 HOYT, R.S., 'The nature and origins of the ancient demesne', *EHR*, 65 (1950), 145–74. Reprinted as chapter 6 of **323**.

325 HOYT, R.S., 'Royal taxation and the growth of the realm in medieval England', *Speculum*, 25 (1950), 36–48. For *regio* and *regnum* in DB, with especial reference to the heading *Dominicatus regis ...* in Exon. Cf. **411**.

326 MAXWELL, I.S., 'The geographical identification of Domesday vills', *Institute of British Geographers, Trans.*, 16 (1950), 95–121. Deals mostly with Yorks., highlighting the possibilities of a geographical approach.

327 FINBERG, H.P.R., 'The Domesday plough-team', *EHR*, 66 (1951), 67–71. Reprinted in H.P.R.Finberg, *Lucerna* (London:

Macmillan, 1964), 181–5. Reaffirmed traditional view that 8 oxen = 1 ploughteam. Cf. **311, 394**.

328 FINN, R.W., 'The evolution of successive versions of Domesday Book', *EHR*, 66 (1951) 561–4. Pointed out that three entries in Exon were written by a curial scribe. See **132**.

329 LENNARD, R., 'The economic position of the bordars and cottars of Domesday Book', *Economic Jour.*, 61 (1951), 342–71.

330 LOYD, L.C., *The origins of some Anglo-Norman families*, ed. C.T.Clay & D.C.Douglas, Harleian Soc., 103 (Leeds: John Whitehead & Son, 1951). A major genealogical work. Invaluable for the Norman origins of many DB landholders.

331 MILLER, E., *The abbey and bishopric of Ely* (Cambridge UP, 1951). An important local study which treats much of general significance on East Anglian DB. Critical of **312, 313**. See further **360**.

332 DARBY, H.C., *The Domesday geography of eastern England* (Cambridge UP, 1952; 2nd edn, 1957; 3rd edn, 1971). The first volume of an indispensable series which sought to map the information in DB. This volume contains an introduction on mapping DB. See **432** for the chief author's conclusions on the series. This volume deals with Lincs., Norfolk, Suffolk, Essex, Cambs., Hunts. Changes in the later editions, though small, should be taken note of. See **344**.

333 HARMER, F.E., *Anglo-Saxon writs* (Manchester UP, 1952). The commentary contains much on the Anglo-Saxon landholders of DB and on terminology. App. IV collects the DB evidence for lost royal writs.

334 POSTAN, M.M., 'Glastonbury estates in the twelfth century', *EcHR*, 2nd ser., 5 (1952–3), 358–67. Reprinted in M.M.Postan, *Essays on medieval agriculture and general problems of the medieval economy* (Cambridge UP, 1973), 249–61. For DB and later surveys, with conclusions of general significance. See further **348, 353, 422, 423**.

335 DOUGLAS, D.C. & GREENAWAY, G.W., *English historical documents 1042–1189*, English Historical Documents, 2 (London: Eyre & Spottiswoode, 1953; repr., 1961). For translations of sections of DB and related surveys.

336 HOYT, R.S., 'The *terrae occupatae* of Cornwall and the Exeter Domesday', *Traditio*, 9 (1953), 155–75.

337 ORDISH, G., *Wine growing in England* (London: Rupert Hart-Davies, 1953).

338 ANON, *Domesday rebound* (London: HMSO, 1954; 2nd edn, 1965). An indispensable study by the Public Record Office of the DB ms. made during the course of rebinding. Of fundamental importance.

339 BERESFORD, M. W., *The lost villages of England* (London: Lutterworth Press, 1954; repr. Gloucester: Alan Sutton, 1983). An early study of DB settlements which have disappeared.

340 DARBY, H. C. & TERRETT, I. B., *The Domesday geography of midland England* (Cambridge UP, 1954; 2nd edn, 1971; repr., 1978). See **412** for comment. Changes in the 2nd edn are small but significant. See further **4335, 4521**.

341 FRANKLIN, T. B., 'Domesday Book', *Amateur historian*, 1 (1954), 261–4, 297–300, 344–7.

342 LENNARD, R., 'Peasant tithe-collectors in Norman England', *EHR*, 69 (1954), 580–96.

343 MASON, J. F. A., 'The date of the Geld Rolls', *EHR*, 69 (1954), 283–9. Supports **322**.

344 POSTAN, M. M., 'The maps of Domesday', *EcHR*, 2nd ser., 7 (1954–5), 98–100. Cf. **332**.

345 DAVIS, R. H. C., 'East Anglia and the Danelaw', *TRHS*, 5th ser., 5 (1955), 23–39. For the distribution of free peasantry.

346 HOSKINS, W. G., *Sheep farming in Saxon and medieval England* (London: Dept. of Education of the International Wool Secretariat, 1955). Reprinted in W. G. Hoskins, *Provincial England: essays in social and economic history* (London: Macmillan, 1964), 1–14.

347 HOYT, R. S., 'Farm of the manor and community of the vill in Domesday Book', *Speculum*, 30 (1955), 147–69. For the few instances of peasants farming manors. Cf. **236**.

348 LENNARD, R., 'The demesnes of Glastonbury abbey in the eleventh and twelfth centuries', *EcHR*, 2nd ser., 8 (1955–6), 355–63. Cf. **334, 353, 422, 423**.

349 SAWYER, P. H., 'The "original returns" and Domesday Book', *EHR*, 70 (1955), 177–97. For the hundredal order of DB. An important article for the making of DB.

350 SAWYER, P. H., 'The place-names of the Domesday manuscripts', *BJRL*, 38 (1955–6), 483–506. Cf. **238, 292**.

351 KOSMINSKY, E. A., *Studies in the agrarian history of England in the thirteenth century* (Oxford: Blackwell, 1956). For some comparisons between DB and the Hundred Rolls.

352 KRAUSE, J., 'The medieval household: large or small?', *EcHR*, 2nd ser., 9 (1956–7), 420–32. For the DB population multiplier. Cf. **318**.

353 POSTAN, M. M., 'Glastonbury estates in the twelfth century: a reply', *EcHR*, 2nd ser., 9 (1956–7), 106–18. Reprinted in M. M. Postan, *Essays on medieval agriculture and general problems of the medieval economy* (Cambridge UP, 1973), 261–77. Cf. **334, 348**.

354 FINN, R. W., 'The immediate sources of the Exchequer Domesday', *BJRL*, 40 (1957–8), 47–78. Contains much valuable material. See especially the textual comparison with Exon (see further **396**).

355 HALLAM, H. E., 'Some thirteenth-century censuses', *EcHR*, 2nd ser., 10 (1957–8), 340–61. Cf. **332** on population density.

356 TROW-SMITH, R., *A history of British livestock husbandry to 1700* (London: Routledge & Kegan Paul, 1957).

357 ASTON, T. H., 'The origins of the manor in England', *TRHS*, 5th ser., 8 (1958), 59–83. Reprinted with 'a postscript' in T. H. Aston *et al* (eds), *Social relations and ideas: essays in honour of R. H. Hilton* (Cambridge UP for the Past & Present Soc., 1983), 1–43.

358 BERESFORD, M. W. & ST JOSEPH, J. K. S., *Medieval England: an aerial survey* (Cambridge UP, 1958; 2nd edn, 1979). See for examples illustrative of DB as a source for settlement.

359 FINN, R. W., 'The Exeter Domesday and its construction', *BJRL*, 41 (1958–9), 360–87. See also **1781, 1911, 3731, 4425**.

360 LENNARD, R., *Rural England 1086–1135* (OUP, 1959). A major publication bringing together years of work on DB. Notable for its discussion of the farming of manors, estate management and the size of peasant holdings.

361 FINN, R. W., 'The *Inquisitio Eliensis* reconsidered', *EHR*, 75 (1960), 385–409.

362 SANDERS, I. J., *English baronies: a study of their origin and descent, 1086–1327* (Oxford: Clarendon Press, 1960). An invaluable source of reference for the holdings of DB tenants and their descent.

363 FINN, R. W., *The Domesday Inquest and the making of Domesday Book* (London: Longmans, 1961). The fullest and most authoritative statement of Finn's views on the making of DB.

364 GALBRAITH, V.H., *The making of Domesday Book* (Oxford: Clarendon Press, 1961). Of outstanding importance for its subject and a development on **303, 317**. See further, **410, 449, 3136**. See also the review by P.H.Sawyer, *EHR*, 79 (1964), 101–5 and **368**.

365 HOLLISTER, C.W., 'The five-hide unit and the Old English military obligation', *Speculum*, 36 (1961), 61–80. For DB and military obligation and the *miles* of Berks. DB. Cf. **366, 371, 379**.

366 HOLT, J.C., 'Feudalism revisited', *EcHR*, 2nd ser., 14 (1961–2), 333–40. Cf. **365, 371, 379**.

367 HOYT, R.S., 'Representation in the administrative practice of Anglo-Norman England', *Studies presented to the International Commission for the History of Representative and Parliamentary Institutions, 24. Album Helen Maud Cam* (Louvain: Publications universitaires de Louvain; Paris: Editions Béatrice-Nauwelaerts, 1961), 13–26. For representation in DB.

368 ASTON, T.H., 'Domesday Book', *The Oxford Magazine* (10 May 1962), 287–9. A notable critique on **364**.

369 DARBY, H.C. & MAXWELL, I.S., *The Domesday geography of northern England* (Cambridge UP, 1962). See **4663, 4669, 4675**.

370 DARBY, H.C. & CAMPBELL, E.M.J., *The Domesday geography of south-east England* (Cambridge UP, 1962). See **1030, 2236**.

371 HOLLISTER, C.W., *Anglo-Saxon military institutions* (Oxford: Clarendon Press, 1962). See **365, 366, 379**.

372 MATTHEW, D.J.A., *The Norman monasteries and their English possessions* (OUP, 1962).

373 SOUTHERN, R.W., 'The place of Henry I in English history', *Proc. British Academy*, 48 (1962), 127–69. See Appendix for royal lands and revenues in DB. Cf. **445**.

374 BARLOW, F., *The English Church 1000–1066* (London: Longmans, 1963; 2nd edn, 1979). For the Church in DB.

375 BARLOW, F., 'Domesday Book: a letter of Lanfranc', *EHR*, 78 (1963), 284–9. Reprinted in F.Barlow, *The Norman Conquest and beyond* (London: Hambledon Press, 1983), 239–44. Added a letter of Lanfranc's to the corpus of material for the making of DB. For an alternative identification of Lanfranc's correspondent 'S.', see **398**. For another edition of the letter, **443**.

376 DARBY, H.C., 'Place-names and the geography of the past', in A.Brown & P.Foote (eds), *Early English and Norse studies* (London: Methuen, 1963), 6–18.

377 FINN, R. W., *An introduction to Domesday Book* (London: Longmans, 1963).

378 FINN, R. W., 'The geld account abstracts in the *Liber Exoniensis*', *BJRL*, 45 (1963), 370–89.

379 HOLLISTER, C. W. & HOLT, J. C., 'Two comments on the problem of continuity in Anglo-Norman feudalism', *EcHR*, 2nd ser., 16 (1963–4), 104–13. See **365, 366, 371**.

380 MASON, J. F. A., 'Roger de Montgomery and his sons (1067–1102)', *TRHS*, 5th ser., 13 (1963), 1–28.

381 MASON, J. F. A., 'The "honour of Richmond" in 1086', *EHR*, 78 (1963), 703–4. For an addition to **265** and suggested corrections to **293**.

382 RICHARDSON, H. G. & SAYLES, G. O., *The governance of medieval England from the Conquest to Magna Carta* (Edinburgh UP, 1963). For DB, 'an inestimable boon to learned posterity, but a vast administrative mistake'.

383 FINN, R. W., *Domesday studies: the Liber Exoniensis* (London: Longmans, 1964). An important and valuable study.

384 LENNARD, R., 'Agrarian history: some vistas and pitfalls', *AgHR*, 12 (1964), 83–98. Reflections on the difficulties of DB interpretation. Critical of **318**.

385 MOORE, J. S., 'The Domesday teamland: a reconsideration', *TRHS*, 5th ser., 14 (1964), 109–30. For a reply, **403**.

386 RUSSELL, J. C., 'A quantative approach to medieval population change', *Jour. Economic History*, 24 (1964), 1–21.

387 BELL, H. E., *Maitland: a critical examination and assessment* (London: Black, 1965).

388 FIFOOT, C. H. S., *The letters of Frederic William Maitland* (London: Selden Soc., 1965).

389 KIEFT, C. van de, 'Domesday Book in het licht van nieuwe onderzoekingen', *Tijdschrift voor Geschiedenis*, 78 (1965), 150–78.

390 LOYN, H. R., *The Norman Conquest* (London: Hutchinson, 1965; 2nd edn, 1968; 3rd edn, 1982). See Table 3 for a valuable tabulation of the relationship of DB and its 'satellites'. Repeated in **447**.

391 SAWYER, P. H., 'The wealth of England in the eleventh century', *TRHS*, 5th ser., 15 (1965), 145–64. For the *censarii* of the Burton abbey surveys and for DB sheep.

392 BUTLER, D., *1066: the story of a year* (London: Blond, 1966). See for DB values and the route of the Conqueror's army. See **201, 393**.

393 LEMMON, C. H., 'The campaign of 1066', in D. Whitelock *et al*, *The Norman Conquest: its setting and impact* (London: Eyre & Spottiswoode, 1966), 77–122. For DB values and the campaign. See also **201, 392**.

394 LENNARD, R., 'The composition of the Domesday *caruca*', *EHR*, 81 (1966), 770–5. Cf. **327**.

395 WIGHTMAN, W. E., *The Lacy family in England and Normandy, 1066–1194* (Oxford: Clarendon Press, 1966). For the extensive DB holdings of the Pontefract and Herefords. Lacy families.

396 DARBY, H. C. & FINN, R. W., *The Domesday geography of south-west England* (Cambridge UP, 1967; repr., 1979). See **3739** for comment. Includes appendices on *Liber Exoniensis* and a comparison of Exon and Exch. DB.

397 FINN, R. W., *Domesday studies: the eastern counties* (London: Longmans, 1967). A comprehensive discussion of the Little DB counties. Emphasises the difficulties of generalisation. See also for IE.

398 GALBRAITH, V. H., 'Notes on the career of Samson bishop of Worcester (1096–1112)', *EHR*, 82 (1967), 86–101. Reprinted in V. H. Galbraith, *Kings and chroniclers: essays in English medieval history* (London: Hambledon Press, 1982), chapter 4. Argues that Samson was 'the man behind Domesday Book'. Cf. **375, 421**.

399 HARVEY, S. P. J., 'Royal revenue and Domesday terminology', *EcHR*, 2nd ser., 20 (1967), 221–8. For the *ora* and methods of payment in coin.

400 MUSSET, L., *Les actes de Guillaume le Conquérant et de la reine Mathilde pour les abbayes caennaises* (Caen: Caron for the Société des Antiquaires de Normandie, 1967). See p. 95 for the *lana regine* in DB.

401 TANN, J., 'Multiple mills', *MA*, 11 (1967), 253–5.

402 COCKS, J. V., 'Length and breadth measurements in Domesday Book', *DCNQ*, 31 (1968–70), 82–4.

403 FINN, R. W., 'The teamland of the Domesday inquest', *EHR*, 83 (1968), 95–101. A reply to **385**.

404 RENN, D. F., *Norman castles in Britain* (London: John Baker, 1968). The Gazeteer contains material on the castles of DB.

405 WALMSLEY, J. F. R., 'The *censarii* of Burton abbey and the Domesday population', *NSJFS*, 8 (1968), 73–80. Suggests that a DB population multiplier of 15 or 16 may be needed. See **196, 225, 251, 3825**. Also **318**.

406 DARBY, H.C., 'Domesday Book: the first land utilisation survey', *The Geographical Magazine*, 42 (1969–70), 416–23. Reprinted with different illustrations in A.R.H.Baker & J.B.Harley (eds), *Man made the land* (Newton Abbot: David & Charles, 1973), 37–45.

407 HARVEY, S.P.J., 'The knight and the knight's fee in England', *Past and Present*, no.49 (1970), 3–43. Essential for the landholdings of DB *milites*.

408 BERESFORD, M.W. & HURST, J.G. (eds), *Deserted medieval villages* (London: Lutterworth Press, 1971). A general review with references to DB.

409 FINN, R.W., *The Norman Conquest and its effects on the economy, 1066–1086* (London: Longmans, 1971). A massive but not entirely successful study of DB values. See **412**.

410 HARVEY, S.P.J., 'Domesday Book and its predecessors', *EHR*, 86 (1971), 753–73. For the suggestion that fiscal documents already in existence assisted the compilation of DB. A contribution of fundamental importance to study of the making of DB. See **364, 426, 449**.

411 WOLFFE, B.P., *The royal demesne in English history* (London: Allen & Unwin, 1971). Cf. **323**.

412 CLARKE, H.B., 'Domesday slavery (adjusted for slaves)', *Midland History*, 1, no.4 (1972), 37–46. For comment on **340, 409**.

413 BERESFORD, M.W. & FINBERG, H.P.R., *English medieval boroughs: a hand-list* (Newton Abbot: David & Charles, 1973).

414 FINN, R.W., *Domesday Book: a guide* (London & Chichester: Phillimore, 1973).

415 KING, E., 'Domesday studies', *History*, 58 (1973), 403–9. A provocative review article.

416 SAWYER, P.H., 'Baldersby, Borup and Bruges: the rise of northern Europe', *University of Leeds Review*, 16 (1973), 75–96. For DB as a source for settlement.

417 GALBRAITH, V.H., *Domesday Book: its place in administrative history* (Oxford: Clarendon Press, 1974).

418 SAWYER, P.H., 'Anglo-Saxon settlement: the documentary evidence', in T.Rowley (ed.), *Anglo-Saxon settlement and landscape*, British

Archaeological Reports, 6 (Oxford: British Archaeological Reports, 1974), 108–19.

419 CAMPBELL, J., 'Observations on English government from the tenth to the twelfth century', *TRHS*, 5th ser., 25 (1975), 39–54. For the Carolingian context of DB.

420 DARBY, H.C. & VERSEY, G.R., *Domesday Gazeteer* (Cambridge UP, 1975). A listing of the DB place-names with suggested identifications and maps. A most useful volume, although one which does not take account of controversies about some of the identifications. Intended as a supplement to the *Domesday Geography* series, it does not perform the function of a DB index. See the County listings below for references to other place-name identifications.

421 HARVEY, S.P.J., 'Domesday Book and Anglo-Norman governance', *TRHS*, 5th ser., 25 (1975), 175–93. An important article. Its arguments on ploughlands are criticised in **453**. On the attempt to identify the mastermind behind DB, see **398**.

422 LENNARD, R., with an introduction by B.F.Harvey and E.Stone, 'The Glastonbury estates: a rejoinder', *EcHR*, 2nd ser., 28 (1975), 517–23. See **334, 348, 353, 423**.

423 POSTAN, M.M., 'The Glastonbury estates: a restatement', *EcHR*, 2nd ser., 28 (1975), 524–7. See **334, 348, 353, 422**.

424 HAMSHERE, J.D. & BLAKEMORE, M.J., 'Computerizing Domesday Book', *Area*, 8 (1976), 289–94.

425 KER, N.R., 'The beginnings of Salisbury cathedral library', in J.J.G.Alexander & M.T.Gibson (eds), *Medieval learning and literature: essays presented to R.W.Hunt* (Oxford: Clarendon Press, 1976), 23–49. Identifies the scribe of two quires of Exon with the scribe employed in making the early collection of books at Salisbury cathedral.

426 KREISLER, F.F., 'Domesday Book and the Anglo-Norman synthesis', in W.C.Jordan *et al* (eds), *Order and innovation in the Middle Ages: essays in honor of Joseph R.Strayer* (Princeton UP, 1976), 3–16, 411–16. For arguments similar to **410**.

427 McINTOSH, M.K., 'The privileged villeins of the English ancient demesne', *Viator*, 7 (1976), 295–328.

428 RACKHAM, 0., *Trees and woodland in the British landscape* (London: Dent, 1976).

429 SAWYER, P.H., 'Introduction: early medieval English settlement', in P.H.Sawyer (ed.), *Medieval settlement: continuity and change*

(London: Edward Arnold, 1976), 1–7. Revised as 'Medieval English settlement: new interpretations', in P. H. Sawyer (ed.), *English medieval settlement* (London: Edward Arnold, 1979), 1–8. A valuable assessment of DB's deficiencies as a source for settlement history.

430 JONES, G. R. J., 'Multiple estates and early settlment', in P. H. Sawyer (ed.), *Medieval settlement: continuity and change* (London: Edward Arnold, 1976), 15–40. Reprinted in P. H. Sawyer (ed.), *English medieval settlement* (London: Edward Arnold, 1979), 9–34. The DB estates discussed are in Sussex and Yorkshire.

431 HARVEY, S. P. J., 'Evidence for settlement study: Domesday Book', in P. H. Sawyer (ed.), *Medieval settlement: continuity and change* (London: Edward Arnold, 1976), 195–200. Reprinted in P. H. Sawyer (ed.), *English medieval settlement* (London: Edward Arnold, 1979), 105–9.

432 DARBY, H. C., *Domesday England* (Cambridge UP, 1977; repr., 1979). The concluding volume of the *Domesday Geography* series. Indispensable. There are numerous statistical appendices, as well as other appendices listing resources and formulae. This volume meets a criticism of earlier volumes in the series with a discussion of DB values. There is a section reflecting on the whole *Domesday Geography* project.

433 KER, N. R., *Medieval manuscripts in British libraries. II Abbotsford – Keele* (Oxford: Clarendon Press, 1977). See pp. 800–7 for a description of the ms. of Exon.

434 ROBERTS, B. K., *Rural settlement in Britain* (London: Dawson, 1977; reissued, London: Hutchinson, 1979).

435 TAYLOR, C. C., 'Polyfocal settlement and the English village', *MA*, 21 (1977), 189–93. A review of discussion of the DB villages.

436 WALMSLEY, J. F. R., 'Another Domesday text', *Mediaeval studies*, 39 (1977), 109–20. A not entirely convincing argument in favour of accepting a text in the Burton cartulary as a pre-DB fiscal list.

437 DODGSHON, R. A., 'The early middle ages, 1066–1350', in R. A. Dodgshon & R. A. Butlin (eds), *An historical geography of England and Wales* (London: Academic Press, 1978), 81–117.

438 LOYN, H. R. & GLASSCOCK, R. E., 'Darby's Domesday Geography', *Jour. Historical Geography*, 4 (1978), 391–7.

439 SOUTHERN, R. W., 'Vivian Hunter Galbraith, 1889–1976', *Proc. British Academy*, 64 (1978), 397–425. For an illuminating section on Galbraith's DB work.

440 BARG, M.A., 'The villeins of the ancient demesne', in *Studi in memoria di Federigo Melis*, 5 vols (Naples: Giannini Editore, 1979), 213–37.

441 CAMPBELL, J., 'The Church in Anglo-Saxon towns', in D. Baker (ed.), *Studies in Church History*, 16 (1979), 119–35.

442 CLANCHY, M.T., *From memory to written record: England, 1066–1307* (London: Edward Arnold, 1979). A provocative assessment of DB's place in the development of literate administration.

443 CLOVER, H.M. & GIBSON, M.T. (eds), *The letters of Lanfranc archbishop of Canterbury*, Oxford Medieval Texts (Oxford: Clarendon Press, 1979). See no. 56 for Lanfranc's letter to 'S.', on which see especially **375, 398**.

444 DARBY, H.C. *et al*, 'The changing geographical distribution of wealth in England: 1086–1334–1525', *Jour. Historical Geography*, 5 (1979), 247–62. Cf. **319**.

445 GREEN, J.A., 'William Rufus, Henry I and the royal demesne', *History*, 64 (1979), 337–52. For a tabulation of DB royal demesne values and a discussion. Cf. **373**.

446 KAPELLE, W.E., *The Norman conquest of the North: the region and its transformation 1000–1135* (London: Croom Helm, 1979).

447 LOYN, H.R., 'Domesday Book', in R.A. Brown (ed.), *Battle, 1 (1978)* (Ipswich: Boydell, 1979), 121–30, 220–2. See **390**.

448 CAMPBELL, J., 'The significance of the Anglo-Norman state in the administrative history of Western Europe', *Francia*, 9 (1980), 117–34.

449 HARVEY, S.P.8J., 'Recent Domesday studies', *EHR*, 95 (1980), 121–33. A valuable review article, especially on its author's differences with V.H. Galbraith.

450 RACKHAM, O., *Ancient woodland: its history, vegetation and uses in England* (London: Edward Arnold, 1980). See chapter 9 for an important discussion of DB woodland.

451 STAFFORD, P.A., 'The "farm of one night" and the organization of king Edward's estates in Domesday', *EcHR*, 2nd ser., 33 (1980), 491–502.

452 BOYDEN, P.B., 'J.H. Round and the beginnings of the modern study of Domesday Book: Essex and beyond', *TEAS*, 3rd ser., 12 (1981), 11–24.

453 GREEN, J.A., 'The last century of Danegeld', *EHR*, 96 (1981), 241–58. An important discussion of hidage and geld collection. Cf. **421**, on ploughlands.

454 HILL, D., *An atlas of Anglo-Saxon England* (Oxford: Blackwell, 1981). Contains numerous valuable maps which use and illustrate the DB evidence.

455 NICOL, A., *Domesday Book: facsimiles with introduction*, PRO Museum Pamphlets, no. 10 (HMSO, 1981). A useful basic introduction.

456 POWELL, W.R., 'J.Horace Round, the county historian: the Victoria County Histories and the Essex Archaeological Society', *TEAS*, 3rd ser., 12 (1981), 25–38. An important survey of Round's contribution to the VCH.

457 WILLIAMS, A., 'Land and power in the eleventh century: the estates of Harold Godwineson', in R.A.Brown (ed.), *Battle, 3 (1980)* (Woodbridge: Boydell, 1981), 171–87, 230–4. Cf. **461**.

458 CANTOR, L. (ed.), *The English medieval landscape* (London: Croom Helm, 1982). A good general survey of current work on DB and the landscape.

459 CHENEY, C.R., 'Service-books and records: the case of the Domesday Monachorum', *BIHR*, 56 (1983), 7–15.

460 DAVIS, R.H.C., 'David Charles Douglas 1898–1982', *Proc. British Academy*, 69 (1983), 513–42.

461 FLEMING, R., 'Domesday estates of the king and the Godwines: a study in late Saxon politics', *Speculum*, 58 (1983), 987–1007. Cf. **457**.

462 GREEN, J.A., 'The sheriffs of William the Conqueror', in R.A.Brown (ed.), *Battle, 5 (1982)* (Woodbridge: Boydell & Brewer, 1983), 129–45. For a table of the values of the estates of sheriffs named in DB and discussion. Cf. **272**.

463 HARVEY, S.P.J., 'The extent and profitability of demesne agriculture in England in the later eleventh century', in T.H.Aston *et al*, *Social relations and ideas: essays in honour of R.H.Hilton* (Cambridge UP for the Past & Present Soc., 1983), 45–72. A provocative discussion of estate management in DB.

464 KEEFE, T.K., *Feudal assessments and the political community under Henry II and his sons* (University of California Press, 1983). For some comment on DB values and *servitia debita* and a correction to **265** at p.231 n.25.

465 KING, D.J.C., *Castellarium Anglicanum*, 2 vols (London: Kraus, 1983). Includes all the DB castles, county by county.

466 TAYLOR, C., *Village and farmstead: a history of rural settlement in England* (London: Philip, 1983). See especially chapters 8 and 10 for an evaluation of archaeology's impact on the value of DB as a source for settlement history.

467 WRIGHT, A.C. & J.A., *Domesday Book: the unwanted bequest* (Chelmsford: the authors, 1983). Proclaims the possibility that DB's statistical information can be defined in terms of modern quantities and is usually logical within each county. Very hastily reasoned and limited in its evidence.

468 BEAUROY, J., 'La conquête cléricale de l'Angleterre', *Cahiers de civilisation médiévale*, 37 (1984), 35–48. A list of the holdings of Norman and French churches and bishops in DB.

469 CONDON, M.M. & HALLAM, E.M., 'Government printing of the public records in the eighteenth century', *Jour. Soc. Archivists*, 7 (1984), 348–88. Essential for the history of the printing of DB.

470 LANGDON, J., 'Horse-hauling: a revolution in vehicle transport in twelfth- and thirteenth-century England?', *Past and Present*, no. 103 (1984), 37–66. See pp. 42–4 for references in DB to horse-hauling.

LOCAL STUDIES

A facsimile of the DB text for each county was produced in the 1860s by the photozincographic method. These are difficult of access. The VCH provide a translation of DB for every county except Cheshire, Gloucestershire and Lincolnshire with an introduction which is usually very valuable. Other VCH volumes can contain important material for DB interpretation, especially those which have been published since the 1950s. The Phillimore edition which is nearing completion provides a text and a translation which is unconvincingly and un-helpfully 'modern' and, in some volumes, valuable commentary. For the DB place-names there are EPNS volumes for most counties and there is also the *Domesday Gazeteer* (**420**) which in addition gives maps of the DB place-names. The latter does not take account of disputed identifications, is indispensable for every county, but must be used in conjunction with items listed below. In the introduction to the General Section attention is drawn to the major studies which should be consulted in relation to most or all counties.

BEDFORDSHIRE

For an early and extensive statistical treatment of Beds. DB, **237**. For the relevant section of the *DB Geography*, **370**. There is an article devoted to the possessions of the abbey of St Nicholas of Angers in Beds., **231**. For DB values and the possible movements of William I's army in 1066, **201, 392, 393**.

1001 C. C. of Biggleswade, 'On the ancient division of counties into hundreds', *Gentleman's Magazine*, 98, pt 2 (1828), 99–102. The earliest known attempt to reconstitute the DB vills of any county.

1002 JAMES, H. (director), *Domesday Book: or the great survey of England of William the Conqueror, A.D. MLXXXVI. Facsimile of the part relating to Bedfordshire* (Southampton: Ordnance Survey Office, 1862). Photo-zincographic edition.

1003 HARVEY, W. M., *The history and antiquities of the hundred of Willey in the county of Bedford* (London: Nichols & Sons, 1872–8).

1004 AIRY, W., *A digest of Domesday Bedfordshire, being an analysis of that portion of the Domesday Survey which relates to the county of Bedford, and a key to the facsimile edition of the same published by Government* (Bedford: The 'Mercury'

Press, 1881). Gives a text, attempts to identify the place-names, and provides a critical commentary of some value.

1005 ROUND, J.H., 'Ely and her despoilers (1072–75)', in J.H. Round, *Feudal England* (London: Swan Sonnenschein, 1895; 2nd edn, London: Allen & Unwin, 1964), 459–61 (1st edn) and 349–50 (2nd edn). For Lisois de Moustiers as the predecessor of Eudo *dapifer*.

1006 NEILSON, N., *Economic conditions on the manors of Ramsey abbey* (Philadelphia: Sherman & Co., 1899).

1007 ROUND, J.H., 'Ingelric the priest and Albert of Lotharingia', in J.H. Round, *The commune of London and other studies* (Westminster: Constable, 1899), 28–38. For Albert's DB holdings in Beds. and five other counties.

1008 ROUND, J.H., 'Introduction to the Bedfordshire Domesday', in *VCH Beds.*, 1, ed. W. Page (London: Constable, 1904), 191–218.

1009 RAGG, F.W., 'Text of the Bedfordshire Domesday', *VCH Beds.*, 1, 221–66.

1010 SKEAT, W.W., *The place-names of Bedfordshire* (London: Bell, 1906). Superseded by EPNS volume (see **1020**).

1011 FOWLER, G.H., 'Domesday notes', *PBedsHRS*, 1 (1913), 63–73; 2 (1914), 265–6. Identifies *Chainhalle* and *Estone* with Ravensdon and Little Staughton. Discusses descent of the estates of Anschil of Ware and Wulmar of Eaton Socon, showing how the pattern of the original settlement had been modified by 1086.

1012 FOWLER, G.H., 'The Beauchamps, barons of Eaton', *PBedsHRS*, 2 (1914), 61–91. Some pertinent points on Eudo *dapifer*'s Beds. DB fief.

1013 AUSTIN, W., 'Markets and fairs of Luton', *PBedsHRS*, 2 (1914), 157–84.

1014 MORRIS, J.E., 'The assessment of knight service in Bedford-shire', *PBedsHRS*, 2 (1914), 185–218; 5 (1920), 1–26. The *milites* of Beds. DB and later surveys.

1015 AUSTIN, W., 'The Domesday water mills of Bedfordshire', *PBedsHRS*, 3 (1916), 207–47. Lists mills and discusses their location.

1016 FOWLER, G.H., 'Domesday notes II – Kenemondwick', *PBedsHRS*, 5 (1920), 61–73. Identifies with Kinwick, a lost place-name in Sandy.

1017 FOWLER, G.H., 'The devastation of Bedfordshire and the neighbouring counties in 1065 and 1066', *Archaeologia*, 72 (1922), 41–50. Cf. **201**.

1018 FOWLER, G.H., *Bedfordshire in 1086: an analysis and synthesis of Domesday Book*, Quarto memoirs of the Bedfordshire Historical Record Society, 1 (Aspley Guise, 1922). Includes maps of hundreds, meadow-land, woodland, mills and Saxon and Norman estates. 'Pioneering work of the first importance' (**370**).

1019 ELLIOT, J.S., 'Stagsden and its manors', *PBedsHRS*, 8 (1924), 1–12 + map.

1020 MAWER, A. & STENTON, F.M., *The place-names of Bedfordshire and Huntingdonshire*, EPNS, 3 (Cambridge UP, 1926).

1021 FARRER, W., with introduction by J.Tait, 'The honour of Old Wardon', *PBedsHRS*, 11 (1927), 1–46. Contains identifications of some DB sub-tenants.

1022 FOWLER, G.H., 'Cartulary of the abbey of Old Wardon', *PBedsHRS*, 13 (1930), 1–418. The notes contain much valuable information on the families of Beds. DB.

1023 RAFTIS, J.A., *The estates of Ramsey abbey* (Toronto: Pontifical Institute of Medieval Studies, 1957). For the abbey's holdings in Beds. and other counties.

1024 DOUGLAS, D.C., 'The Domesday tenant of Hawling', *TBGAS*, 84 (1965), 28–30. Brief discussion of the DB holdings of the Chocques ('de Cioches') family.

1025 GODBER, J., *History of Bedfordshire, 1066–1888* (Luton: Beds. County Council, 1969). Makes full use of DB material with numerous maps. Dependent to a considerable extent on **1018**.

1026 KING, E., *Peterborough abbey 1086–1310* (Cambridge UP, 1973). For the abbey's holdings in Beds. and other counties.

1027 HARVEY, B., *Westminster abbey and its estates in the middle ages* (Oxford: Clarendon Press, 1977). For the abbey's holdings in Beds. and other counties.

1028 MORRIS, J. (ed., from a draft translation by V.Sankaran and D.Sherlock), *Domesday Book. 20. Bedfordshire* (Chichester: Phillimore, 1977).

1029 RABAN, S., *The estates of Thorney and Crowland. A study in medieval monastic land tenure*, University of Cambridge, Dept. of Land Economy, Occasional Paper, no. 7 (Cambridge, 1977).

1030 OWEN, D., 'Bedfordshire chapelries: an essay in rural settlement history', *PBedsHRS*, 57 (1978), 9–20. For deficiencies in the recording of woodland in Beds. DB. Cf. **370**.

1031 BIGMORE, P., *The Bedfordshire and Huntingdonshire landscape* (London: Hodder & Stoughton, 1979).

BERKSHIRE

Freeman selected Berkshire for special treatment in vol. 4 of his *Norman Conquest*, **115**. For an early and extensive statistical treatment of Berks. DB, **237**, and for a statistical tabulation of values, **236**. Baring also dealt with the evidence of DB values for the possible movement of William I's army in 1066 and the hidation of Berks. DB, **201, 203**. For the former see also, **392, 393**. For the relevant section of the *DB Geography*, **370**. For churches omitted from Berks. DB, **159**. For the Lacy family and Westminster abbey landholdings, **395, 1027**. The status of *unus miles* of the customs of Berkshire recorded in DB has been much discussed, see **279, 365, 366, 371, 379**.

1101 JAMES, H. (director), *Domesday Book: or the great survey of England of William the Conqueror, A.D. MLXXXVI. Facsimile of the part relating to Berkshire* (Southampton: Ordnance Survey Office, 1863). Photozincographic edition.

1102 RICHARDSON, W. H., 'Notes on Blewbury', *Trans. Newbury District Field Club*, 4 (1886–95), 35–72.

1103 MONEY, W., 'Notes on Enbourne', *Trans. Newbury District Field Club*, 4 (1886–95), 165–216.

1104 MONEY, W., *The history of the ancient town and borough of Newbury in the county of Berks.* (London: Parker & Co., 1887). See chapter 4 for a brief analysis of the DB hundred of Thatcham. *Ulvrintone* is identified as Newbury.

1105 ANON (Mr Mowat), 'Berkshire – resumé of Domesday holders and holdings', *Quarterly Jour. Berks. Arch. and Archit. Soc.*, 3 (1894–5), 138–43, 167, 195–200; *BBOAJ*, 1 (1895), 26–8, 61, 75–8; 2 (1896), 19–22, 59–60, 86–9, 113–15. The author is identified by J. E. Field (**1106**).

1106 FIELD, J. E., 'Some notes on the Domesday survey of Berkshire', *BBOAJ*, 10 (1904), 81–6.

1107 ROUND, J. H., 'Introduction to the Berkshire Domesday' in *VCH Berks.*, 1, ed. P. H. Ditchfield & W. Page (London: Constable,

1906), 285–323. Suggested corrections were made by H. Peake in *BBOAJ*, 13 (1907), 102–5.

1108 RAGG, F.W., 'Translation of the Berkshire Domesday', in *VCH Berks.*, 1, 324–69.

1109 ROUND, J.H., 'The tenure of Draycote-under-Needwood', *CHS*, ns, 10, pt 1 (1907), 3–10. Identifies Roger *venator* of Berks. DB with the Roger who held Boyleston (Derbys.).

1110 SKEAT, W.W., *The place-names of Berkshire* (Oxford: Clarendon Press, 1911). Superseded by EPNS volume (**1122**).

1111 STENTON, F.M., *The place-names of Berkshire: an essay*, (Reading: University College, 1911). Superseded by EPNS volume (**1122**).

1112 TREACHER, L., 'The origins of the Berkshire villages', *BBOAJ*, 23 (1917), 54–61. Suggests locations for two DB mills in Sonning.

1113 FARRER, W., 'The honour of Wallingford', in H. E. Salter (ed.), *The Boarstall cartulary* (Oxford: Clarendon Press, for the Oxford Historical Soc., 1930). For the holdings of Robert d'Ouilly and Miles Crispin.

1114 HUNTINGFORD, G.W.B., 'Berkshire place-names', *Berks.AJ*, 38 (1934), 109–27; 39 (1935), 11–34, 198–9.

1115 MORGAN, F.W., 'The Domesday geography of Berkshire', *Scottish Geographical Magazine*, 51 (1935), 353–63.

1116 PEAKE, H.E.J., 'Roeburgh hundred and its associations', *Trans. Newbury District Field Club*, 8 (1938), 63–70. The modern name is Rowbury.

1117 YATES, E.M., 'The settlement of north-west Sussex', *Sociological Review*, 2 (1954), 209–27. For comparative statistics of DB peasantry in Berks., Kent, and N.E. Sussex.

1118 BIDDLE, M., 'The deserted medieval village of Seacourt, Berkshire', *Oxoniensia*, 36–7 (1961–2), 70–201. See pp. 80–1 for a discussion of the DB economy of Seacourt.

1119 BERESFORD, M.W. & HURST, J.G., 'Introduction to a first list of deserted medieval village sites in Berkshire', *Berks.AJ*, 60 (1962), 92–7.

1120 KEMP, B.R., 'The mother church of Thatcham', *Berks.AJ*, 63 (1965–6), 15–22. A discussion of minster churches which has more than local significance (see especially **360, 374**). Identifies *Acenge* with East Ginge.

1121 BROOKS, J., 'Eaton Hastings: a deserted medieval village', *Berks.AJ*, 64 (1969), 1–8.

1122 GELLING, M., *The place-names of Berkshire*, 3 vols, EPNS, 49–51 (Cambridge UP, 1973–6).

1123 LINGHAM, B. F., *The long years of obscurity. A history of Didcot, vol. 1 to 1841* (Didcot: Gem Graphic Services, 1978). Argues that *Wibalditone* is Didcot against all major Berks. DB authorities.

1124 MORGAN, P. (ed., from a draft translation by A. Hawkins), *Domesday Book. 5. Berkshire* (Chichester: Phillimore, 1979). For additions and corrections, see **4523**.

BUCKINGHAMSHIRE

Serious critical study of Bucks. DB began unusually late. In contrast, there is a relatively high number of good modern studies which seek to illuminate the DB text through local knowledge and geography. Baring contributed a major statistical survey of Bucks. DB, **237**, as well as studies of the values in order to plot the possible movements of William I's army in 1066 and of the hidation of Berks. DB, **201, 203**. For the movements of the army, see also **392, 393**. For the relevant section of the *DB Geography*, see **370**. There are studies of the holdings of the abbeys of St Nicholas of Angers and La Couture of Le Mans in Bucks., **231**; of the estates of the two branches of the Lacy family, **395**; of the lands of Westminster abbey, **1027**; and of the fees of Robert d'Ouilly and Miles Crispin, **1113**.

1201 BAWDWEN, W., *Dom. Boc. A translation of the record called Domesday, so far as it relates to the counties of Middlesex, Hertford, Buckingham, Oxford and Gloucester* (Doncaster: Sheardown, 1812). Bawdwen produced a rather unsatisfactory translation of the whole of DB (British Library, Add. ms. 27769), of which only sections were published. See also **1601**.

1202 LIPSCOMB, G., *The history and antiquities of the county of Buckingham*, 4 vols (London: J.W.Robins, 1847). Translated and transcribed portions of the DB text in his descriptions of parishes.

1203 JAMES, H. (director), *Domesday Book: or the great survey of England of William the Conqueror, A.D. MLXXXVI. Facsimile of the part relating to Buckinghamshire* (Southampton: Ordnance Survey Office, 1862). Photo-zincographic edition.

1204 BOYLE, J.R., 'Who was Eddeva?', *Trans, East Riding Ant. Soc.*, 4 (1896), 11–22. For the DB holdings of Edith the Fair in Bucks. and six other counties.

1205 BARING, F.H., 'Note on the hidation of Buckinghamshire', *EHR*, 15 (1900), 199. A correction to the Bucks. section of **203**.

1206 DAVIES, A.M., 'The ancient hundreds of Buckinghamshire', *The Home Counties Magazine*, 6 (1904), 134–44. Reprinted with corrections in *RB*, 9 (1909), 104–19. Davies' map was used by the VCH (**1207**).

1207 ROUND, J.H., 'Introduction to the Buckinghamshire Domesday', in *VCH Bucks.*, 1, ed. W. Page (London: Constable, 1905), 207–29.

1208 RAGG, F.W., 'Text of the Buckinghamshire Domesday', *VCH Bucks.*, 1, 230–77.

1209 DAVIES, A.M., 'Eleventh century Buckinghamshire', *RB*, 10 (1916), 69–74. A commentary on **237**.

1210 MAWER, A. & STENTON, F.M., *The place-names of Buckinghamshire*, EPNS, 2 (Cambridge UP, 1925).

1211 JENKINS, J.G., *History of the parish of Penn in the county of Buckingham* (London: St Catherine Press, 1935). At pp. 5–6 corrects VCH (**1208**) and confirms EPNS on the identification of *Dilehurst*. See also **1225**.

1212 KISSAN, B.W., 'Lanfranc's alleged division of lands between archbishop and community', *EHR*, 54 (1939), 285–93. For the DB account of Canterbury's lands in nine counties.

1213 DAVIES, A.M., 'Abefeld and Achamsted', *RB*, 15 (1947–52), 166–71. Suggests identifications for unidentified estates.

1214 DAVIES, A.M., 'The hundreds of Buckinghamshire and Oxfordshire', *RB*, 15 (1947–52), 231–49. A reappraisal of **1206** in the light of Assize Roll evidence. Compares the two counties.

1215 BERESFORD, M.W., 'Glebe terriers and open-field Buckinghamshire, with a summary list of deserted villages of the county', *RB*, 16 (1953–60), 5–28.

1216 ELVEY, G.R., 'Buckinghamshire in 1086', *RB*, 16 (1953–60), 342–62. A useful survey, with an important appendix devoted to anonymous estates and lost and doubtful names. There is an interesting reconstruction of DB Amersham with a map.

1217 ASHFORD, L.J., *The history of the borough of High Wycombe from its origins to 1880* (London: Routledge & Kegan Paul, 1960). Includes a map of the DB hundred of Desborough.

1218 ELVEY, E.M., 'The abbot of Missenden's estates in Chalfont St Peter', *RB*, 17 (1961–65), 20–40. A piece of local DB geography.

1219 CHIBNALL, A.C., *Sherington: fiefs and fields of a Buckinghamshire village* (Cambridge UP, 1965).

1220 TULL, G.K., 'Land utilisation in the Newport hundreds at the time of the Domesday survey', *Wolverton Arch. Soc. Jour.*, 2 (1969), 32–48.

1221 BROWN, O.F., 'Cleyley in Domesday', *Wolverton Arch. Soc. Jour.*, 2 (1969), 49–58.

1222 HAY, D. & J., *Hilltop villages of the Chilterns* (London & Chichester: Phillimore, 1971). See chapter 8 for settlements not recorded in DB.

1223 BULL, L., 'The ancient saltway from Droitwich to Princes Risborough', *RB*, 20 (1975–78), 87–92.

1224 REED, M., 'Markets and fairs in medieval Buckinghamshire', *RB*, 20 (1975–8), 563–85. Discussion of the indirect evidence thereof in Bucks. DB.

1225 MORRIS, J. (ed., from a draft translation by E. Teague and V. Sankaran), *Domesday Book. 13. Buckinghamshire* (Chichester: Phillimore, 1978).

1226 CHIBNALL, A.C., *Beyond Sherington: the early history of the region of Buckinghamshire lying to the north-east of Newport Pagnell* (London and Chichester: Phillimore, 1979).

1227 REED, M., *The Buckinghamshire landscape* (London: Hodder & Stoughton, 1979).

CAMBRIDGESHIRE

For Cambs. DB it is essential to take account of the editions of IE and ICC, **11, 12**. See also **16, 149**, and the translation cited below, **1316**. Baring made a study of the county's hidation, **203**, but see also **1326**. On hidation, see also **216**. For the Cambs. evidence for commendation, **316**. On the Cambs. *terra regis*, **323**. There are numerous studies devoted to the monastic landholders of the county, the abbeys of Crowland, Ely, Ramsey, Thorney and St Sergius of Angers, **1005, 1006, 231, 331, 1023, 1029**, in addition to those mentioned below. For the estates of Edith the Fair in Cambs. and six other counties, **1204**.

1301 JAMES, H. (director), *Domesday Book: or the great survey of England of William the Conqueror, A.D. MLXXXVI. Facsimile of the part relating to Cambridgeshire* (Southampton: Ordnance Survey Office, 1862). Photo-zincographic edition.

1302 WALKER, B., 'On the measurements and valuations of the Domesday of Cambridgeshire', *PCAS*, 5 (1884), 93–129 + supplement.

1303 BARBER, H., 'Place-names of East Anglia', *The East Anglian*, ns, 6 (1895–6), 65–9, 93–5, 124–7, 196–9, 237–40, 281–5; 7 (1897–8), 9–11, 29–31, 41–4, 52–5, 157–60, 181–4, 204–6. Included little more than the DB names.

1304 MAITLAND, F. W., *Township and borough* (Cambridge UP, 1898; repr., 1964). Relates to Cambridge.

1305 SKEAT, W. W., *The place-names of Cambridgeshire* (London: Bell, 1901; 2nd edn, 1911). Selective. Superseded by **1318**.

1306 EVELYN-WHITE, C. H. & H. G., *The Cambridgeshire portion of the great survey of England* (London: Elliot Stock; Norwich: Goose & Son; Cambridge: Bowes & Bowes, 1910). Reprinted from *The East Anglian*, ns, 11 (1905–6), 65–71, 92–5, 110–11, 116–19, 134–7, 150–3, 174–5, 180–1, 204–5, 218–19, 232–5, 248–51, 262–5, 282–5, 292–5, 314–17, 328–33, 342–7, 362–5, 380–5; ns, 12 (1907–8), 4–9, 26–9, 40–5, 58–61, 74–7, 84–7, 100–3, 120–3, 140–1, 150–1, 170–3, 188–91, 206–7, 220–1, 236–7, 248–9, 272–5, 286–9, 318–19, 328–9, 346–9. Gives a text with abbreviations extended and a translation made by Bawdwen (see **1201**) which is not entirely reliable.

1307 STOKES, D., 'The old mills of Cambridge', *PCAS*, 14 (1910), 180–233. See pp. 181–3 for the DB mills.

1308 FARRER, W., *Feudal Cambridgeshire* (Cambridge UP, 1920). Important for Cambs. DB manors and their descent.

1309 GRAY, A., *The town of Cambridge: a history* (Cambridge: Heffer, 1925). See chapter 4 for DB Cambridge.

1310 FOWLER, G., 'Fenland waterways, past and present. South Level district. Part I', *PCAS*, 33 (1931–2), 108–28. See Appendix IV for the fisheries of Cambs. DB.

1311 CAM, H. M., 'The origin of the borough of Cambridge', *PCAS*, 35 (1933–4), 33–53. Reprinted in H. M. Cam, *Liberties and communities in medieval England* (Cambridge UP, 1944), 1–18. Cf. **282**.

1312 DARBY, H. C., 'The Domesday geography of Cambridgeshire', *PCAS*, 36 (1934–5), 35–57.

1313 PAGE, F. M., *The estates of Crowland abbey* (Cambridge UP, 1934). For DB estates in five counties. See also **1029**.

1314 SALZMAN, L.F., 'Introduction to the Cambridgeshire Domesday', in *VCH Cambs. and the Isle of Ely*, 1, ed. L.F. Salzman (Oxford UP, for the Institute of Historical Research, 1938), 335–57.

1315 OTWAY-RUTHVEN, J., 'Translation of the text of Cambridgeshire Domesday', *VCH Cambs.*, 1, 358–99.

1316 OTWAY-RUTHVEN, J., 'Translation of *Inquisitio Comitatus Cantabrigiensis*', in *VCH Cambs.*, 1, 400–27.

1317 DARBY, H.C., *The medieval fenland* (Cambridge UP, 1940; repr. Newton Abbot: David & Charles, 1974).

1318 REANEY, P.H., *The place-names of Cambridgeshire and the Isle of Ely*, EPNS, 19 (Cambridge UP, 1943).

1319 DARBY, H.C., 'Domesday Cambridgeshire', in *VCH Cambs. and the Isle of Ely*, 2, ed. L.F. Salzman (Oxford UP, for the Institute of Historical Research, 1948), 49–58. An abbreviation of **1312** with maps of population, mills, woodland, etc.

1320 FINN, R.W., 'Some reflections on the Cambridgeshire Domesday', *PCAS*, 53 (1959), 29–38. Mostly devoted to the transfer of estates from English to Normans.

1321 BLAKE, E.O. (ed.), *Liber Eliensis*, Camden Soc., 3rd ser., 92 (London: Royal Historical Soc., 1962). See pp. 419–32 for the abbey of Ely's estates in this and six other counties.

1322 SPUFFORD, M., *A Cambridgeshire community: Chippenham from settlement to enclosure*, Dept. of English Local History, Occasional papers, no. 20 (Leicester UP, 1965).

1323 HART, C., *The early charters of eastern England* (Leicester UP, 1966). For the DB estates of Turkil of Harringworth in five counties.

1324 MILLER, E., 'Some twelfth-century documents concerning St Peter's church at Babraham', *PCAS*, 59 (1966), 113–23. Second part of the article is mainly devoted to DB Babraham and its tenants.

1325 TAYLOR, C., *The Cambridgeshire landscape* (London: Hodder & Stoughton, 1973).

1326 HART, C., *The hidation of Cambridgeshire*, Dept. of English Local History, occasional papers, 2nd ser., no. 6 (Leicester UP, 1974). Of fundamental importance for the structure of Cambs. DB. Discussion bears on wider questions about the making of DB.

1327 HART, C., 'Hereward "the Wake" ', *PCAS*, 65 (1974), 28–40. For well-known material on Hereward's DB lands and for the holdings of Turkil of Harringworth in five counties.

1328 OWEN, A. E. B., 'Medieval saltmaking and the coastline in Cambridgeshire and north-west Norfolk', in K. W. de Brisay & K. A. Evans (eds), *Salt: the study of an ancient industry* (Colchester: Colchester Archaeological Group, 1975), 42–4.

1329 DARBY, H. C., *Medieval Cambridgeshire* (Cambridge: Oleander Press, 1977).

1330 RUMBLE, A. (ed., from a draft translation by J. Fellows & S. Keynes), *Domesday Book. 18 Cambridgeshire* (Chichester: Phillimore, 1981). Contains text, translation, valuable notes and the names of the hundred-juries from ICC and IE. Also comparisons with and discussion of ICC and IE.

1331 OWEN, A. E. B., 'A fenland frontier: the establishment of the boundary between Cambridgeshire and Lincolnshire', *Landscape History*, 4 (1982), 41–6.

CHESHIRE

Cheshire DB included material for modern Lancashire, Cumbria and north Wales. Editions and translations of Cheshire DB therefore include entries for these areas. The studies listed below relate only to the modern county of Cheshire. See separate sections for Lancashire and Wales. There is so far no VCH translation and introduction to Cheshire DB, although **1424** was in fact prepared for the VCH and not published there. The new VCH DB will be published shortly. For the relevant section of the *DB Geography*, **369**. For the suggestion that Cheshire DB values reflect the Conqueror's devastation of the N.W. Midlands, **281**.

1401 SQUIRE, Mr, 'A transcript of Cheshire at large, out of the Greater Domesday-Book, remaining on record in the Tally-Office at Westminster', in Leycester, P., *Historical antiquities in two books. The first treating in general of Great Britain and Ireland. The second containing particular remarks concerning Cheshire* (London: W.L. for Robert Clavell, 1673).

1402 ORMEROD, G., *The history of the county palatine and city of Chester*, 3 vols (London: Lackington, Hughes, Harding, Mavor & Jones, 1819. 2nd edn, revised and enlarged, London: George Routledge, 1875–82). Much descriptive use of DB material.

1403 ROBSON, J., 'On the early charters of St Werburgh's in Chester', *THSLC*, 11 (1858–9), 187–98. A brief survey of St Werburgh's DB holdings.

1404 EARLE, J., 'The ethnology of Cheshire, traced chiefly in the local names', *Arch. Jour.*, 17 (1860), 93–116. Includes a list of the place-names in DB under their several hundreds.

1405 JAMES, H. (director), *Domesday Book: or the great survey of England of William the Conqueror, A.D. MLXXXVI. Facsimile of the part relating to Cheshire and Lancashire* (Southampton: Ordnance Survey Office, 1861). Photo-zincographic edition.

1406 BEAMONT, W., *A literal extension and translation of the portion of Domesday Book relating to Cheshire and Lancashire, and to parts of Flintshire and Denbighshire, Cumberland, Westmoreland and Yorkshire* (London: Vacher & Sons, 1863; 2nd edn, Chester: Minshull & Hughes, 1882). Superseded by later editions.

1407 BARNS, T., 'The architectural antiquities of the parish church of St Wilfrid, Grappenhall, co. Chester', *THSLC*, 33 (1880–1), 85–122. See pp. 90–2 for the DB church at Lymm which the author suggests served Grappenhall in 1086.

1408 ESDAILE, G., 'Cheshire in Domesday and the Domesday of Chester', *Cheshire N&Q*, 6 (1886), 184–6.

1409 ESDAILE, G., 'Lancashire and Cheshire Domesday', *TLCAS*, 4 (1886), 35–49. Mainly devoted to arguing the author's belief that Cheshire DB was 'a précis'.

1410 IRVINE, W. F., 'Place names in the hundred of Wirral', *THSLC*, 53–4 (1891–2), 279–304.

1411 IRVINE, W. F., 'Notes on the Domesday survey, so far as it relates to the hundred of Wirral', *JCNW*, 5 (1893–5), 72–84. A useful survey which has something to say about many important matters. Identified *Salhale* with Saughall Massey against **1402**. But see **1424** at p. 147.

1412 IRVINE, W. F., 'Note on the ancient parish of Bidston', *THSLC*, 45 (1894), 33–80. Identification of *Salhale*. See **1411**.

1413 TAIT, J., 'Wirral place-names', *The Athenaeum*, no. 3551 (16 Nov. 1895), 681–2; no. 3554 (7 Dec. 1895), 792. A criticism of **194**. See **1414**.

1414 ROUND, J. H., 'Wirral place-names', *The Athenaeum*, no. 3552 (23 Nov. 1895), 718; no. 3555 (14 Dec. 1895), 835.

1415 BROWNBILL, J., 'Cheshire in Domesday Book', *THSLC*, 51 (1899), 1–26. Still has many useful points.

1416 BROWNBILL, J., 'Some notes on the Cheshire Domesday', *Cheshire Sheaf*, 3 (1901), 85–8, 89–90, 94–7; 4 (1903), 54, 56, 61, 64, 67, 69, 72, 76–7, 79, 81, 84, 87, 90, 92, 94–7, 100, 102–3, 105, 108, 110–11, 113–14, 115–16, 118–19, 121–2, 124–5, 125–6, 130, 132–3, 135–6. Description of the hundreds, some identifications, areas of manors. A wide-ranging discussion of many DB topics.

1417 IRVINE, W.F., 'Notes on the old halls of Wirral', *THSLC*, 53 (1901), 93–130. At pp. 101–2 locates a DB mill.

1418 IRVINE, W.F. & BEAZLEY, F.C., 'Notes on the parish of Woodchurch', *THSLC*, 53 (1901), 139–78. Suggests that the church mentioned in DB under Landican was Woodchurch.

1419 BROWNBILL, J., 'Ancient church dedications in Cheshire and South Lancashire', *THSLC*, 54 (1902), 19–44. See pp. 40–44 for a list of the dedications of the DB churches.

1420 LUMBY, J.H., 'Chester, Birkenhead, and Liverpool in the patent and close rolls of the three Edwards', *THSLC*, 54 (1902), 45–72. See p. 60 for the marten skins mentioned in the Chester DB entry.

1421 HARRISON, W., 'Ancient forests, chases, and deer parks in Cheshire', *TLCAS*, 20 (1902), 1–28.

1422 IRVINE, W.F., 'Notes on the history of St Mary's nunnery, Chester', *JCNW*, ns, 13 (1907), 67–109. Discussion of the *monasterium sancte Marie* of the Chester DB entry. Argues that it was a small church near St John's, pp. 67–9.

1423 STEWART-BROWN, R., 'The royal manor and park of Shotwick', *THSLC*, 64 (1912), 82–137. See pp. 85–7 for discussion of the extent of DB Shotwick.

1424 TAIT, J., *The Domesday survey of Cheshire*, Chetham Soc., ns, 75 (Manchester, 1916). Contains text, translation, a valuable introduction and notes. Of fundamental importance.

1425 TAIT, J. (ed.), *The chartulary or register of the abbey of St Werburgh, Chester*, 2 vols, Chetham Soc., ns, 79, 82 (Manchester, 1920, 1923). Contains much of value.

1426 HEWITT, H.J., *Medieval Cheshire*, Chetham Soc., ns, 88 (Manchester, 1929). Some commentary on DB material, although mostly on the 13th and 14th centuries.

1427 BROWNBILL, J., 'A history of the old parish church of Bidston, Cheshire', *THSLC*, 87 (1935), 133–99. See especially pp. 156–9. There is a map of Wirral DB manors opposite p. 137.

1428 CRUMP, W. B., 'Saltways from the Cheshire Wiches', *TLCAS*, 54 (1939), 84–142.

1429 STEWART-BROWN, R., 'Bridge-work at Chester', *EHR*, 54 (1939), 83–7. Suggests an amendment to **1424**.

1430 WAINWRIGHT, F. T., 'North-west Mercia, A.D. 871–924', *THSLC*, 94 (1942), 3–55. See pp. 33–5 for a list of Scandinavian personal names in Cheshire DB, correcting **1424**.

1431 TERRETT, I. B., 'The Domesday woodland of Cheshire', *THSLC*, 100 (1948), 1–7.

1432 SYLVESTER, D., 'Rural settlement in Cheshire', *THSLC*, 101 (1949), 1–37. Includes maps of DB population and plough-teams. See especially pp. 6–10.

1433 RICHARDS, R., 'The chapels of the blessed virgin Mary and St John at High Legh, Cheshire, with some account of the Cornwall-Legh and Egerton Leigh families', *THSLC*, 101 (1949), 97–138. A rather muddled discussion of possible English continuity over 1066 and of a DB church at pp. 101, 105, 113–15.

1434 VARLEY, W. J., 'Excavations of the castle ditch, Eddisbury, 1935–38', *THSLC*, 102 (1950), 1–68. See p. 63 for DB Eddisbury.

1435 BARRACLOUGH, G., 'The earldom and county palatine of Chester', *THSLC*, 103 (1953), 23–57. Examines DB evidence that earl Hugh held a specially privileged position in the county and finds none.

1436 SYLVESTER, D., 'The open fields of Cheshire', *THSLC*, 108 (1956), 1–33. Discussion of the extent of cultivation recorded in DB. A map of the DB ploughlands.

1437 SYLVESTER, D., 'Cheshire woodland in the Middle Ages', *The Cheshire Historian*, 7 (1957), 7–13.

1438 SYLVESTER, D. & NULTY, G. (eds), *The historical atlas of Cheshire* (Chester: Cheshire Community Council, 1958). Includes 3 DB maps: waste and woodland, population of manors, agriculture and industry.

1439 BURNE, R. V. H., 'Domesday Book and Cheshire', *JCNW*, 49 (1962), 19–26. A derivative and general account of mediocre quality.

1440 SYLVESTER, D., 'Cheshire in the Dark Ages: a map study of the Celtic and Anglian settlement', *THSLC*, 114 (1962), 1–22. See p. 2 for a map of the suggested extent of DB woodland compared to that of modern woodland and deduced extent of earlier woodland. Discussion at pp. 4–5.

1441 SYLVESTER, D., 'Parish and township in Cheshire and N.E. Wales', *Jour. Chester Arch. Soc.*, 54 (1967), 23–35. Contains map of DB churches and priests and of churches in later surveys.

1442 SYLVESTER, D., *The rural landscape of the Welsh borderland* (London: Macmillan, 1969).

1443 DODGSON, J. McN., *The place-names of Cheshire*, 6 vols, EPNS, 44–8, 54 (Cambridge UP, 1970–81). In progress.

1444 BU'LOCK, J. D., *Pre-Conquest Cheshire, 386–1066* (Chester: Cheshire Community Council, 1972).

1445 HUSAIN, B. M. C., *Cheshire under the Norman earls* (Chester: Cheshire Community Council, 1973). A general and sometimes misguided account of DB Cheshire.

1446 MORGAN, P. (ed., from a draft translation by A. Rumble), *Domesday Book. 26. Cheshire* (Chichester: Phillimore, 1978). For additions and corrections, **2838**.

1447 OXLEY, J., 'Nantwich: an eleventh-century salt town and its origins', *THSLC*, 131 (1981), 1–19.

1448 LEWIS, C. P., 'Herbert the Jerkin-maker: a Domesday tenant identified', *THSLC*, 131 (1981), 159–60. For the tenants and extent of Upton-by-Chester.

1449 THACKER, A. T., 'Chester and Gloucester: early ecclesiastical organisation in two Mercian burhs', *NH*, 18 (1982), 199–211.

CORNWALL

All studies of Cornwall DB must take account of the numerous publications dealing with Exon DB, on which see especially **383**. For Cornwall see also **336**. For the relevant section of the *DB Geography*, **396**. For woodland in Cornwall, **289**, and for plough-teams, **311**. For revenues deriving from the hundreds, **263**. For villeins from comital manors, **257**. For the holdings of Tavistock abbey in Cornwall, **1778**.

1501 COUCH, J., 'Translations from Domesday', *Trans. Nat. Hist. & Ant. Soc. of Penzance*, 2 (1851–5), 110–25, 167–85, 244–69. A complete translation of the Exch. DB text.

1502 JAMES, H. (director), *Domesday Book: or the great survey of England of William the Conqueror, A.D. MLXXXVI. Facsimile of the part relating to Cornwall* (Southampton: Ordnance Survey Office, 1861). Photozincographic edition.

1503 CARNE, J., 'Identification of the Ridwri of the Tregothnan charter', *JRIC*, 1, no. 2 (1864), 1–3; with a letter from L. H. Courtney, 3–4. Carne identifies *Ritwore* of DB with Roseworthy in Gwinear. See further *JRIC*, 1, no. 3 (1865), 41–4.

1504 CARNE, J., 'An attempt to identify the Domesday manors', *JRIC*, 1 (1865), 11–59; 2 (1867), 219–22. See also *JRIC*, 4 (1876) for some notes and corrections. A valuable work.

1505 ANON, ed. J. Polsue, *A complete history of the county of Cornwall*, 4 vols (Truro & London: W. Lake & J. C. Hotten, 1867–72. Reprinted by E. P. Publishing Ltd. in collaboration with Cornwall County Library, 1974). Made great use of DB, but place-name identifications are not always to be relied upon.

1506 JAMES, H., *A literal translation of the part of Domesday Book relating to the county of Cornwall to accompany the facsimile copy photozinco-graphed at the Ordnance Survey Office, Southampton* (Southampton: Ordnance Survey Office, 1875).

1507 SINCOCK, W., 'Principal landowners in Cornwall, A.D. 1165', *JRIC*, 10 (1890–1), 150–68. Much material on DB sub-tenants.

1508 WHITLEY, H. M., 'The Cornish Domesday and the geld inquest', *JRIC*, 13 (1898), 548–75. A translation and analysis of the Cornwall *Inquisitio Gheldi* and a tabulation of DB entries.

1509 TAYLOR, T., 'Blohin: his descendants and lands', *The Ancestor*, 60 (1904), 20–7.

1510 TAYLOR, T., 'St Michael's Mount and the Domesday Survey', *JRIC*, 17 (1907–8), 230–5. Cf. **1547**.

1511 ROWE, J. H., 'The forty mythical brewers of Cornwall', *DCNQ*, 6 (1910–11), 39–41. On *cervisarii* in DB. See **1517**.

1512 ROWE, J. H., 'B and G confused in Domesday and Feudal Aids', *N&Q*, 11th ser., 3 (1911), 443–4. For *Gluston* (Exch.) and *Glustona* (Exon.). Cf. **1520, 1552**.

1513 RUTTER, J.A., 'Cornish acres in Domesday', *N&Q*, 12th ser., 7 (1920), 392, 437, 471–2.

1514 ROWE, J.H., 'The boundaries of hundreds, ancient and modern', *DCNQ*, 11 (1920–1), 256–7; 12 (1923), 325–6.

1515 CHOPE, R.P., 'Domesday mills in Devon and Cornwall', *DCNQ*, 12 (1922–3), 21–3.

1516 ROWE, J.H., 'Domesday manors in Cornwall', *DCNQ*, 12 (1922–3), 56–7, 135–6. For identifications of *Boten, Polscat, Carbihan*.

1517 CHOPE, R.P., 'Cornish brewers in Domesday Book', *DCNQ*, 12 (1922–3), 57, 137. See **1511**.

1518 ROWE, J.H., 'The hundreds of Cornwall', *DCNQ*, 12 (1922–3), 325–6.

1519 SALZMAN, L.F., 'The Domesday Survey for Cornwall. Introduction', in *VCH Cornwall*, 2, pt 8, ed. W.Page (London: St Catherine Press, 1924), 45–59.

1520 TAYLOR, T., 'The Domesday survey for Cornwall. Translation of the text', in *VCH Cornwall*, 2, pt 8, 61–103.

1521 DEXTER, T.F.G., *Cornish names* (London: Longmans, 1926. Reprinted, Truro: D.Bradford Burton, 1968). DB place-name forms given alongside some others.

1522 GOVER, J.E.B., 'Cornish place-names', *Antiquity*, 2 (1928), 319–27.

1523 ALEXANDER, J.J., 'The Devon-Cornwall boundary', *DCNQ*, 15 (1929), 270–4.

1524 HENDERSON, C., 'The cult of S. Pieran or Perran and S. Keverne in Cornwall', in G.H.Doble, *Saint Perran, Saint Keverne and Saint Kerrian*, Cornish Saints series, no. 29 (Long Compton: The 'King's Stone' Press, 1931), 36–68. See pp. 38–9 for a suggested identification of *Tregrebri*. See further **420**.

1525 ALEXANDER, J.J., 'The hundreds of Cornwall', *DCNQ*, 18 (1934–5), 177–82.

1526 ADAMS, J.H., 'Landelech in Domesday', *DCNQ*, 18 (1934–5), 196–8. Identifies with Landulph on the basis of arguments by C.Henderson in *Truro Diocesan Gazette* (June 1929) (not traced).

1527 HENDERSON, C., 'A note on the hundreds of Power and Pyder', in C. Henderson, *Essays in Cornish history*, ed. A. L. Rowse & M. I. Henderson (Oxford: Clarendon Press, 1935), 108–24.

1528 PICKEN, W. M. M., 'Domesday Book and east Cornwall', *Old Cornwall*, 2 (1936), 24–7.

1529 GOVER, J. E. B., 'The element *Ros* in Cornish place-names', *London medieval studies*, 1, pt 2 (1938), 249–64. Lists the relevant DB names and identifies *Rosminuet*.

1530 POUNDS, N. J. G., 'The Domesday geography of Cornwall', *Annual report of the Royal Cornwall Polytechnic Society*, 109 (1942), 68–81.

1531 POUNDS, N. J. G., 'The identification of the Domesday manors of Cornwall', *Old Cornwall*, 3 (1942), 458–63.

1532 POUNDS, N. J. G., 'The ancient woodland of Cornwall', *Old Cornwall*, 3 (1942), 523–8. Contains a map of places with DB woodland.

1533 FINBERG, H. P. R., 'A Domesday identification', *DCNQ*, 22 (1942–6), 95. For *Heli* in DB and *Elent* in *Terrae occupatae*.

1534 FINBERG, H. P. R., 'The early history of Werrington', *EHR*, 59 (1944), 237–51. Subsequently revised as 'The making of a boundary', in W. G. Hoskins & H. P. R. Finberg (eds), *Devonshire studies* (London: Jonathan Cape, 1952), 19–39. This revision reprinted in H. P. R. Finberg, *Lucerna* (London: Macmillan, 1964), 204–21. For the DB survey and the boundary between Cornwall and Devon.

1535 BEST, W. S., 'Notes on the church lands in the Domesday survey of Cornwall', *Old Cornwall*, 4 (1946), 148–51.

1536 FINBERG, H. P. R., 'Childe's tomb', *RTDA*, 78 (1946), 265–80. For the DB manor of Antony.

1537 VIVIAN, S., 'The Domesday geography of Cornwall', *Annual report of the Royal Cornwall Polytechnic Society*, 113 (1946), 27–32.

1538 PICKEN, W. M. N., 'Charaton and Penhawger', *DCNQ*, 23 (1948), 202–5.

1539 FINBERG, H. P. R., 'The castle of Cornwall', *DCNQ*, 23 (1949), 123. Identified with Launceston castle.

1540 BALCHIN, W. G. V., *Cornwall: a history of the landscape* (London: Hodder & Stoughton, 1954).

1541 HENDERSON, C., 'The 109 ancient parishes of the four western hundreds of Cornwall' and 'The ecclesiastical history of the 109 western parishes of Cornwall', *JRIC*, ns, 2, pt 3 (1955), 1–210.

1542 HENDERSON, C., 'The ecclesiastical antiquities of the 109 parishes of West Cornwall', *JRIC*, ns, 3, pt 2 (1958), 211–382; 3, pt 4 (1960), 383–497.

1543 THOMAS, C., 'Settlement history in early Cornwall. I. The antiquity of the hundreds', *Cornish Archaeology*, 3 (1964), 70–9.

1544 FINBERG, H. P. R., 'Boiton, Elent, Trebican, Trewant', *DCNQ*, 22 (1965), 95.

1545 PICKEN, W. M. M., 'The names of the hundreds of Cornwall', *DCNQ*, 30 (1965–7), 36–40.

1546 MATTHEW, D. J. A., 'Mont Saint-Michel and England', in Dom. J. Laporte (ed.), *Millenaire monastique du Mont Saint-Michel, 1, histoire et vie monastique* (Paris: Lethielleux, 1966), 677–700.

1547 HULL, P. L., 'The foundation of St Michael's Mount in Cornwall, a priory of Mont St-Michel', in Dom. J. Laporte (ed.), *Millenaire monastique du Mont St-Michel, 1, histoire et vie monastique* (Paris: Lethielleux, 1966), 703–24. For St Michael's Mount in DB. Cf. **1510**.

1548 WITHERICK, M. E., 'The medieval boroughs of Cornwall – an alternative view of their origins', Southampton Research Series in Geography, 4 (1967), 41–60. Argues that the form of Cornwall DB conceals the presence of settlements which became towns.

1549 PICKEN, W. M. M., 'The manor of Tremaruustel and the honour of St Keus', *JRIC*, ns, 7, pt 3 (1975–6), 220–30. Identifies *Tremaruustel* and *honor S. Chei* of Exon. Accepted by **1552**. Cf. **1520, 420**.

1550 SOULSBY, I. N., 'Richard fitz Turold, lord of Penhallam Cornwall', *MA*, 20 (1976), 146–8.

1551 DITMAS, E. M. R., 'Breton settlers in Cornwall after the Norman Conquest', *Trans. Hon. Soc. Cymmrodorion* (1977), 11–39.

1552 THORN, C. & F., *Domesday Book. 10. Cornwall* (Chichester: Phillimore, 1979). Valuable notes on place-name identifications, hundreds, Exon DB, with tabulated details of lordship. For additions and corrections, **2838, 4523**.

1553 POOL, P. A. S., 'The tithings of Cornwall', *JRIC*, ns, 8 (1981), 275–337. The tithings and the DB manors discussed and presented in tabular form.

DERBYSHIRE

Stenton's famous studies of the Danelaw are important for Derbys. DB, **241, 256**. So also are the numerous works on the Burton abbey surveys, **196, 225, 251, 405, 436, 3825**. For the relevant section of the *DB Geography*, **369**. For statistical tables of villeins and sokemen in Derbys. DB, **236**. For the suggestion that falls in values of estates reflect the Conqueror's devastation of the N.W. Midlands, **281**. And for the identification of the sub-tenant at Boyleston, see **1109**.

1601 BAWDWEN, W., *Dom. Boc. A translation of the record called Domesday, so far as relates to the county of York, including also Amounderness, Lonsdale, and Furness, in Lancashire; and such parts of Westmoreland and Cumberland as are contained in the survey. Also the counties of Derby, Nottingham, Rutland, and Lincoln, with an introduction, glossary and indexes* (Doncaster: Sheardown, 1809). See also **1201**.

1602 JAMES, H. (director), *Domesday Book: or the great survey of England of William the Conqueror, A.D. MLXXXVI. Facsimile of the part relating to Derbyshire* (Southampton: Ordnance Survey Office, 1862). Photozincographic edition.

1603 JEWITT, L. F. W., *Domesday Book of Derbyshire. Temp. William the Conqueror, 1068; extended latin text; and the literal translation* (London: Bemrose & Sons, 1871).

1604 DAVIS, F., 'The etymology of some Derbyshire place-names', *JDANHS*, 2 (1880), 33–71. Lists and identifies Derbys. DB place-names. Follows **1603** in most cases and is not especially helpful. Cf. **1607**.

1605 YEATMAN, J. P., SITWELL, G. R. & FOLJAMBE, C. J. S., *The feudal history of the county of Derby*, 6 vols (London: Bemrose & Sons, 1886–1907). Vol. 1 contains the DB text, with a translation and introduction. See **1611**.

1606 YEATMAN, J. P., *The Domesday Book for the county of Derby* (London: Bemrose & Sons, 1886). Reprinted from **1605**. Not in general a very reliable work.

1607 BARBER, H., 'Etymologies of Derbyshire place-names', *JDANHS*, 19 (1897), 53–79. Gives DB place-names and indentifications.

1608 BRYAN, B., 'The lost manor of Metesforde', *JDANHS*, 23 (1901), 77–82. Suggests, against **1603**, that *Metesforde* should be identified with the neighbourhood of Matlock Bridge.

1609 STENTON, F. M., 'Introduction to the Derbyshire Domesday', in *VCH Derbys.*, 1, ed. W. Page (London: Constable, 1905), 293–326.

1610 STENTON, F.M., 'Text of the Derbyshire Domesday', *VCH Derbys.*, 1, 327–55.

1611 ROUND, J.H., 'The origin of the Shirleys and of the Gresleys', *JDANHS*, 27 (1905), 151–84. Corrects **1605**. The under-tenant of the later Gresley lands was Nigel de Stafford, not Nigel d'Aubigny. See **2713**.

1612 WALKER, B., 'The place-names of Derbyshire', *JDANHS*, 36 (1914), 123–284; 37 (1915), 97–244. A useful study, but omitted many DB names and failed to identify some place-names. See **1616, 1619**.

1613 STATHAM, S.P.H., 'Notes on the Domesday tenants and under-tenants in Derbyshire', *JDANHS*, ns, 1 (1924–5), 152–99. Important.

1614 STATHAM, S.P.H., 'The family of Duckmanton', *JDANHS*, ns, 1 (1924–5), 201–5. Suggests that Geoffrey Ridel was the under-tenant of Ralph fitz Hubert at Duckmanton. See also **1613**.

1615 STATHAM, S.P.H., 'Later descendants of Domesday holders of land in Derbyshire', *JDANHS*, ns, 2 (1926–7), 51–106, 233–328; 3 (1928–9), 48–70.

1616 WILLIAMSON, F., 'Notes on Walker's place-names of Derbyshire', *JDANHS*, ns, 2 (1926–7), 143–98; ns, 3 (1928–9), 1–47. Important. The first serious attempt to identify many of the DB place-names.

1617 STATHAM, S.P.H., 'Later descendants of Domesday tenants in Derbyshire', *JDANHS*, ns, 5 (1931), 27–56.

1618 CARTER, W.F. & WILKINSON, R.F., 'Notes on the family of Lisures', *YAJ*, 35 (1943), 183–200. For the DB holdings of Fulk de Lisours in Derbys., Notts. and Yorks.

1619 CAMERON, K., *The place-names of Derbyshire*, 3 vols, EPNS, 27–9 (Cambridge UP, 1959).

1620 FULLER, G.J., 'Early lead smelting in the Peak District: another look at the evidence', *The East Midland Geographer*, 5 (1970), 1–8. Also printed in R.H. Osborne *et al*, *Geographical essays in honour of K.C. Edwards* (University of Nottingham, 1970), 1–8. Suggests that *plumbaria* should be translated as 'smelting works'.

1621 HALL, R.A., 'The pre-Conquest burgh of Derby', *Derbys. Arch. Jour.*, 94 (1974), 16–23. Some comment on the Derby DB entry.

1622 TURBUTT, G., 'Court Rolls and other papers of the manor of Stretton', *Derbys. Arch. Jour.*, 95 (1975), 12–36.

1623 CAMERON, K., 'Scandinavian settlement in the territory of the Five Boroughs: I, the place-name evidence; II, place-names in thorp; III, the Grimston-hybrids', in K. Cameron (ed.), *Place-name evidence for the Anglo-Saxon invasion and Scandinavian settlements* (EPNS, 1977), 115–71. For discussion and maps of DB place-names.

1624 JENSEN, G. F., *Scandinavian settlement names in the East Midlands* (Copenhagen: I Kommission hos Akademisk Forlag, 1978).

1625 MORGAN, P. (ed., from a draft translation by S. Wood), *Domesday Book. 27. Derbyshire* (Chichester: Phillimore, 1978).

1626 HART, C. R., *The north Derbyshire archaeological survey to A.D. 1500* (Chesterfield: The North Derbyshire Archaeological Trust, 1981). Contains material on settlement which is valuable for DB interpretation and two DB maps.

1627 CROOK, D., 'The establishment of the Derbyshire county court, 1256', *Derbys. Arch. Jour.*, 103 (1983), 98–106. Confirms DB on Derbys. and Notts. sharing a shire court.

DEVON

All work on Devon DB must take account of the numerous publications on Exon DB, of which see especially **383**. For the relevant section of the *DB Geography*, **396**. Material from Devon DB was used in a general article on DB by Pollock, **190**. For revenues deriving from the hundreds, **252, 263**. On woodland in Devon DB, **289**, and on plough-teams, **311, 327**. There are two discussions of the DB inquest and changes in the Cornwall-Devon boundary, **1523, 1534**. For villeins on comital manors, **257**. For 'the castle of Cornwall' (Launceston) which appears in Devon DB, **1539**. The Phillimore edition of Devon DB had not appeared when this bibliography was passed to the publishers.

1701 JAMES, H. (director), *Domesday Book: or the great survey of England of William the Conqueror, A.D. MLXXXVI. Facsimile of the part relating to Devonshire* (Southampton: Ordnance Survey Office, 1862). Photozincographic facsimile.

1702 DAVIDSON, J. B., 'Remarks on old Teign bridge', *RTDA*, 16 (1884), 444–52. For DB evidence for bridges.

1703 WORTH, R. N., 'President's address at the opening of the session 1882–83', *Annual reports and trans. of the Plymouth Institution and Devon & Cornwall Nat. Hist. Soc.*, 8 (1884), 181–220 + 2 tables. An attempt to survey the DB evidence for pre-1066 Devon.

1704 AMERY, J.S. *et al*, *The Devonshire Domesday and Geld Inquest* (Plymouth: Brendon & Son, for the Devonshire Assoc., 1884–92). Exch. and Exon. texts and translations given on opposite pages. For critical comment and omissions, see **1706, 197**.

1705 PENGELLY, W., 'Notes on slips connected with Devonshire. Part VIII. Clovelly and Domesday Book', *RTDA*, 17 (1885), 313–16.

1706 PHEAR, J.B., 'On the Association's English version of the Devonshire Domesday', *RTDA*, 25 (1893), 229–308. See **1704**.

1707 WORTH, R.N., 'The identifications of the Domesday manors of Devon', *RTDA*, 25 (1893), 309–42.

1708 REICHEL, O.J., 'Some suggestions to aid in identifying the place-names in Devonshire Domesday', *RTDA*, 26 (1894), 133–67. Issued separately (nd, ?1894).

1709 REICHEL, O.J., 'The Leuca or Lug of Domesday', *RTDA*, 26 (1894), 308–12. Issued separately (nd, ?1894).

1710 REICHEL, O.J., 'The hundred of Hartland and the Geld Roll', *RTDA*, 26 (1894), 416–18. Issued separately (nd, ?1894).

1711 REICHEL, O.J., 'The Devonshire Domesday. II. The Devonshire Domesday and Geld Roll; III Berry Pomeroy and Stockleigh Pomeroy. A contribution to the economic history of the cultivating classes in "Domesday"; IV. The "Domesday" churches of Devon; V. The hundreds of Devon; VI. "Domesday" identifications. Part I', *RTDA*, 27 (1895), 165–98; 28 (1896), 362–90; 30 (1898), 258–315; 33 (1901), 554–602, 603–39; 34 (1902), 715–31. Issued in one volume (nd, ?1902).

1712 ROUND, J.H., 'The Conqueror at Exeter', in J.H.Round, *Feudal England* (London: Swan Sonnenschein, 1895; 2nd edn, London: Allen & Unwin, 1964), 431–55 (1st edn) and 330–46 (2nd edn). For Exeter in DB. Cf. **115**.

1713 WORTH, R.N., 'Domesday identifications – the hundreds', *RTDA*, 27 (1895), 374–403.

1714 AMERY, P.F.S., 'A tangle in the history of Ashburton', *RTDA*, 28 (1896), 209–27. For *Aisbertona* and *Essebretona* in Exon. See **1782**.

1715 REICHEL, O.J., 'The "Domesday" hundreds. II The hundred of Listone. V. The hundred of Teignbridge. III. The hundred of North Tawton. VI. The hundred of Witheridge. VII & VIII. The hundreds of Bampton and Ufculm', *RTDA*, 28 (1896), 464–93; 29 (1897), 225–74; 30 (1898), 391–457. Issued in one volume (nd, ?1898).

1716 WHALE, T.W., 'Exchequer tax books and Domesday identification', *RTDA*, 29 (1897), 216–24.

1717 WHALE, T.W., 'Principles of the "Domesday" survey and "Feudal Aids" ', *RTDA*, 32 (1900), 521–51.

1718 CHOPE, R.P., 'The early history of the manor of Hartland', *RTDA*, 34 (1902), 418–54.

1719 WHALE, T.W., 'Analysis of the Exon. "Domesday" in hundreds', *RTDA*, 35 (1903), 662–712; 36 (1904), 156–72. See **1720** for criticisms.

1720 REICHEL, O.J., 'Some doubtful and disputed "Domesday" identifications', *RTDA*, 36 (1904), 347–79. Issued separately (nd, ?1904). Cf. **1719**.

1721 REICHEL, O.J., 'Walter de Douai's Domesday fief', *Devon N&Q*, 3 (1904–5), 206–7.

1722 REICHEL, O.J., 'Introduction to the Devonshire Domesday', in *VCH Devon*, 1, ed. W. Page (London: Constable, 1906), 375–402.

1723 REICHEL, O.J., 'Translation of the Devonshire Domesday', *VCH Devon*, 1, 403–549. Used Exon collated with Exch. DB.

1724 REICHEL, O.J., 'Feudal baronage', *VCH Devon*, 1, 551–72.

1725 BURNARD, R., 'The ancient population of the forest of Dartmoor', *RTDA*, 39 (1907), 198–207. See pp. 201–7 for DB population.

1726 REICHEL, O.J., 'The hundred of Haytor in the time of "Testa de Nevil", A.D. 1244', *RTDA*, 40 (1908), 110–36. Issued separately (nd, ?1908). See for DB estates.

1727 REICHEL, O.J., 'The hundreds of Devon. XI. Materials for the hundred of Hairidge in early times', *RTDA*, 42 (1910), 215–57. Issued separately (nd, ?1910).

1728 REICHEL, O.J., 'The hundreds of Devon. XII. The early history of the hundred of Colridge', *RTDA*, 43 (1911), 190–236.

1729 REICHEL, O.J., 'The hundreds of Devon. XIII. The Domesday hundred of Wenford or Wonford', *RTDA*, 44 (1912), 278–311. Issued separately with **1731** (1912).

1730 REICHEL, O.J., 'Early descents of the manors in Wonford hundred', *RTDA*, 44 (1912), 312–42.

1731 REICHEL, O.J., 'The hundreds of Devon. XIV. The hundred of South Tawton in early times', *RTDA*, 44 (1912), 343–65. See **1729**.

1732 REICHEL, O.J., 'The hundreds of Devon. XV. The hundred of Stanborough or Dippeforda in the time of Testa de Nevil, A.D. 1243', *RTDA*, 45 (1913), 169–218. Issued separately (nd, ?1913).

1733 REICHEL, O.J., 'The hundred of Lifton in the time of Testa de Nevil, A.D. 1243', *RTDA*, 46 (1914), 185–219, 238–55. Issued separately with **1734** (nd, ?1914).

1734 REICHEL, O.J., 'The hundred of Tavistock in early times', *RTDA*, 46 (1914), 220–37, 242–55. See **1733**.

1735 REICHEL, O.J., 'The hundred of Exminster in early times', *RTDA*, 47 (1915), 194–209, 237–47. Issued separately with **1736** (1915).

1736 REICHEL, O.J., 'The early history of the principal manors in Exminster hundred', *RTDA*, 47 (1915), 210–47. See **1735**.

1737 REICHEL, O.J., 'Barnstaple and its three sub-manors, part of the inland hundred of Braunton', *RTDA*, 49 (1917), 376–88. Issued separately (nd, ?1917). Cf. **1740**.

1738 CHANTER, J.F., 'Devonshire place-names. Part I. The parishes', *RTDA*, 50 (1918), 503–32. Superseded by **1753**.

1739 WATKIN, H.R., 'Dittisham parish and church', *RTDA*, 50 (1918), 37–50. For the identification of a sub-tenant.

1740 ROUND, J.H., 'The *tertius dernarius* of a borough', *EHR*, 34 (1919), 62–4. For DB Barnstaple. Cf. **1737**.

1741 REICHEL, O.J., 'The manor and hundred of Crediton', *RTDA*, 54 (1923), 146–81.

1742 ALEXANDER, J.J., 'An Irish invasion of Devon', *RTDA*, 55 (1924), 125–30. DB values and the invasions of 1068 and 1069.

1743 PRIDEAUX, F.B., '*Alfelmestone* manor', *DCNQ*, 14 (1926–7), 300–4. Not Yealmpstone, but Traine in Wembury. See also **1791**.

1744 ALEXANDER, J.J. 'The early boroughs of Devon', *RTDA*, 58 (1927), 275–87.

1745 CHOPE, R.P., 'Hartland abbey', *RTDA*, 58 (1927), 49–112. See pp. 53–4 for DB holding of Gerald the chaplain.

1746 TAPLEY-SOPER, H., 'Thirteenth report on manuscripts and records existing in, or relating to Devonshire', *RTDA*, 59 (1927), 173–95. For the papers of O.J. Reichel.

1747 CARTER, G.E.L., 'History of the hundred in Devon', *RTDA*, 60 (1928), 313–28.

1748 REICHEL, O.J., *The hundred of Tiverton in early times*, ed. F.B. Prideaux, Supplements to the Trans. Devonshire Assoc., 1 (1928), 1–31.

1749 BLOMÉ, B., *The place-names of northern Devonshire* (Uppsala: Applebergs Boktryckeri Aktiebolag, 1929). See **1753**.

1750 REICHEL, O.J., *The hundreds of Hemyock and Halberton in early times*, ed. F.B. Prideaux, Supplements to the Trans. Devonshire Assoc., 2 (1929), 35–63.

1751 REICHEL, O.J., *The hundreds of South Molton and Roborough in early times*, ed. F.B. Prideaux, Supplements to the Trans. Devonshire Assoc., 3 (1930), 65–132.

1752 ALEXANDER, J.J., 'The beginnings of Lifton', *RTDA*, 63 (1931), 349–58.

1753 GOVER, J.E.B., MAWER, A. & STENTON, F.M., *The place-names of Devon*, 2 vols, EPNS, 8–9 (Cambridge UP, 1931–2). Addenda and corrigenda printed in *DCNQ*, 18 (1934–5), 127–30.

1754 REICHEL, O.J., *The hundreds of Axminster and Axmouth in early times*, ed. F.B. Prideaux, Supplements to the Trans. Devonshire Assoc., 4 (1931), 133–85.

1755 ALEXANDER, J.J., 'The Saxon conquest and settlement', *RTDA*, 64 (1932), 75–112. See p. 94 for comments on the relationship of DB place-names to early settlement.

1756 REICHEL, O.J., *The hundred of Black Torrington in early times*, ed. F.B. Prideaux, Supplements to the Trans. Devonshire Assoc., 5 (1932), 187–243.

1757 CARTER, G.E.L., 'Anglo-Saxon Devon. 1. The early boroughs of Devon', *RTDA*, 64 (1932), 519–38.

1758 SCANES, J., 'The Pomeroys of Berry Pomeroy', *RTDA*, 64 (1932), 257–71.

1759 REICHEL, O.J., *The hundreds of Plympton and Ermington in early times*, ed. F.B. Prideaux, Supplements to the Trans. Devonshire Assoc., 6 (1933), 245–332.

1760 REICHEL, O.J., *The hundred of Colyton and Clyston in early times*, ed. F.B. Prideaux, Supplements to the Trans. Devonshire Assoc., 7 (1934), 333–85.

1761 REICHEL, O.J., *The hundreds of Braunton, Shirwell and Fremington in early times*, ed. F.B. Prideaux, Supplements to the Trans. Devonshire Assoc., 8 (1935), 387–520.

1762 REICHEL, O.J., *The one-time hundreds of North Molton and Molland in early times*, ed. F.B. Prideaux, Supplements to the Trans. Devonshire Assoc., 9 (1936), 521–31.

1763 ROSE-TROUP, F., 'Newton St Cyres and Norton', *RTDA*, 68 (1936), 221–31.

1764 SPIEGELHALTER, C., 'Surnames of Devon. Part I', *RTDA*, 68 (1936), 397–410. See pp. 398–9 for Exon.

1765 REICHEL, O.J., *The hundred of Shebbear in early times*, ed. W.H. Rogers, Supplement to the Trans. Devonshire Assoc., 10 (1938), 533–84.

1766 ALEXANDER, J.J., 'Tenth report on early history. II. The hundreds of Devon', *RTDA*, 71 (1939), 117–24.

1767 REICHEL, O.J., 'The church and the hundreds in Devon', *RTDA*, 71 (1939), 331–42. A criticism of **247**.

1768 MORGAN, F.W., 'The Domesday geography of Devon', *RTDA*, 72 (1940), 305–31.

1769 ALEXANDER, J.J., 'Early barons of Torrington and Barnstaple', *RTDA*, 73 (1941), 153–79.

1770 REICHEL, O.J., *Index of personal and place names in the 'hundreds of Devon' contributed to the Transactions of the Association*, ed. J.J. Alexander, W.H. Rogers & H. Tapley-Soper (Plymouth: Devonshire Association, 1942).

1771 FINBERG, H.P.R., 'Ancient demesne in Devonshire', *DCNQ*, 22 (1942–6), 178–9. See mainly for the identification of *Tavestok* in an ancient demesne suit of 1279.

1772 FINBERG, H.P.R., 'Morwell', *RTDA*, 77 (1945), 157–71. For DB Tavistock.

1773 FINBERG, H. P. R., 'The Devon-Cornwall boundary', *DCNQ*, 23 (1947–9), 104–7. A summary of **1534**.

1774 FINBERG, H. P. R., 'The manor of Roborough', *DCNQ*, 23 (1947–9), 241. An addition to **1772**.

1775 NORRIS, C., 'Hard facts in the Domesday Book', *Buckfast Abbey chronicle*, 19 (1949), 79–84, 132–6. For Buckfast abbey in DB.

1776 ADAMS, E. A., 'Forests and forestry in Devon', *RTDA*, 82 (1950), 29–43.

1777 HOSKINS, W. G., 'A Domesday identification (Leigh Barton, Silverton)', *DCNQ*, 24 (1950–1), 111–12.

1778 FINBERG, H. P. R., *Tavistock Abbey* (Cambridge UP, 1951; 2nd edn, Newton Abbot: David & Charles, 1969).

1779 FINBERG, H. P. R., 'Uffculme', in W. G. Hoskins & H. P. R. Finberg (eds), *Devonshire studies* (London: Jonathan Cape, 1952), 59–77. Reprinted in H. P. R. Finberg, *Lucerna* (London: Macmillan, 1964), 204–21.

1780 MARTIN, W. K., 'A short history of Coffinswell', *RTDA*, 87 (1955), 165–90. For DB *Willa*.

1781 FINN, R. W., 'The making of the Devonshire Domesdays', *RTDA*, 89 (1957), 93–123. Of general significance for the making of DB.

1782 HANHAM, H. J., 'A tangle untangled: the lordship of the manor and borough of Ashburton', *RTDA*, 94 (1962), 440–57. For *Aisbertona* and *Essebretona* in Exon. Cf. **1714**.

1783 LINEHAN, C. D., 'A forgotten manor in Widecombe-in-the-Moor', *RTDA*, 94 (1962), 463–92. Identifies *Depdona* with Jordan in Widecombe-in-the-Moor.

1784 FRENCH, H. & LINEHAN, C. D., 'Abandoned medieval sites in Widecombe-in-the-Moor', *RTDA*, 95 (1963), 168–79. Identifies *Blackeslac* (Exon) and *Blackestach* (Exch.) with Blackslade Manor in Dunstone.

1785 HOSKINS, W. G., 'The highland zone in Domesday Book', in W. G. Hoskins (ed.), *Provincial England: essays in social and economic history* (London: Macmillan, 1964), 15–52. An important discussion of the topography of Devon DB, demonstrating the considerable number of separate settlements, including isolated farms, recorded therein.

1786 WALKER, H.H., 'Some medieval demesne boundaries in Torquay', *RTDA*, 97 (1965), 194–211.

1787 LINEHAN, C.D., 'Deserted sites and rabbit-warrens on Dartmoor, Devon', *MA*, 10 (1966), 113–44.

1788 COCKS, J.V.S., 'Dartmoor and Domesday Book', *DCNQ*, 30 (1965–7), 290–3.

1789 ANNETT, N., 'North Molton: the pre-census population', *RTDA*, 108 (1976), 69–125.

1790 PHILLIPS, M.C. & WILSON, R.E., 'Water mills in East Devon', *DCNQ*, 33 (1977), 13–17, 51–6, 80–4, 126–30, 170–5, 262–4, 304–6; 34 (1977–81), 32–6, 75–80, 113–19, 139–44.

1791 ROWLAND, R.C., 'Traine Farm, Wembury, Devonshire', *Jour. EPNS*, 10 (1977–8), 40. For *Alfelmestone*. A correction to **1753, 420**. See also **1743**.

1792 BERESFORD, G., with contributions by P.Brandon & C.D. Linehan, 'Three deserted medieval settlements on Dartmoor: a report on the late E.Marie Minter's excavations', *MA*, 23 (1979), 98–158.

DORSET

All work on Dorset DB must take account of the numerous publications devoted to Exon DB, of which see especially **383**. For the relevant sections of the *DB Geography*, **396**. For woodland, **289**, and for villeins on comital manors, **257**.

1901 HUTCHINS, J., *History and antiquities of the county of Dorset ... with a copy of Domesday Book, and the Inquisitio Gheldi for the County*, 2 vols (London: W.Bowyer & J.Nichols, 1774. 2nd edn, ed. R.Gough and J.B.Nichols, 4 vols, London: J.Nichols, 1796–1815. 3rd edn, ed. W.Shipp and J.W.Hodson, 4 vols, Westminster: J.Nichols, 1861–73). 1st edn contained a Latin text of DB and the *Inquisitio*, together with an introduction. Vol.4 of 2nd edn added a translation by Bawdwen which was removed in the 3rd edn.

1902 JAMES, H. (director), *Domesday Book: or the great survey of England of William the Conqueror, A.D. MLXXXVI. Facsimile of the part relating to Dorset* (Southampton: Ordnance Survey Office, 1862). Photozincographic edition.

1903 PLANCHÉ, J.R., 'On the family and connexions of Robert Fitzgerald, the Domesday tenant of Corfe', *JBAA*, 28 (1872), 113–22. Some comment on DB Corfe.

1904 EYTON, R. W., *A key to Domesday: an analysis and digest of the Dorset survey showing the method and exactitude of its mensuration, and the precise meaning of its more usual formulae. The subject being exemplified by an analysis and digest of the Dorset survey* (London & Dorchester: Taylor & Co., James Foster, 1878). A major study, although its ideas on DB measurements and many of its identifications are not now accepted.

1905 MOULE, H.J., 'Domesday return for Dorchester', *N&Q for Somerset and Dorset*, 2 (1891), 225.

1906 MOORE, M.F., 'The feudal aspect of the Domesday survey of Somerset and Dorset in connection with the Barony of Moiun (Dunster castle) and other analogous feudal estates', *BIHR*, 9 (1932), 49–52.

1907 FÄGERSTEN, A., *The place-names of Dorset* (Uppsala: Lundequistska Bokhandeln, 1933. Reprinted East Ardsley: E.P. Publishing, 1978). Superseded by **1918**.

1908 ARKELL, W.J., 'Some topographical names in south Dorset', *PDNHAS*, 62 (1940), 39–49.

1909 ARKELL, W.J., 'Further notes on topographical names in South Dorset', *PDNHAS*, 63 (1941), 33–40.

1910 DREW, C.D., 'The manors of the Iwerne Valley, Dorset. A study of early country planning', *PDNHAS*, 69 (1947), 45–50. An attempt to trace the bounds of DB manors.

1911 FINN, R.W., 'The making of the Dorset Domesday', *PDNHAS*, 81 (1959), 150–7.

1912 DEWAR, H.S.L., 'The windmills, watermills and horse-mills of Dorset', *PDNHAS*, 82 (1961), 109–32. Includes a list and map of DB watermills.

1913 TAYLOR, C.C., 'The pattern of medieval settlement in the forest of Blackmoor', *PDNHAS*, 87 (1965), 251–4.

1914 TAYLOR, C.C., 'Lost Dorset place-names', *PDNHAS*, 88 (1966), 207–15. Discussion of several DB holdings.

1915 WILLIAMS, A., 'Introduction to the Dorset Domesday' and 'Introduction to the Dorset Geld Rolls', in *VCH Dorset*, 3, ed. R.B. Pugh (Oxford UP, for the Institute of Historical Research, 1968), 1–60, 115–23.

1916 WILLIAMS, A., 'Translation of the text of the Dorset Domesday', 'Text and translation of the Dorset Geld Rolls', and

'Summaries of fiefs in Exon Domesday', *VCH Dorset*, 3, 61–114, 124–48, 148–9.

1917 TAYLOR, C., *The making of the English landscape: Dorset* (London: Hodder & Stoughton, 1970; repr., 1975).

1918 MILLS, A.D., *The place-names of Dorset*, 2 vols, EPNS, 52–3 (Cambridge UP, 1977–80). In progress. Two more volumes expected.

1919 GOOD, R., *The lost villages of Dorset* (Wimborne: Dovecote Press, 1979).

1920 THORN, C. & F. (ed., from a draft translation by M.Newman), *Domesday Book. 7. Dorset* (Chichester: Phillimore, 1983).

1921 BARKER, K., 'Sherborne in Dorset: an early ecclesiastical settlement and its estate', in S.C.Hawkes, J.Campbell & D.Brown (eds), *Anglo-Saxon studies in archaeology and history*, 3 (Oxford: Oxford University Committee for Archaeology, 1984), 1–34.

ESSEX

For a comprehensive and valuable discussion of the Little DB counties, see **397**. For IE and Essex, see **1005, 331, 1321**, as well as the studies mentioned below. For an early and entirely superseded study of the place-names of Essex DB, **1303**. Vinogradoff compiled statistical tables of Essex villeins and sokemen, **236**. For revenues deriving from the hundreds, **270**, and for commendation, **316**. For the relevant section of the *DB Geography*, **332**. For a study of J.H.Round's work on DB Essex, see **452** in addition to **2068** below. There are several studies of the estates of Essex landholders who also held in other counties. For Lisois de Moustiers and the descent of his lands to Eudo *dapifer*, **1005**; for Edith the Fair, **1204**, for the archbishopric of Canterbury, **1212**, for Westminster abbey, **1027**, and for the family of earl Godwine, **461**.

2001 MORANT, P., *The history and antiquities of the county of Essex*, 2 vols (London: T.Osborne, J.Whiston, S.Baker, L.Davis, C.Reymers, 1768). Attempted to identify many DB places and landholders. Very erratic, but of considerable importance.

2002 GURNEY, D., *The record of the house of Gournay* (London: Nichols & Nichols, 1848). For the DB estates of the Gournai family in Essex and Somerset.

2003 JAMES, H., *Domesday Book: or the great survey of England of William the Conqueror, A.D. MLXXXVI. Facsimile of the part relating to Essex* (Southampton: Ordnance Survey Office, 1862). Photozincographic edition.

2004 CHISENHALE-MARSH, T.C., *Domesday Book relating to Essex* (Chelmsford: W.D.Burrell; London: Vacher & Son, 1864). A translation with place-name identifications and some notes. 'Of remarkable excellence for its date' (Round, **2014**).

2005 'A MEMBER OF THE SOCIETY', 'The early history of Stratford and the surrounding villages', *TEAS*, 2 (1864), 93–101.

2006 FRY, Miss, 'Some account of Suene of Essex, his family and estates', *TEAS*, 5 (1873), 101–15.

2007 FRY, Miss, 'Some account of Robert Gernon and his successors, the barons Montfichet', *TEAS*, 5 (1873), 173–207.

2008 ROUND, J.H., 'The Domesday of Colchester', *The Antiquary*, 5 (1882), 244–50; 6 (1882), 5–9, 95–100, 251–6.

2009 FENTON, J., 'The Domesday of Colchester', *The Antiquary*, 6 (1882), 37–8.

2010 WALLER, W.C., 'Essex Domesday', *N&Q*, 7th ser., 10 (1890), 484. Identifies *Alvertuna* with Alderton and *Tippedena* with Debden in Laughton. Confirms **2004**.

2011 ROUND, J.H., 'Pleshy', *TEAS*, ns, 5 (1895), 83–6. Corrects Morant's identification of *Plesinchou*. See **2001, 2010, 2019, 2030**.

2012 ROUND, J.H., 'The honour of Ongar', *TEAS*, ns, 7 (1900), 142–52.

2013 ROUND, J.H., 'Essex vineyards in Domesday', *TEAS*, ns, 7 (1900), 249–51. See **337** for criticism.

2014 ROUND, J.H., 'Introduction to the Essex Domesday', in *VCH Essex*, 1, ed. W.Page (Westminster: Constable, 1903), 333–426. The greatest of Round's VCH introductions.

2015 ROUND, J.H., 'Text of the Essex Domesday', *VCH Essex*, 1, 427–578.

2016 ROUND, J.H., 'The Colchester mint in Norman times', *EHR*, 18 (1903), 305–15. A critique of **211** and its treatment of DB, based on local evidence.

2017 ROUND, J.H., 'Helion of Helion's Bumpstead', *TEAS*, ns, 8 (1903), 187–91. The DB holding of Tihel de Helléan.

2018 ROUND, J.H., 'The manor of Colne Engaine', *TEAS*, ns, 8 (1903), 192–8. The DB holding of Walter de Caen.

2019 ROUND, J.H., 'Wethersfield, Pleshey and "Plesingho" ', *TEAS*, ns, 8 (1903), 332–4. See **2011, 2030**.

2020 FOWLER, R.C., 'The "Curlai" of Domesday', *TEAS*, ns, 9 (1906), 415. Locates near Hoe Mill in Woodham Walter.

2021 ROUND, J.H., 'The Essex Sackvilles', *Arch. Jour.*, 64 (1907), 217–26. Reprinted (London: Harrison & Sons, nd). Identifies under-tenant at Great Braxted as Richard de Sauqueville.

2022 ROUND, J.H., 'Heydon and Great Chishall', *TEAS*, ns, 10 (1909), 348. Identifies *Haindena*.

2023 FOWLER, R.C., 'Blackmore and Fingrith', *TEAS*, ns, 11 (1911), 167.

2024 ROUND, J.H., 'Stow Maries', *TEAS*, ns, 11 (1911), 267. For DB *Fenne, Phenna, Eistanes, Haintuna*.

2025 ROUND, J.H., ' "Hobrige" and "Glasene" ', *TEAS*, ns, 11 (1911), 267–9.

2026 ROUND, J.H., 'The early lords of Shelley', *TEAS*, ns, 11 (1911), 362–5.

2027 RICKWORD, G., 'The kingdom of the East Saxons and the Tribal Hidage', *TEAS*, ns, 11 (1911), 246–65. An attempt to explain the DB hidage of Essex. Cf. **2031**.

2028 RICKWORD, G., 'The East Saxon kingdom', *TEAS*, ns, 12 (1913), 38–50. An attempt to work backwards from DB material.

2029 CHRISTY, Mrs A., 'The "ings" and "gings" of the Domesday survey especially Fryerning', *TEAS*, ns, 12 (1913), 94–100.

2030 WALLER, W.C., 'Plessingho: Plesynghow', *TEAS*, ns, 12 (1913), 352. Manages a closer location than **2019**.

2031 ROUND, J.H., 'The Domesday hidation of Essex', *EHR*, 29 (1914), 477–9. Critical of **2027**.

2032 ROUND, J.H., 'The "Haymesocne" in Colchester', *TEAS*, ns, 15 (1921), 77–81. Locates the DB holding of Haimo *dapifer* in Colchester.

2033 ROUND, J.H., 'Bradwell juxta mare', *TEAS*, ns, 16 (1923), 52–4. Identifies *Hacflet*.

2034 BEAUMONT, G.F., 'Domesday Book: Colne', *TEAS*, ns, 16 (1923), 55–6. Suggests a location for an anonymous holding of 22 acres in Colne, held by Turbern. This suggestion is not noted in **2069**.

2035 FOWLER, R.C., 'Utlesford hundred, east and west', *TEAS*, ns, 16 (1923), 183–6. Demonstrates details of division of Utlesford hundred. Suggests same may be true of Dengie hundred. This has implications for modern views on the making of DB, see **1326** at 15 note 2, and **364** at 158–9.

2036 REANEY, P.H., 'A survey of Essex place-names', *TEAS*, ns, 16 (1923), 251–7.

2037 FOWLER, R.C., 'Blacham', *TEAS*, ns, 17 (1926), 44.

2038 ROUND, J.H., 'The making of Brentwood', *TEAS*, ns, 17 (1926), 69–74. See p.72 for a DB sub-tenant.

2039 REANEY, P.H., 'The place-names of Rochford hundred', *Trans. Southend-on-Sea Ant. & Hist. Soc.*, 2 (1926–34), 103–12.

2040 FOWLER, R.C., 'Chelveston', *TEAS*, ns, 18 (1928), 68–9.

2041 FOWLER, R.C., 'Liffildewella', *TEAS*, ns, 18 (1928), 69. See **2050, 2069** for a more precise identification.

2042 CHRISTY, M., 'The Essex hundred-moots: an attempt to identify their meeting-places', *TEAS*, ns, 18 (1928), 172–97.

2043 REANEY, P.H., 'Thunreslau', *TEAS*, ns, 19 (1930), 63.

2044 REANEY, P.H., 'Essex place-name study', *TEAS*, ns, 19 (1930), 90–6.

2045 REANEY, P.H., 'Derleghe', *TEAS*, ns, 19 (1930), 133–4.

2046 LANDON, L., 'The barony of Little Easton and the family of Hastings', *TEAS*, ns, 19 (1930), 174–9. On the DB estates of Walter the deacon.

2047 WOOLRIDGE, S.W. & SMETHAM, D.J., 'The glacial drifts of Essex and Hertfordshire, and their bearing upon the agricultural and historical geography of the region', *Geog. Jour.*, 78 (1931), 243–69.

2048 ROUND, J.H., 'The Thurrocks', *TEAS*, ns, 20 (1933), 41–6.

2049 COLES, R., 'Past history of the forest of Essex', *Essex Naturalist*, 24 (1935), 115–33.

2050 REANEY, P.H., *The place-names of Essex*, EPNS, 12 (Cambridge UP, 1935).

2051 REANEY, P.H., 'Some identifications of Essex place-names', *TEAS*, ns, 21 (1937), 56–72.

2052 ROUND, J.H., 'The Horkesleys of Little Horkesley', *TEAS*, ns, 21 (1937), 284–91. For Godebold, DB tenant of Sweyn of Essex.

2053 RAIMES, A.L., 'The family of Reymes of Wherstead in Suffolk, with some notes on the descendants of Roger de Rames of 1086', *PSIANH*, 23 (1939), 89–115. For DB estates in Essex and Suffolk.

2054 FISHER, J.L., 'Thurstan, son of Wine', *TEAS*, ns, 22 (1940), 98–104. Discussion of a great Anglo-Saxon landowner's will and DB. His widow is identified in DB.

2055 LENNARD, R., 'The destruction of woodland in the eastern counties under William the Conqueror', *EcHR*, 15 (1945), 36–43. Cf. **3127, 3128**.

2056 REANEY, P.H., 'The face of Essex: a study in place-names', *Essex Review*, 58 (1949), 10–21.

2057 POWELL, W.R., 'The making of Essex parishes', *Essex Review*, 62 (1953), 6–18. Contains a list of Essex DB churches.

2058 REANEY, P.H., 'A Saxon land-owner of Essex birth', *TEAS*, ns, 25 (1955–60), 109–10. On Alwin *Godtuna*. Cf. **292, 295**.

2059 POWELL, W.R., 'The Essex fees of the honour of Richmond', *TEAS*, 3rd ser., 1 (1961–5), 179–89.

2060 FINN, R.W., 'The Essex entries in the *Inquisitio Eliensis*', *TEAS*, 3rd ser., 1 (1961–5), 190–5.

2061 CARTER, H.M., 'The manors of Tolleshunta', *TEAS*, 3rd ser., 1 (1961–5), 239–46. A complex problem of identification.

2062 HART, C., *The early charters of Essex: the Norman period*, Dept. of English Local History, Occasional papers, no. 11 (Leicester UP, 1957). For DB related material.

2063 FINN, R.W., 'Changes in the population of Essex 1066–1086', *TEAS*, 3rd ser., 4 (1972), 128–33.

2064 BOYDEN, P.B., 'Archaeological notes: *nemus de Eduluesnasa* in 1127', *TEAS*, 3rd ser., 4 (1972), 146–7. Demonstrates that DB *Aedulvesnasa* was included in the later parish of Kirby.

2065 LORAM, S., 'The Dengie hundred and the Domesday survey of 1086', *Burnham-on-Crouch and District Local History Society Bulletin*, 4 (1978), 8–12.

2066 ANON, 'Domesday Thurrock', *Panorama*, 23 (1980), 30–5.

2067 MORTIMER, R., 'The beginnings of the honour of Clare', in R. A. Brown (ed.), *Battle, 3 (1980)* (Woodbridge: Boydell, 1981), 119–41, 220–1. An important study of a DB fee, concentrating on Essex, Kent, Suffolk and Surrey. See also **2070**.

2068 POWELL, W. R., 'Norman Essex and its historian', *Essex Jour.*, 18 (1983), 26–38. A useful survey of Essex DB and an assessment of the work of J. H. Round. See also **452, 456**.

2069 RUMBLE, A. (ed., from a draft translation by J. Plaister & V. Sankaran), *Domesday Book. 32. Essex* (Chichester: Phillimore, 1983). Text, translation and notes. There are special notes on the hundreds and half-hundreds and an appendix on IE. For some criticisms, see P. B. Boyden in *TEAS*, 3rd ser., 15 (1983), 181–2.

2070 WARD, J. C., 'The place of the honour in twelfth-century society: the honour of Clare 1066–1217', *PSIANH*, 35 (1983), 191–202. For the Clare DB estates in Essex, Kent, Suffolk and Surrey. See also **2067**.

GLOUCESTERSHIRE

There is an early translation of Glos. DB by Bawdwen, **1201**, but as yet no VCH. For the relevant section of the *DB Geography*, **340**. On the hidation of Glos., see **203**. For the estates of Evesham abbey, see **281** in addition to the studies mentioned below. For the holdings in Glos. of Walter the Deacon, the Chocques ('de Cioches') family, the Lacy family and Westminster abbey, see **2046, 1024, 395, 1027**. For an estate in Glos. DB which is now in Worcs., **4507**.

2101 HALE, M., *The primitive organisation of mankind, considered and examined according to the light of nature* (London: William Godbid for William Shrewsbery, 1677). Made use of DB statistics from Glos. to demonstrate an increase in population in later times at pp. 236–7.

2102 RUDDER, S., *A new history of Gloucestershire* (Cirencester: the author, 1779). Contains a text of the DB folios for the county.

2103 JAMES, H. (director), *Domesday Book: or the great survey of England of William the Conqueror, A.D. MLXXXVI. Facsimile of the part relating to*

Gloucestershire (Southampton: Ordnance Survey Office, 1862). Photo-zincographic edition.

2104 FULLER, E.A., 'Tenures of land, by the customary tenants in Cirencester', *TBGAS*, 2 (1877–8), 285–319. Some discussion of DB for Cirencester and its relationship to the record of customs and services in the Cirencester cartulary of *c.* 1155.

2105 ELLIS, A.S., 'On the manorial history of Clifton', *TBGAS*, 3 (1878–9), 211–31. See also for Clifton-on-Teme (Worcs.) mentioned in the Westbury-on-Severn entry. See **2116**.

2106 ELLIS, A.S., 'On the landholders of Gloucestershire named in Domesday Book', *TBGAS*, 4 (1879–80), 86–198. Also printed as *Some account of the landholders of Gloucestershire named in Domesday Book, A.D. 1086* (privately printed, 1880). Of variable quality. A collection of material about the DB tenants.

2107 BARKLY, H., 'On an alleged instance of the fallibility of Domesday in regard to "ancient demesne" ', in P.E.Dove (ed.), *Domesday Studies: being the papers read at the meetings of the Domesday commemoration 1886*, 2 vols (London: Longmans, 1888–91), 471–83. Deals with Nympsfield and a supposed contradiction between charter evidence and DB.

2108 TAYLOR, C.S., *An analysis of the Domesday survey of Gloucestershire* (Bristol: C.T.Jeffries & Sons, for the Bristol & Gloucestershire Arch. Soc., 1889). A large-scale analysis of the contents of Glos. DB in the manner of Eyton's work on Dorset and Somerset. The treatment of statistics is not always reliable.

2109 TAYLOR, C.S., 'The pre-Domesday hide of Gloucestershire', *TBGAS*, 18 (1893–4), 288–319.

2110 HALL, A., 'Bibury', *N&Q*, 9th ser., 5 (1899), 384. Suggests identification of *Alvredintune* with Ablington in Bibury. But see **2141**.

2111 TAYLOR, C.S., 'Deerhurst, Pershore, and Westminster', *TBGAS*, 25 (1902), 230–50. Deals mainly with Deerhurst hundred.

2112 HARVEY, A., *Bristol: a historical and topographical account of the city* (London: Methuen, 1906). A brief discussion of the DB entry.

2113 TAYLOR, C.S., 'The northern boundary of Gloucestershire', *TBGAS*, 32 (1909), 109–39. Reprinted in shortened form in H.P.R. Finberg (ed.), *Gloucestershire studies* (Leicester UP, 1957), 17–51.

2114 BAZELEY, M.L., 'The Forest of Dean and its relations with the Crown during the twelfth and thirteenth centuries', *TBGAS*, 33 (1910), 153–286. Discusses DB evidence. See **2123, 2125**.

2115 BADDELEY, W. St C., *Place-names of Gloucestershire: a handbook* (Gloucester: John Bellows, 1913). Superseded by **2133**.

2116 TAYLOR, C. S., 'Note on the entry in Domesday Book relating to Westbury-on-Severn', *TBGAS*, 36 (1913), 782–90. Several identifications, of which several are in Herefords. and Worcs. See **2105**.

2117 TAYLOR, C. S., 'The Norman settlement of Gloucestershire', *TBGAS*, 40 (1917), 57–88.

2118 HOUGHTON, F. T. S., 'The family of Muchgros', *TBAS*, 47 (1921), 8–34. For the DB holdings of the Mussegros family in Glos. and other counties.

2119 THOMPSON, A. H., 'The jurisdiction of the archbishops of York in Gloucestershire', *TBGAS*, 43 (1921), 85–180. For DB and the lands of the former monastery of St Oswald's, Gloucester.

2120 OMAN, C., 'Concerning some Gloucestershire boundaries', in H. W. C. Davis (ed.), *Essays in history presented to Reginald Lane Poole* (Oxford: Clarendon Press, 1927), 86–97.

2121 FULLER, E. A., 'Medieval Cirencester', *TBGAS*, 54 (1932), 107–15.

2122 FULLBROOK-LEGATT, L. E. W. O., 'Saxon Gloucestershire', *TBGAS*, 57 (1935), 110–35. Contains material on DB place-names and hundreds.

2123 GRUNDY, G. B., 'The ancient woodland of Gloucestershire', *TBGAS*, 58 (1936), 65–155; 59 (1937), 205–9. For maps and discussion of DB woodland. Cf. **2125**.

2124 HART, C. E., 'The origin and the geographical extent of the hundred of St Briavels in Gloucestershire', *TBGAS*, 66 (1945), 138–65. Reprinted in C. E. Hart, *The extent and boundaries of the Forest of Dean and hundred of St Briavels* (Woodgate near Coleford: the author, 1947), 1–28.

2125 HART, C. E., 'The metes and bounds of the Forest of Dean', *TBGAS*, 66 (1945), 166–207. Reprinted in C. E. Hart, *The extent and boundaries of the Forest of Dean and hundred of St Briavels* (Woodgate near Coleford: the author, 1947), 29–70. Uses DB evidence to discuss and map the Forest of Dean, which is not mentioned in DB. See also **2123**.

2126 HILTON, R. H., 'Winchcombe abbey and the manor of Sherborne', *University of Birmingham Hist. Jour.*, 2 (1949–50), 31–52.

2127 FINBERG, H. P. R., *Roman and Saxon Withington: a study in continuity*, Dept. of English Local History, Occasional papers, no. 8 (Leicester UP, 1955; repr., 1959).

2128 FINBERG, H. P. R., *Gloucestershire: an illustrated essay on the history of the landscape* (London: Hodder & Stoughton, 1955). Revised as *The Gloucestershire landscape* (London: Hodder & Stoughton, 1975).

2129 FINBERG, H. P. R., 'The genesis of the Gloucestershire towns', in H. P. R. Finberg (ed.), *Gloucestershire studies* (Leicester UP, 1957), 52–88.

2130 WALKER, D., 'Miles of Gloucester, earl of Hereford', *TBGAS*, 77 (1958), 66–84. See pp. 81–2 for *Alwintune* in Herefords. DB as Alvington (Glos.).

2131 WALKER, D., 'The "honours" of the earls of Hereford in the twelfth century', *TBGAS*, 79 (1960), 174–211. For the DB holdings of Durand, sheriff of Glos., and his nephew Walter fitz Roger in Glos. and other counties.

2132 WIGHTMAN, W. E., 'The palatine earldom of William fitz Osbern in Gloucestershire and Worcestershire (1066–1071)', *EHR*, 77 (1962), 6–17.

2133 SMITH, A. H., *The place-names of Gloucestershire*, 4 vols, EPNS, 38–41 (Cambridge UP, 1964–5).

2134 CLARKE, H. B., 'The Norman conquest of the West Midlands', *Vale of Evesham Historical Soc.: research papers*, 1 (1967), 17–26.

2135 KEMP, B. R., 'The churches of Berkeley Hernesse', *TBGAS*, 87 (1968), 96–110. Several points about DB Berkeley.

2136 BOND, C. J., 'The estates of Evesham abbey: a preliminary survey of their medieval topography', *Vale of Evesham Historical Soc.: research papers*, 4 (1973), 1–62.

2137 COX, D. C., 'The Vale estates of the church of Evesham, c. 700–1086', *Vale of Evesham Historical Soc.: research papers*, 5 (1975), 25–50.

2138 BOND, C. J., 'The medieval topography of the Evesham abbey estates: a supplement', *Vale of Evesham Historical Soc.: research papers*, 5 (1975), 51–60.

2139 WALKER, D., 'Gloucester and Gloucestershire in Domesday Book', *TBGAS*, 94 (1976), 107–16.

2140 DYER, C., *Lords and peasants in a changing society: the estates of the bishopric of Worcester, 680–1540*, Past and Present Publications (Cambridge UP, 1980). For landholdings in Glos., Warws. and Worcs.

2141 MOORE, J. S., *Domesday Book. 15. Gloucestershire* (Chichester: Phillimore, 1982). Text, translation and valuable notes. An appendix describes the sections of the Evesham and Worcester satellites and surveys which are relevant to Glos. DB.

2142 WARMINGTON, A., 'The Domesday manor of Langeberge cum Mene', *Jour.EPNS*, 16 (1983–4), 38–49. Identifies as Longborough. Cf. **2133, 2141**.

HAMPSHIRE

For the relevant section of the *DB Geography*, **370**. For woodland, **289**. On DB Hants values and the possible movements of the Conqueror's army in 1066, see **201, 392, 393**, in addition to Baring's work cited below. On the holdings of Durand, sheriff of Glos., and his nephew Walter fitz Roger, and the lands of Westminster abbey, **2131, 1027**.

2201 CAMDEN, W., *Britannia*, ed. R.Gough, 1 (London: 1789; 2nd edn, London: John Stockdale, 1806). See 1st edn, 129–30 and 2nd edn, 181–4 for tables of the New Forest entries.

2202 WARNER, R., *Topographical remarks relating to the south-western parts of Hampshire*, 2 vols (London: R.Blamire, 1793). See 1, 163–215 for tables of the New Forest entries.

2203 WARNER, R., *Hampshire – extracted from Domesday Book, with an accurate English translation, a preface, and an introduction … to which is added a glossary* (London: Faulder of Bond Street, etc., 1789). Reissued in *Collections for the history of Hampshire and the bishoprick of Winchester, including the Isles of Wight, Jersey, Guernsey, and Sark, by D.Y., with the original Domesday Book of the county, etc. by R.Warner*, 2 (London: Rivington, Cadell & Davies, Law, Sewel, 1795).

2204 LEWIS, P., *Historical inquiries concerning forests and forest laws, with topographical remarks upon the ancient and modern state of the New Forest* (London: T.Payne, 1811). See pp.167–72 for tables of the New Forest entries.

2205 MOODY, H., *Hampshire in 1086. Alphabetical list of such of the present parishes, tythings and manors, with the exception of those in the Isle of Wight as are mentioned in the Domesday Book* (1845). Not located.

2206 MOODY, H., 'The Domesday Book: Hampshire and Wiltshire', in H.Moody, *Notes and essays, archaeological, historical and topographical, relating to the counties of Hants. and Wilts.* (London, Winchester, Salisbury: Simpkin & Marshall, Jacob & Johnson, G.Brown, 1851), 12–24.

2207 JAMES, H. (director), *Domesday Book: or the great survey of England of William the Conqueror, A.D. MLXXXVI. Facsimile of the part relating to*

Hampshire (Southampton: Ordnance Survey Office, 1861). Photozinco-graphic edition.

2208 MOODY, H., *Hampshire in 1086: an extension of the latin text and an English translation of the Domesday Book as far as it relates to Hampshire, with explanatory notes to accompany facsimile photo-zincographed under the direction of Col. Sir H. James at the Ordnance Survey Office* (Winchester: John T. Doswell; London: J. Russell Smith, 1862).

2209 WISE, J. R. de C., *The New Forest: its history and its scenery* (London: H. Southeran & Co., 1883). See chapter 3.

2210 SHORE, T. W., 'Early boroughs in Hampshire', *Arch. Rev.*, 4 (1890), 286–91.

2211 ROUND, J. H., 'Introduction to the Hampshire Domesday', in *VCH Hants*, 1, ed. H. A. Doubleday (Westminster: Constable, 1900), 399–447.

2212 ROUND, J. H., 'The text of the Hampshire Domesday', *VCH Hants*, 1, 448–526.

2213 BARING, F. H., 'The making of the New Forest', *EHR*, 16 (1901), 427–38. Reprinted in **237**.

2214 MOENS, W. J. C., 'The New Forest: its afforestation, ancient area, and law in the time of the Conqueror and his successors. Did William I devastate the New Forest district and destroy churches there and had it been previously afforested as related by the early chroniclers?', *Arch. Jour.*, 60 (1903), 30–50.

2215 RAVENSCROFT, W., 'Notes on the origin of "Milford", and the Domesday records', *Milford-on-Sea Record Society. Occasional Magazine*, 1, no. 1 (1909), 14–16.

2216 BARING, F. H., 'The making of the New Forest', *PHFCAS*, 6 (1910), 309–17.

2217 PARKER, F. H. M., 'The forest laws and the death of William Rufus', *EHR*, 27 (1912), 26–38. Little specific about the DB evidence. Cf. **2218**.

2218 BARING, F. H., 'The making of the New Forest', *EHR*, 27 (1912), 513–15. Cf. **2217**. A note argues that DB values suggest that in 1066 William's army may have crossed the Thames at Hampton.

2219 BARING, F. H., 'William the Conqueror's march through Hampshire in 1066', *PHFCAS*, 7, pt 2 (1915), 33–9.

2220 SYKES, W.S., 'The reference to Milford church in Domesday Book', *Milford-on-Sea Record Society. Occasional Magazine*, 2, no. 3 (1917), 33–45. Suggests a correction to **2212**.

2221 SUCKLING, Mrs, 'Some notes on the manor of East Tytherley', *PHFCAS*, 9 (1920–25), 1–22.

2222 GRAS, N.S.B. & GRAS, E.C., *The economic and social history of an English village (Crawley, Hampshire) A.D. 909–1928*, Harvard economic studies, no. 34 (Cambridge, Mass.: Harvard UP, 1930).

2223 HAWKES, C.F.C., MYRES, J.N.L. & STEVENS, C.G., 'Saint Catherine's Hill, Winchester', *PHFCAS*, 11 (1930), 1–310. See pp. 192–3 for the nine DB churches of Chilcomb.

2224 HOFMANN, M., *Die Französierung des Personennamenschatzes im Domesday Book der Graftschafen Hampshire und Sussex*, Inaugural-Dissertation zur erlangung der doktorwürde der philosophischen Fakultät (I. sektion) der Ludwig-Maximilians-Universität zu Munchen (Murnau, 1934). See **292** for severe criticism.

2225 KARSLAKE, J.B., 'The water mills of Hampshire', *PHFCAS*, 14 (1938), 3–8. Brief on DB mills.

2226 KÖKERITZ, H., *The place-names of the Isle of Wight* (Uppsala: Appelbergs Boktryckeriaktiebolag, 1940).

2227 STONE, G., 'The place-names of the Test Valley', *PHFCAS*, 18 (1953), 154–6. Simply a list of DB place-names and unspecific Anglo-Saxon references.

2228 SHAW, A.K., 'Windmills and water mills in Hampshire', *PHFCAS*, 21, pt 2 (1959), 107–9; pt 3 (1960), 125–33. See pt 3 for some DB mills.

2229 BURGESS, L.A., *The origins of Southampton*, Dept. of English Local History, Occasional papers, no. 16 (Leicester UP, 1964). See pp. 16–20.

2230 LLOYD, A.T., 'The place-names of Hampshire', in F.J. Monkhouse (ed.), *A survey of Southampton and its region* (Southampton: British Association for the Advancement of Science, 1964), 177–88. Derivative and uncritical.

2231 LLOYD, A.T., 'The salterns of the Lymington area', *PHFCAS*, 24 (1967), 86–102. A brief discussion and list of Hants DB salt pans.

2232 ELLIS, C.M., 'A gazeteer of the water, wind and tide mills of Hampshire', *PHFCAS*, 25 (1968), 119–40. A list of surviving mill sites, with some material on the location of DB mills.

2233 COLLINS, F. & OLIVER, J., 'Lomer: a study of a deserted medieval village', *PHFCAS*, 28 (1971), 67–76.

2234 CUNLIFFE, B., 'Saxon and medieval settlement-pattern in the region of Chalton, Hampshire', *MA*, 16 (1972), 1–12.

2235 ADDYMAN, P.V. & LEIGH, D., 'The Anglo-Saxon village at Chalton, Hampshire: second interim report', *MA*, 17 (1973), 1–25. For DB estates and land use.

2236 STAGG, D., 'The New Forest in Domesday Book', in *Hampshire Field Club, New Forest Section, report no.13* (1974), 20–4. Modifies **370** through further place-name identifications.

2237 BIDDLE, M. *et al* (eds), *Winchester in the early middle ages* (Oxford: Clarendon Press, 1976). For DB Hants in general.

2238 HILL, R.M.T., 'The manor of Stockbridge', *PHFCAS*, 32 (1975), 93–101. Identifies *Sumburne* as Stockbridge. See also *idem*, 'The borough of Stockbridge', *PHFCAS*, 33 (1976), 79–88 where the same point is made.

2239 STAGG, D.J., *New Forest documents A.D. 1244–A.D. 1334*, Hants Rec. Ser., 3 (Hampshire County Council, 1979). Brief discussion of DB evidence.

2240 RUMBLE, A.R., '*Hamtun* alias *Hamwic* (Saxon Southampton): the place-name traditions and their significance', in D.A. Hinton (ed.), *Excavations at Melbourne Street, Southampton, 1971–76* (London: Council for British Archaeology, 1980), 7–20. For the spellings of *Hantone*, *Hantune* and *Hantescire* in DB.

2241 HOAD, M., 'The origins of Portsmouth', in J. Webb, N. Yates & S. Peacock (eds), *Hampshire studies presented to Dorothy Dymond, CBE, MA, DLitt on the occasion of her ninetieth birthday* (Portsmouth: Portsmouth City Records Office, 1981), 1–30. Tabulation and full discussion of the DB evidence for Portsdown hundred.

2242 MUNBY, J. (ed., from a draft translation by J. Mothersill, P. Osmund & J. Jenkyns), *Domesday Book. 4. Hampshire* (Chichester: Phillimore, 1982). Text, translation and valuable notes. A bibliographical note on the New Forest. An appendix on the ms. of Hants DB and the way in which the DB compiler left space for the New Forest section is an important contribution to the making of DB.

2243 STAMPER, P.A., 'The medieval forest of Pamber, Hampshire', *Landscape History*, 5 (1983), 41–52.

HEREFORDSHIRE

Essential for the study of Herefords. DB is the edition of the 'Herefordshire Domesday' of the 1160s, **19**. For the relevant section of the *DB Geography*, **340**. For the landholdings of Albert the Lotharingian, Roger de Mussegros, Durand, sheriff of Glos., and his nephew Walter fitz Roger, the Lacy family, and the family of earl Godwine, see **1007, 2118, 2131, 395, 461**. For the identification of Kingstone in Weston under Penyard, **2116**. For a general essay in historical geography which makes some use of DB material, **1442**.

2301 DUNCUMB, J., *Collections towards the history and antiquities of the county of Hereford*, 1 (Hereford: E.C.Wright, 1804). See pp.59–65 for 'Names of places and of landed proprietors in Domesday Book'.

2302 JAMES, H. (director), *Domesday Book: or the great survey of England of William the Conqueror, A.D. MLXXXVI. Facsimile of the part relating to Herefordshire* (Southampton: Ordnance Survey Office, 1862). Photozincographic edition.

2303 BULL, H.G., 'Ewyas Harold, its name, its castle, and its priory', *TWNFC* (1869), 28–33. Prints and discusses the DB entry.

2304 ROBINSON, C.J., 'The Domesday survey of Herefordshire', *TWNFC*, (1871–3), 94–9.

2305 BANKS, R.W., 'Herefordshire and its Welsh border during the Saxon period', *Arch. Camb.*, 4th ser., 13 (1882), 19–39.

2306 BANNISTER, A.T., *The history of Ewyas Harold, its castle, priory and church* (Hereford: Jakeman & Carver, 1902).

2307 BANNISTER, A.T., 'The Herefordshire Domesday', *TWNFC* (1902–4), 318–25. Notes the lack of publications on Herefords. DB at this date. Useful work.

2308 ROUND, J.H., 'Introduction to the Herefordshire Domesday', in *VCH Herefords.*, 1, ed. W.Page (London: Constable, 1908), 263–307.

2309 WOOD, J.G. & ROUND, J.H., 'Translation of the Herefordshire Domesday', *VCH Herefords.*, 1, 309–45.

2310 WOOD, J.G., 'Some Domesday place-names in the neighbourhood of Dean Forest', *TWNFC* (1905–7), 244–50.

2311 BADDELEY, W. St C., 'Herefordshire place-names', *TBGAS*, 39 (1916), 87–200. Critical of **2312**.

2312 BANNISTER, A. T., *The place-names of Herefordshire: their origin and development* (Cambridge UP, for the author, 1916). The author's copy with additional annotations is in Hereford Record Office.

2313 READE, H., 'Welsh and English place-names in south Herefordshire', *TWNFC* (1921–3), 18–29.

2314 ROBINSON, S., 'The forests and woodland areas of Herefordshire', *TWNFC* (1921–3), 193–220. Identifies woods mentioned in DB.

2315 GALBRAITH, V. H., 'An episcopal land-grant of 1085', *EHR*, 44 (1929), 353–72. For DB Holme Lacy (Herefords.) and Onibury (Shrops.). Also for the phrase *de victu* (*canonicorum, monachorum*, etc.) in DB.

2316 ROYAL COMMISSION ON HISTORICAL MONUMENTS, ENGLAND, *Herefordshire*, 3 vols (London: HMSO, 1931–4). See 3, 52–3 for the *domus defensabilis* at Eardisley. Also a brief essay by F. M. Stenton, 'Pre-Conquest Herefordshire', 3, lv–lxi; reprinted in D. M. Stenton (ed.), *Preparatory to Anglo-Saxon England* (Oxford: Clarendon Press, 1970), 193–202.

2317 MARSHALL, G., 'The Norman occupation of the lands in the Golden Valley, Ewyas, and Clifford and their motte and bailey castles', *TWNFC* (1936–8), 141–58. A useful account with a map.

2318 RENNELL OF RODD, F. J. R., Rodd, Baron, 'The manors of Rodd, Nash and Little Brampton, near Presteigne: a note on a possible Domesday Book identification', *TRS*, 14 (1944), 24–9. For *Hercope*, cf. **420**.

2319 HART, C. E., 'The Herefordshire portion of the ancient Forest of Dene', *TWNFC*, 32 (1946–8), 24–31.

2320 MARTIN, S. H., 'Edvin Loach', *TWNFC*, 34 (1952–4), 293–4. In Worcs. until 1893.

2321 RENNELL OF RODD, F. J. R., Rodd, Baron, 'Aids to the Domesday geography of north-west Herefordshire', *Geog. Jour.*, 120 (1954), 458–67. This and the author's other contributions are based on thorough local knowledge.

2322 RENNELL OF RODD, F. J. R., Rodd, Baron, 'The Domesday manors in the hundreds of Hezetre and Elsedune in Herefordshire', in *Herefordshire, its natural history, archaeology, and history: chapters written to celebrate the centenary of the Woolhope Naturalists' Field Club, founded in 1851* (Gloucester: Bristol Publishing Co., nd, probably 1954; repr. East Ardsley: E. P. Publishing Co., 1971), 130–58.

2323 JACKSON, J.N., 'The historical geography of Herefordshire, from Saxon times to the Act of Union, 1536', in *Herefordshire, its natural history, archaeology and history* (Gloucester: Bristol Publishing Co., nd, probably 1954; repr. East Ardsley: E.P. Publishing Co., 1971), 180–90.

2324 LENNARD, R., 'The hidation of "demesne" in some Domesday entries', *EcHR*, 2nd ser., 7 (1954–5), 67–70. Concerned mainly with Herefords. and Worcs.

2325 RENNELL OF RODD, F.J.R., Rodd, Baron, *Valley on the March: a history of a group of manors on the Herefordshire march of Wales* (London: OUP, 1958). Study of the Hindwell and Lugg valley manors in N.W. Herefordshire. See especially chapters 2 and 3.

2326 WALKER, D., 'The descent of Westwood in Llanwarne in the eleventh and twelfth centuries', *TWNFC*, 36 (1958–60), 191–5. Resolves apparent contradictions between the DB entries for Westwood and the charters and list of donations of the abbey of Gloucester.

2327 RENNELL OF RODD, F.J.R., Rodd, Baron, 'The boundaries of the Saxon manor of Staunton on Arrow in a charter of king Edgar of 958 A.D.', *TWNFC*, 36 (1958–60), 279–91. Discussion of the four *Stantone* or *Standune* in Herefords. DB.

2328 CHARLES, B.G., 'The Welsh, their language and place-names in Archenfield and Oswestry', in *Angles and Britons*, O'Donnell Lectures (Cardiff: University of Wales Press, 1963), 85–110.

2329 NOBLE, F., 'Further excavations at Bleddfa church, and associated problems of the history of the lordship of Bleddfa', *TRS*, 33 (1963), 57–63. Queried the identification of *Hech* with Nash. Cf. **2333**.

2330 RENNELL OF RODD, F.J.R., Rodd, Baron, 'The land of Lene', in I.Ll. Foster & L. Alcock (eds), *Culture and environment: essays in honour of Sir Cyril Fox* (London: Routledge & Kegan Paul, 1963), 303–26. See for DB Leominster.

2331 WOOD, A.S., 'The Domesday *More*', *TWNFC*, 37 (1963), 329–30.

2332 NOBLE, F., 'Medieval boroughs of west Herefordshire', *TWNFC*, 38 (1964–6), 62–70.

2333 RENNELL OF RODD, F.J.R., Rodd, Baron, 'A note on *Hech* in the Domesday Book', *TRS*, 34 (1964), 63–4. Cf. **2329**.

2334 NELSON, L.H., *The Normans in South Wales, 1070–1171* (Austin & London: University of Texas Press, 1966). Uncritical and often misleading. Deals with Herefords., Shrops. and parts of Wales in DB.

2335 STANFORD, S.C., 'The deserted medieval village of Hampton Wafer, Herefordshire', *TWNFC*, 39 (1967–9), 71–92. See especially p.89. For comment **2337**.

2336 WALKER, D., 'William fitz Osbern and the Norman settlement in Herefordshire', *TWNFC*, 39 (1967–9), 402–12. See especially pp.408–11

2337 RENNELL OF RODD, F.J.R., Rodd, Baron, 'Note on certain pre-Domesday estates east of Leominster', *TWNFC*, 39 (1967–9), 469–73. A comment on **2335**.

2338 WALKER, D., 'Hereford and the laws of Breteuil', *TWNFC*, 40 (1970–2), 55–65. Mainly on the 12th and 13th centuries.

2339 GWYNNE, T.A., 'Domesday society in Herefordshire', *TWNFC*, 41 (1973–5), 22–33.

2340 COPLESTONE-CROW, B., 'The Baskervilles of Herefordshire, 1086–1300', *TWNFC*, 43 (1979), 18–39. Full discussion of the DB holdings of Robert and Ralph de Bacqueville.

2341 THORN, F. & C. (eds, from a draft translation by V.Sankaran), *Domesday Book. 17. Herefordshire*, (Chichester: Phillimore, 1983). Contains notes on the Welsh border, castles, the county boundary, Hereford-shire Domesday (see **19**), place-name identification, the hundreds and forest.

HERTFORDSHIRE

There is an early translation of Herts. DB by Bawdwen, **1201**. For IE and the lands of the abbey of Ely in Herts., see **1005, 331, 1321**, in addition to **2418**. For the relevant section of the *DB Geography*, **370**. For Herts. DB statistics, **237**, and also for a tabulation of values, **236**. For an early essay in DB historical geography, **2047**. There are numerous studies of the lands in Herts. of landholders there and in other counties. For Edith the Fair, Ramsey abbey, Roger de Mussegros, the archbishopric of Canterbury, the Chocques ('de Cioches') family and Westminster abbey, see **1204, 1006, 1023, 2118, 1212, 1024, 1027**. For DB values and the possible movements of the Conqueror's army in 1066, see **201, 392, 393**.

2401 CHAUNCY, H., *The historical antiquities of Hertfordshire*, 2 vols (London: Griffin, Keble, Browne, Midwinter & Leigh, 1700. Repr., Bishops Stortford & London: Mullinger & Holdsworth, 1826; Dorking: Kohler & Coombes, 1975). Transcribed and translated the

DB entries, identified many place-names, and reassembled the entries on a geographical basis.

2402 CLUTTERBUCK, R., *The history and antiquities of the county of Hertford*, 3 vols (London: Nichols & Bentley, 1815–27). Translated the DB entries and provided a transcription of the Latin text.

2403 JAMES, H. (director), *Domesday Book: or the great survey of England of William the Conqueror, A.D. MLXXXVI. Facsimile of the part relating to Hertford-shire* (Southampton: Ordnance Survey Office, 1863). Photozinco-graphic edition.

2404 SKEAT, W. W., *The place-names of Hertfordshire* (Hertford: Stephen Austin & Sons, for the East Herts. Arch. Soc., 1904). Superseded by **2415**.

2405 GOULD, I. C., 'Some notes on Wymondley in Domesday', *TEHAS*, 3 (1905) 12–13.

2406 ROUND, J. H., 'Introduction to the Hertfordshire Domesday', in *VCH Herts.*, 1, ed. W. Page (London: Constable, 1902), 263–99.

2407 RAGG, F. W., 'Text of the Hertfordshire Domesday', *VCH Herts.*, 1, 300–44.

2408 SKEAT, W. W., 'Place-names of Hertfordshire. Tring. Stevenage. Royston', *TEHAS*, 4 (1908–11), 179–81.

2409 ANDREWS, H. C., 'Bygrave: its owners, rectors, and legends', *TEHAS*, 4 (1908–11), 279–99.

2410 ANDREWS, H. C., 'Broxbourne: its churches and builders', *TEHAS*, 8 (1928–33), 116–26. See p. 117 for a suggestion for the site of a DB church.

2411 ANDREWS, H. C., 'Shephall Bury', *TEHAS*, 9 (1934–6), 112–3. A problem of DB commendation.

2412 ANDREWS, H. C. & BUSHBY, G. H., 'Wormley and Wormley-bury', *TEHAS*, 9 (1934–6), 113–18.

2413 HUNT, E. M., 'William Vallans, poet, and Ware', *TEHAS*, 9 (1934–6), 271–7. Suggests location for a DB mill.

2414 ANDREWS, H. C., 'Weston', *TEHAS*, 10 (1937–9), 109–11. Suggests that the two priests of DB Weston served churches in Weston and Baldock.

2415 GOVER, J. E. B., MAWER, A. & STENTON, F. M., *The place-names of Hertfordshire*, EPNS, 15 (Cambridge UP, 1938).

2416 ANDREWS, H.C., 'Early Bengeo manor lords and Hertford churches', *TEHAS*, 11 (1940–4), 77–88.

2417 JOHNSON, W.B., 'Hertfordshire nine hundred years ago', *Hertfordshire countryside*, 8 (1953), 68, 95. Notes include a count of DB population, pigs and mills.

2418 MORRIS, J. (ed., from a draft translation by M.Newman & S.Wood), *Domesday Book. 12. Hertfordshire* (Chichester: Phillimore, 1976). An appendix deals with IE for Herts. For additions and corrections, see **1028**.

2419 MUNBY, L.M., *The Hertfordshire landscape* (London: Hodder & Stoughton, 1977).

HUNTINGDONSHIRE

The EPNS and the History of the English Landscape volumes for Hunts. were combined with Beds., see **1020, 1031**. For the relevant section of the *DB Geography*, **332**. On IE for Hunts. and the holdings of the abbey of Ely, **1005, 331, 1321**. For the estates of the abbeys of Ramsey, Crowland, Thorney and Peterborough in Hunts. and other counties, see **1006, 1023, 1313, 1029, 1026**. For the TRE holdings of Turkil of Harringworth in Hunts. and other counties, **1323, 1327**.

2501 JAMES, H. (director), *Domesday Book: or the great survey of England of William the Conqueror, A.D. MLXXXVI. Facsimile of the part relating to Huntingdonshire* (Southampton: Ordnance Survey Office, 1863). Photozincographic edition.

2502 ANON (Revd G. Johnstone, see **332**), *Translation of Domesday Book or the Great Survey of England of William the Conqueror, A.D. MLXXXVI, with notes and explanations, so far as relates to Huntingdonshire* (Huntingdon: Robert Edis, 1864).

2503 ROUND, J.H., 'The knights of Peterborough', in J.H.Round, *Feudal England* (London: Swan Sonnenschein, 1895; 2nd edn, London: Allen & Unwin, 1964), 157–68 (1st edn) and 131–9 (2nd edn). Valuable for identifying DB sub-tenants in Hunts., Lincs. and Northants.

2504 SKEAT, W.W., 'The place-names of Huntingdonshire', *PCAS*, 10 (1898–1903), 317–60. Superseded by **1020**.

2505 PARSONS, D.M., 'A hitherto unprinted charter of David I', *Scottish Hist. Rev.*, 14 (1917), 370–1. Identifies the three unnamed berewicks in Great Paxton.

2506 STENTON, F. M., 'Introduction to the Huntingdonshire Domesday', in *VCH Hunts.*, 1, ed. W. Page & G. Proby (London: St Catherine Press, 1926), 315–36.

2507 STENTON, F. M., 'Text of the Huntingdonshire Domesday', *VCH Hunts.*, 1, 337–55.

2508 LADDS, S. I., 'The borough of Huntingdon and Domesday Book', *Trans. Cambs. & Hunts. Arch. Soc.*, 5 (1931–6), 105–12 + map.

2509 DARBY, H. C., 'Domesday woodland in Huntingdonshire', *Trans. Cambs & Hunts. Arch. Soc.*, 5 (1931–6), 269–73.

2510 HART, C., 'The church of St Mary of Huntingdon', *PCAS*, 59 (1966), 105–11. Attempts to unravel the three DB refs. to this church.

2511 HART, C., 'The hidation of Huntingdonshire', *PCAS*, 61 (1968), 55–66.

2512 DEWINDT, E. B., *Land and people in Holywell-cum-Needingworth* (Toronto: Pontifical Institute of Medieval Studies, 1972). See p. 9 for a settlement omitted from DB.

2513 MORRIS, J. (ed., from a draft translation by S. Harvey), *Domesday Book. 19. Huntingdonshire* (Chichester: Phillimore, 1975). Text, translation and brief notes. For additions and corrections, **3837**.

KENT

The study of Kent DB relies a great deal upon the survival of 'satellites' from Christ Church and St Augustine's, Canterbury. For printed texts, **14, 18**. The main commentaries on these texts are **21, 364, 410, 426**. For the relevant section of the *DB Geography*, **370**. For DB values and the possible movements of the Conqueror's army in 1066 in Kent, **201, 392, 393**. For comparative statistics of DB peasantry in Berks., Kent and N.E. Sussex, **1117**. On the DB estates of Richard fitz Gilbert in Kent and other counties, **2067, 2070**. For the archbishopric of Canterbury, **1212**, as well as the other studies below. On the lands of Albert the Lotharingian in Kent and other counties, **1007**.

2601 SOMNER, W., *The antiquities of Canterbury* (London: J.L., for R. Thrale, 1640). 2nd edn, revised and enlarged by N. Batteley (London: R. Knaplock, 1703; reprinted with an introduction by W. Urry, Wakefield: E.P. Publishing Ltd., 1977).

2602 HARRIS, J., *The history of Kent* (London: D. Midwinter, 1719). Contains many attempts to identify DB manors. Not very accurate.

2603 HASTED, E., *The history and topographical survey of the county of Kent*, 4 vols (Canterbury: Simmons & Kirkby, 1778–99). 2nd edn, corrected and continued, 12 vols (Canterbury: W. Bristow, 1797–1801). Identifications are much sounder than **2602**.

2604 HENSHALL, S., *Specimens and parts: containing a history of the county of Kent* (London: R. Faulder & F. and C. Rivington, 1798). Has elaborate tables of the DB entries and lengthy commentaries thereon. Also a map of DB place-names on which lathes, hundreds and mills were marked.

2605 HASTED, E., *The history of the ancient and metropolitical city of Canterbury* (Canterbury: Simmons & Kirkby, 1799; 2nd edn, 2 vols, Canterbury: Bristow, 1801).

2606 HENSHALL, S. & WILKINSON, J., *Domesday; or an actual survey of South-Britain* (London: Bye & Law, 1799). A translation of Kent DB with no attempt to identify place-names.

2607 HUSSEY, A., *Notes on the churches of Kent, Sussex and Surrey mentioned in Domesday Book and those of more recent date including comparative lists of the churches and some account of the sepulchral memorials and other antiquities* (London: J. R. Smith, 1852).

2608 JAMES, H. (director), *Domesday Book: or the great survey of England of William the Conqueror, A.D. MLXXXVI. Facsimile of the part relating to Kent* (Southampton: Ordnance Survey Office, 1863). Photozincographic edition.

2609 ELTON., C. I., *The tenures of Kent* (London: James Parker & Co., 1867). See chapter 6 for DB.

2610 LARKING, L. B., *The Domesday Book of Kent* (London: Toovey, 1869). A facsimile copy of Kent DB, with an extension, concordance, translation and notes. Place-names are identified.

2611 FURLEY, R., *A history of the Weald of Kent*, 2 vols (London and Ashford: J. R. Smith & H. Igglesden, 1871–4). Maps and lists DB place-names lying partly or wholly within the Weald.

2612 FURLEY, R., 'An outline of the history of Romney Marsh', *Arch. Cant.*, 13 (1880), 178–200.

2613 ROBERTSON, S., 'Romney, old and new. The Saxon ville of St Martin', *Arch. Cant.*, 13 (1880), 349–73.

2614 FURLEY, R., 'The early history of Ashford', *Arch. Cant.*, 16 (1886),161–78.

2615 VINOGRADOFF, P., 'Sulung and hide', *EHR*, 19 (1904), 282–6.

2616 FROST, R.C., 'The Domesday Book and its times', *Woolwich and District Ant. Soc. Annual Report*, 12 (1907), 67–71. An uncritical appreciation of **2610**.

2617 KNOCKER, H.W., ' "The Valley of Holmesdale". Its evolution and development', *Arch. Cant.*, 31 (1915), 155–77. Much DB material and a map of DB manors.

2618 NEILSON, N., *The cartulary and terrier of the priory of Bilsington, Kent*, Records of the social and economic history of England and Wales, 7 (London: OUP for the British Academy, 1928). See the introduction for the Weald in DB.

2619 JOLLIFFE, J.E.A., 'The hidation of Kent', *EHR*, 44 (1929), 612–18.

2620 HAINES, C.R., *Dover priory* (Cambridge UP, 1930). For the DB holding of the canons of St Martin's, Dover.

2621 WARD, G., 'A note on the yokes of Otford', *Arch. Cant.*, 42 (1930), 147–56.

2622 WALLENBERG, J.K., *Kentish place-names* (Uppsala: A.B. Lundequistska Bokhandeln, 1931). See **2633**.

2623 NEILSON, N., 'Introduction to the Kent Domesday', in *VCH Kent*, 3, ed. W.Page (London: St Catherine Press, 1932), 177–200.

2624 RAGG, F.W., 'Text of the Kent Domesday', *VCH Kent*, 3, 203–52.

2625 NEILSON, N., 'The Domesday Monachorum', in *VCH Kent*, 3, 253–69. A mediocre translation. See further **18**.

2626 SALTER, G., 'Social and economic history', in *VCH Kent*, 3, 319–70. See pp.321–4 for the ploughlands, sulungs and yokes of Kent DB.

2627 WARD, G., 'The list of Saxon churches in the Textus Roffensis', *Arch. Cant.*, 44 (1932), 39–59. Important for DB and evidence of settlement in the Weald.

2628 DOUGLAS, D.C., 'Odo, Lanfranc, and the Domesday survey', in *Historical essays in honour of James Tait*, ed. J.G.Edwards, V.H.Galbraith & E.F.Jacob (Manchester: printed for the subscribers, 1933), 47–57. See **2646, 2653**.

2629 JOLLIFFE, J. E. A., 'The origin of the hundred in Kent', in *Historical essays in honour of James Tait*, ed. J. G. Edwards, V. H. Galbraith & E. F. Jacob (Manchester: for the subscribers, 1933), 155–68.

2630 JOLLIFFE, J. E. A., *Pre-feudal England: the Jutes* (OUP, 1933). For sulungs and lathes. See review by G. Ward in *Arch. Cant.*, 45 (1933), 290–4.

2631 MUHLFELD, H. E., *A survey of the manor of Wye* (New York: Columbia UP; London: King, 1933).

2632 WARD, G., 'The lists of Saxon churches in the Domesday Monachorum and White Book of St Augustine', *Arch. Cant.*, 45 (1933), 60–89.

2633 WALLENBERG, J. K., *The place-names of Kent* (Uppsala: Appelbergs Boktryckeriaktiebolag, 1934). Supplements **2622**. For critical comment see **2641**. This and **2622** need to be used together and with caution.

2634 WARD, G., 'The lathe of Aylesford in 975', *Arch. Cant.*, 46 (1934), 7–26. For the list of manors contributing to the upkeep of Rochester bridge and DB.

2635 WARD, G., 'The origins of Whitstable', *Arch. Cant.*, 57 (1944), 51–5. Suggests an identification for *Dodeham* in DMon.

2636 EVANS, J. H., 'Archaeological horizons in the North Kent marshes. Appendix D. The Wicks', *Arch. Cant.*, 66 (1953), 144–5.

2637 BLOXAM, R. N., 'A Surrey charter of king John', *SurreyAC*, 54 (1955), 58–65. Suggests an identification for an unnamed holding of 6 acres in Somerdon hundred. See also **2659**.

2638 GOODSALL, R. H., 'Watermills on the River Len', *Arch. Cant.*, 71 (1957), 106–29. See also **2649**.

2639 URRY, W., 'The Normans in Canterbury', *Annales de Normandie*, 8 (1958), 119–38.

2640 DUMBRECK, W. V., 'The lowy of Tonbridge', *Arch. Cant.*, 72 (1958), 138–47. See also **2067**.

2641 REANEY, P. H., 'A survey of Kent place-names', *Arch. Cant.*, 73 (1959), 62–74.

2642 REANEY, P. H., 'Place-names and early settlement in Kent', *Arch. Cant.*, 76 (1961), 58–74. Maps the DB vills and discusses some DB place-names.

2643 DU BOULAY, F. R. H., 'Dens, droving and danger', *Arch. Cant.*, 76 (1961), 75–87. For DB denes. See also **2651**.

2644 COLVIN, H. M., 'A list of the archbishop of Canterbury's tenants by knight-service in the reign of Henry II', in F. R. H. Du Boulay (ed.), *Kent records: documents illustrative of medieval Kentish society* (Ashford: Kent Arch. Soc., 1964), 1–40. A list of 1171 compared with the DMon list and the holdings of Canterbury knights in DB.

2645 BAKER, A. R. H., 'The Kentish *iugum*: its relationship to soils at Gillingham', *EHR*, 81 (1966), 74–9.

2646 DU BOULAY, F. R. H., *The lordship of Canterbury: an essay on medieval society* (London: Nelson, 1966).

2647 STOYEL, A. D., 'Watermill sites at Kemsing and Otford', *Arch. Cant.*, 81 (1966), 244–5.

2648 URRY, W., *Canterbury under the Angevin kings* (London: Athlone Press, 1967). Discussion and maps of the Canterbury DB entry.

2649 SPAIN, R. J., 'The Len water-mills', *Arch. Cant.*, 82 (1967), 32–104. See also **2638**.

2650 STOYEL, B. D. & A. J., 'The Old Mill, Bexley', *Arch. Cant.*, 83 (1968), 105–10.

2651 WITNEY, K. P., *The Jutish forest: a study of the Weald of Kent from 450 to 1380 A.D.* (London: Athlone Press, 1976).

2652 EVERITT, A. M., 'The making of the agrarian landscape of Kent', *Arch. Cant.*, 92 (1976), 1–31. For DB evidence and the Weald.

2653 BATES, D. R., 'The land pleas of William I's reign: Penenden Heath revisited', *BIHR*, 51 (1978), 1–19. For DB and the Kent land pleas. See **2628, 2646**.

2654 ROLLASON, D. W., 'The date of the parish-boundary of Minster-in-Thanet (Kent)', *Arch. Cant.*, 95 (1979), 7–17.

2655 BAMPING, Z., 'A Domesday name identified?', *Kent Arch. Rev.*, 61 (1980), 6–7. For DB *Sonnings*.

2656 BROOKS, N. P., 'Romney Marsh in the early middle ages', in T. Rowley (ed.), *The evolution of marshland landscapes: papers presented to a conference on marshland landscapes held in Oxford in December 1979* (Oxford: Oxford University Dept. for External Studies, 1981), 74–95.

2657 TATTON-BROWN, T., 'The topography and buildings of Horton manor', *Arch. Cant.*, 98 (1982), 77–105.

2658 LAWRENCE, M., 'A Saxon royal manor, Burr's Oak Farm, East Peckham', *Arch Cant.*, 98 (1982), 253–5. For DMon *Stokenbury.*

2659 MORGAN, P. (ed.), *Domesday Book. 1. Kent* (Chichester: Phillimore, 1983). Includes notes on place-names, hundreds and lathes.

2660 BROOKS, N.P., *The early history of the church of Canterbury* (Leicester UP, 1984). See also **2646, 2653**.

LANCASHIRE

(including Cumberland and Westmorland)

The text of DB for Lancashire was included with Cheshire and Yorkshire. It is therefore necessary to consult the sections for those two counties for editions and translations. See especially, **1405, 1406, 1424, 1445, 4609, 4617, 4618**. There is an early translation of DB covering Lancs. by Bawdwen, **1601**. For the relevant section of the *DB Geography*, **369**. For a general study of DB for northern England, **446**. For a mediocre article dealing with both Cheshire and Lancs., **1409**.

2701 ROBSON, J., 'On the *Walintune* of Domesday Book', *THSLC*, 27 (1874–5), 180–3.

2702 ESDAILE, G., 'The charters of Manchester and Salford', *TLCAS*, 5 (1887), 242–8. See for Manchester's near-omission from DB.

2703 GRAY, A. E. P., 'The Domesday record of the land between Ribble and Mersey', *THSLC*, 39 (1887), 35–48.

2704 MAITLAND, F. W., 'Northumbrian tenures', *EHR*, 5 (1890), 625–32. For thegns and 'drengs' between Ribble and Mersey.

2705 FARRER, W., 'Notes on the Domesday survey of the land between Ribble and Mersey', *TLCAS*, 16 (1898), 1–38.

2706 FISHWICK, H., 'Places in Lancashire destroyed by the sea', *THSLC*, 49 (1897), 87–96. Demonstrated that land in Furness and West Derby had not disappeared by the time of DB. Identified *Erengermeles* with a part of North Meols. Cf. **2732**.

2707 FARRER, W., 'The Domesday survey of north Lancashire and the adjacent parts of Cumberland, Westmorland and Yorkshire', *TLCAS*, 18 (1900), 88–113.

2708 LUMBY, J. H., 'The Domesday survey of south Lancashire', *THSLC*, 52 (1900), 53–76.

2709 WILSON, J., 'Introduction to the Cumberland Domesday, early pipe rolls and Testa de Nevill', in *VCH Cumberland*, 1. ed. J. Wilson (Westminster: Constable, 1901), 295–335.

2710 WILSON, J., 'The text of the Cumberland Domesday', *VCH Cumberland*, 1, 336.

2711 FARRER, W., 'The barony of Grelley', *THSLC*, 53 (1901), 23–58. For DB holdings of Albert Greslet.

2712 SEPHTON, J., 'Notes on the south Lancashire place-names in Domesday Book', *Otia Merseiana*, 4 (1904), 65–74. Superseded by **2720**.

2713 FARRER, W., 'Introduction to the Lancashire Domesday', in *VCH Lancs.*, 1, ed. W. Farrer & J. Brownbill (London: Constable, 1906), 269–83.

2714 FARRER, W., 'Text of the Lancashire Domesday', *VCH Lancs.*, 1, 283–90.

2715 FARRER, W., 'Feudal baronage', *VCH Lancs.*, 1, 291–376.

2716 WYLD, H.C.K. & HIRST, T.O., *The place-names of Lancashire: their origin and history* (London: Constable, 1911). See **2720**.

2717 SEPHTON, J., *A handbook of Lancashire place-names* (Liverpool: Henry Young & Sons, 1913). See **2720**.

2718 SEDGEFIELD, W.J., *The place-names of Cumberland and Westmorland*, University of Manchester publications, English ser. no. 7 (Manchester UP, 1915). Superseded by **2733**.

2719 CHIPPINDALL, W.H., 'The lost manor of Thirnby', *THSLC*, 73 (1921), 225–7. Further material is in *THSLC*, 75 (1923), 238–58. A lost DB place-name.

2720 EKWALL, E., *The place-names of Lancashire*, Publications of the University of Manchester, English ser. no. 11 (Manchester UP, 1922).

2721 DEMAREST, E.B., '*Inter Ripam et Mersham*', *EHR*, 38 (1923), 161–70. Deals with the hundred and the geld. For criticism, **263**.

2722 JOLLIFFE, J.E.A., 'Northumbrian institutions', *EHR*, 41 (1926), 1–42. For *inter Ripam et Mersham*.

2723 LONGFORD, W.W., 'Some notes on the family history of Nicholas Longford, sheriff of Lancashire in 1413', *THSLC*, 86 (1934), 47–71. See pp. 48–50 for an attempt to support Farrer's argument (**2713**) that the Nigel who held of Roger the Poitevin in Salford hundred was Nigel de Stafford.

2724 WALKER, F., *Historical geography of southwest Lancashire before the Industrial Revolution*, Chetham Soc., ns, 103 (Manchester, 1939).

2725 McNULTY, J., 'Clitheroe castle and its chapel: their origins', *THSLC*, 93 (1941), 45–53. Doubts whether Clitheroe castle is mentioned in DB. But see **243, 404**.

2726 WAINWRIGHT, F.T., 'The Anglian settlement of Lancashire', *THSLC*, 93 (1941), 1–44. Some comment on the location of DB manors.

2727 SKELTON, J., 'Anglo-Norman territorial claims in south Westmoreland and north Lancashire', *TCWAAS*, ns, 42 (1942), 159–69.

2728 ARMSTRONG, A.M., MAWER, A., STENTON, F.M. & DICKINS, B., *The place-names of Cumberland*, 3 vols, EPNS, 20–2 (Cambridge UP, 1950–2).

2729 MILLWARD, R., *Lancashire: an illustrated essay on the history of the landscape* (London: Hodder & Stoughton, 1955).

2730 SMITH, E.H., 'Lancashire long measure', *THSLC*, 110 (1958), 1–14. See especially pp. 1–2, 12–13, for discussion of Lancs. land measurements and for the DB survey.

2731 SMITH, R.B., *Blackburnshire: a study in early Lancashire history*, Dept. of English Local History, Occasional papers, no. 15 (Leicester UP, 1961).

2732 ROLLINSON, W., 'The lost villages and hamlets of Low Furness', *TCWAAS*, ns, 63 (1963), 160–9. Cf. **2706**. A discussion of four unidentified DB place-names.

2733 SMITH, A.H., *The place-names of Westmorland*, 2 vols, EPNS, 42–3 (Cambridge UP, 1967).

2734 BOLTON, G.L., 'Domesday revisited', *Lancashire Local Historian*, 2 (1984), 9–13. For Leyland hundred and manor. Not entirely accurate.

LEICESTERSHIRE

Stenton's studies of the Danelaw include Leics., **241, 256**, and are important for Leics. DB. There are two modern specialist studies of Scandinavian place-names in Leics., **1623, 1624**. For the relevant section of the *DB Geography*, **340**. For the suggestion that Leics. DB values reflect devastation in 1065, **281**. On the landholdings of Crowland, Peterborough and Thorney abbeys, **1313, 1026, 1029**.

2801 NICHOLS, J., *History and antiquities of the county of Leicester*, 4 vols (London: J. Nichols, 1795–1811). Vol. 1 included a text of the Leics. folios and an English translation.

2802 JAMES, H. (director), *Domesday Book: or the great survey of England of William the Conqueror, A.D. MLXXXVI. Facsimile of the part relating to Leicestershire* (Southampton: Ordnance Survey Office, 1862). Photozincographic edition.

2803 ANON, *A literal extension of the Latin text, and an English translation of Domesday Book in relation to the county of Leicestershire* (Leicester: J. & T. Spencer; London: Vacher & Sons, 1864).

2804 THOMPSON, J., 'The secular history of Lutterworth', *TLAAS*, 4 (1878), 159–70.

2805 STEVENSON, W. H., 'The hundreds of Domesday', *EHR*, 5 (1890), 95–100. Argued that the hides of Leics. DB were a scribal error for hundreds of 12 geld carucates. See **200, 340, 2809, 2834**.

2806 ROUND, J. H., 'The Leicestershire survey (1124–1129)', in J. H. Round, *Feudal England* (London: Swan Sonnenschein, 1895; 2nd edn, London: Allen & Unwin, 1964), 196–214 (1st edn) and 160–74 (2nd edn). Prints and discusses text. Numerous DB insights. See **2807, 2808, 2811, 2826**.

2807 FLETCHER, W. G. D., 'Survey of Leicestershire, 1124–1129', *TLAAS*, 8 (1896), 142–4. Appears to be critical of **2806** and some of the place-name identifications, but makes no specific corrections.

2808 BOYD, W. K., 'Survey of Leicestershire', *TLAAS*, 8 (1896), 179–83. The text and a photographic copy. See **2806, 2811, 2826**.

2809 STENTON, F. M., 'Introduction to the Leicestershire Domesday', *VCH Leics.*, 1, ed. W. Page (London: Constable, 1907), 277–305.

2810 STENTON, F. M., 'Translation of the Leicestershire Domesday', *VCH Leics.*, 1, 306–38.

2811 STENTON, F. M., 'Leicestershire survey (twelfth century)', *VCH Leics.*, 1, 339–54. Introduction and translation.

2812 ROUND, J. H., 'The origin of Belvoir castle', *EHR*, 22 (1907), 508–10. For DB tenures on Robert de Tosny's fief.

2813 WATTS, W., 'The place-names of Leicestershire', *AASRP*, 31 (1911–12), 225–42. Descriptive, relying heavily on DB forms.

2814 FARNHAM, G., 'Rothley. II. The descent of the manor', *TLAAS*, 12 (1921–2), 35–98. See p. 36 for the soke of Rothley.

2815 FRANCIS, H. J., 'Hugh de Grentemesnil and his family', *TLAAS*, 13 (1923–4), 155–97. Discusses DB holdings.

2816 BILLSON, C. J., 'The open fields of Leicester', *TLAAS*, 14 (1925–6), 1–29. For DB Leicester and its surrounds.

2817 FARNHAM, G. F., 'Charnwood Forest and its historians', *TLAAS*, 15 (1927–8), 1–32. See p. 17. Supports traditional view that *Cernelega* is Charley.

2818 DARE, M. P., ' "Aldeby": a suggested identification in the Leicestershire Domesday, with a note on the site and church', *TLAAS*, 15 (1927–8), 333–6. Proposes an identification not accepted by **420, 2838**. But see **2822**.

2819 FARNHAM, G. F., *Leicestershire medieval village notes*, 6 vols (Leicester: W. Thornley & Son, 1929–33). A collection of material gathered by an industrious local antiquarian. Each village section includes the DB entry.

2820 HOLLY, D., 'The Domesday geography of Leicestershire', *TLAAS*, 20 (1938–9), 167–202.

2821 HOSKINS, W. G., ' A short history of Galby and Frisby', *TLAAS*, 22 (1944–5), 174–210. Reprinted as 'Galby and Frisby' in W. G. Hoskins, *Essays in Leicestershire history* (Liverpool UP, 1950), 24–66.

2822 HOSKINS, W. G., 'The deserted villages of Leicestershire', *TLAAS*, 22 (1944–5), 241–64. Reprinted with additions in W. G. Hoskins, *Essays in Leicestershire history* (Liverpool UP, 1950), 67–107. See **2818**.

2823 HOSKINS, W. G., 'The origin and rise of Market Harborough', *TLAAS*, 25 (1949), 56–68. Market Harborough was a 12th-century plantation. See for Leics. villages omitted from DB and for DB Great Bowden. Reprinted in W. G. Hoskins, *Provincial England: essays in social and economic history* (London: Macmillan, 1964), 53–67.

2824 HILTON, R. H., 'Medieval agrarian history', in *VCH Leics.*, 2, ed. W. G. Hoskins assisted by R. A. McKinley (OUP, for the Institute of Historical Research, 1954), 145–98. See pp. 148–55.

2825 SMITH, C. T., 'Population', in *VCH Leics.*, 3, ed. W. G. Hoskins & R. A. McKinley (OUP, for the Institute of Historical Research, 1955), 129–217. See pp. 129–32, 156–62 including a map and tables.

2826 SLADE, C. F., *The Leicestershire survey c. A.D. 1130*, Dept. of English Local History, Occasional papers, no. 7 (Leicester UP, 1956). See **2806, 2811**. The definitive modern edition, which adds new material to that used by previous editors. There is an important commentary devoted to vills, hundreds, landholders, purpose and compilation.

2827 HOSKINS, W. G., 'Seven deserted village sites in Leicestershire', *TLAAS*, 32 (1956), 36–51. Reprinted in W. G. Hoskins, *Provincial England: essays in social and economic history* (London: Macmillan, 1964), 115–30.

2828 HOSKINS, W. G., *Leicestershire: an illustrated essay on the history of the landscape* (London: Hodder & Stoughton, 1957).

2829 HOSKINS, W. G., 'The population of an English village, 1086–1801: a study of Wigston Magna', *TLAAS*, 33 (1957), 15–35. Reprinted in *Provincial England: essays in social and economic history* (London: Macmillan, 1964), 181–208.

2830 HOSKINS, W. G., *The midland peasant: the economic and social history of a Leicestershire village* (London: Macmillan, 1957). Deals with Wigston Magna.

2831 DALE, M. K., 'The city of Leicester: social and economic history, 1066–1509', in *VCH Leics.*, 4, ed. R. A. McKinley (OUP, for the Institute of Historical Research, 1958). See pp. 31–2.

2832 MOORE, J. S., 'The Domesday teamland in Leicestershire', *EHR*, 78 (1963), 696–703. Cf. **432**.

2833 DESERTED MEDIEVAL VILLAGE RESEARCH GROUP, 'Provisional list of deserted medieval villages in Leicestershire', *TLAHS*, 39 (1963–4), 24–33.

2834 HUGHES, C. J., 'Hides, carucates and yardlands in Leicestershire: the case of Saddington', *TLAHS*, 43 (1967–8), 19–23. The problem of the number of carucates in a hide in Leics. See **2805, 2809**.

2835 COX, B. H., 'Leicestershire moot-sites: the place-name evidence', *TLAHS*, 47 (1971–2), 14–21. Discusses the DB wapentakes.

2836 MARTIN, G. H., 'Church life in medieval Leicester', in A. E. Brown (ed.), *The growth of Leicester* (Leicester UP, 1972), 27–37.

2837 PHYTHIAN-ADAMS, C., *Continuity, fields and fission: the making of a midland parish*, Dept. of English local history, Occasional papers, 3rd ser., no. 4 (Leicester UP, 1978). For Claybrooke Magna and Claybrooke Parva.

2838 MORGAN, P. (ed. from a draft translation by M. Griffin), *Domesday Book. 22. Leicestershire* (Chichester: Phillimore, 1979). Some new place-name identifications. Cf. **2818**.

2839 POSTLES, D., 'Barkby 1086–1524', *TLAHS*, 56 (1980–1), 46–61.

2840 SQUIRES, A. E., 'History of the Charnwood Forest landscape', in J. Crocker (ed.), *Charnwood Forest: a changing landscape* (London & Wisbech: Balding & Mansell, for Loughborough Naturalists' Club, 1981), 20–129.

LINCOLNSHIRE

There is no VCH translation of Lincs. DB and as yet no Phillimore edition. For the present, see **2919**, which is work of notable quality. There is an early translation of Lincs. DB by Bawdwen, **1601**. Stenton's studies of the Danelaw are important for Lincs. DB, **241, 256**. For the relevant sections of the *DB Geography*, **332**. There are two studies of Scandinavian place-names in Lincs., **1623, 1624**. H. C. Darby has published a study of the Fenland, **1317**. On the Cambs./Lincs. boundary, **1331**. Vinogradoff made a statistical survey of the correspondence between geld assessments and estimates of ploughlands, **236**. There are numerous studies of Lincs. DB landholders. For Peterborough abbey and its tenants, **1026, 2503**. For Ramsey abbey, **1006, 1023**. For the abbey of St Calais, **231**. For Crowland and Thorney abbeys, **1029, 1313**. For the TRE holdings of Turkil of Harringworth, **1323, 1327**. For the Lacy family, **395**. For Westminster abbey, **1027**.

2901 JAMES, H. (director), *Domesday Book: or the great survey of England of William the Conqueror, A.D. MLXXXVI. Facsimile of the part relating to Lincolnshire* (Southampton: Ordnance Survey Office, 1862). Photozincographic edition.

2902 SMITH, C. G., *A translation of that portion of Domesday Book which relates to Lincolnshire and Rutlandshire* (London: Simpkin, Marshall & Co., 1870). Place-name identifications are often untrustworthy. Appears to have relied on Bawdwen (see **1601**), but at times to have guessed where he left a blank.

2903 WATERS, R. E. C., 'Roll of landowners in Lindsey temp. Henry I (Cotton ms. Claudius, C.5)', *AASRP*, 16 (1881–2), 166–230. Translates the Lindsey survey and compares its contents with DB. See **2919**.

2904 STREATFIELD, G. S., *Lincolnshire and the Danes* (London: Kegan Paul, Trench & Co., 1884). An early attempt to identify the Scandinavian element in Lincs. DB place-names.

2905 ROUND, J.H., 'The Lindsey survey', *The Academy*, no.676 (18 Apr. 1885), 275. See **2906**.

2906 WATERS, R.E.C., 'The Lindsey survey', *The Academy*, no.680 (16 May 1885), 347–8. A reply to **2905**.

2907 MASSINGBERD, W.O., *History of the parish of Ormsby-cum-Ketsby, in the hundred of Hill and county of Lincoln* (Lincoln: James Williamson, nd [1893]).

2908 'W.O.M.', 'Early records of Bag Enderby', *Lincs. N&Q*, 3 (1893), 238–41. Corrects an identification in **2902**.

2909 ROUND, J.H., 'The Lindsey survey (1115–1118)', in J.H. Round, *Feudal England* (London: Swan Sonnenschein, 1895; 2nd edn, London: Allen & Unwin, 1964), 181–95 (1st edn) and 149–59 (2nd edn).

2910 WELBY, A.C.E., 'Clergy and religious houses in Domesday', *Lincs. N&Q*, 5 (1896–8), 54–7.

2911 GOULDING, R.W., 'Notes on the lords of the manor of Burwell', *AASRP*, 24 (1897–8), 62–94. Some material on the DB tenant Ansgot of Burwell. See further *Lincs. N&Q*, 6 (1900–1), 111–15.

2912 ANON, 'Lincolnshire names', *Lincs. N&Q*, 6 (1900–1), 20–8, 41–5, 67–71, 172–5, 203–6, 228–31; 7 (1902–3), 4–7, 50–3, 71–4, 106–8. Interest is primarily etymological, but relies exclusively on DB forms.

2913 MASSINGBERD, W.O., 'The Lincolnshire sokemen', *EHR*, 20 (1905), 699–703. Counts sokemen and discusses distribution and status.

2914 TATHAM, E.H.R., 'Notes on the history of Well', *AASRP*, 30 (1909–10), 343–66. Suggests a location for a DB mill.

2915 WELBY, A.C.E., 'Ulf of Lincolnshire, before and after the Conquest', *Lincs. N&Q*, 14 (1917), 196–200. The DB estates of a Jerusalem pilgrim.

2916 STENTON, F.M., 'Sokemen and the village waste', *EHR*, 33 (1918), 344–7. For Kirkby Green and Scopwick.

2917 FOSTER, C.W., *Final concords for the county of Lincoln*, Lincs. Rec. Soc., 17 (Horncastle: W.K. Morton for the Lincs. Rec. Soc., 1920). See pp. l–lxv for DB vills which have disappeared.

2918 CRASTER, H.H.E., 'The origin of the Nevilles of Burreth', *AASRP*, 37 (1923–5), 233–8. Suggested identification of a knight of

Peterborough abbey in the Lincs. *clamores* with a tenant of the bishop of Lincoln.

2919 FOSTER, C.W. & LONGLEY, T., with an introduction by F.M.Stenton, *The Lincolnshire Domesday and the Lindsey survey* (Lincs. Rec. Soc., 19, 1924; repr. 1976). A translation of Lincs. DB, with the Latin text of the boroughs and *clamores*. Also a translation of the Lindsey survey. Stenton's introduction is very valuable. Foster contributed an appendix on places mentioned in DB which have since disappeared. At the moment the definitive edition for identification of Lincs. DB place-names.

2920 HILL, J.W.F., 'The manor of Hungate, or Beaumont fee, in the city of Lincoln', *AASRP*, 38 (1926–7), 175–208. Suggests a location for Alvred of Lincoln's DB holding in the city.

2921 FOSTER, C.W., *A history of the villages of Aisthorpe and Thorpe in the Fallows* (Lincoln: J.W.Ruddock, 1927).

2922 HILL, J.W.F., 'Lincoln castle: the constables and the guard', *AASRP*, 40 (1930–1), 1–14. See p.6 for the identification of Coleswegen of Lincoln's DB holding in Lincoln.

2923 HILL, J.W.F., 'Danish and Norman Lincoln', *AASRP*, 41 (1932–3), 7–22.

2924 CLAY, C.T., 'The family of Amundeville', *RPLAAS*, ns, 3 (1945–7), 109–36. Identifies the Goislan (Goslin, Gocelin) who held of the bishops of Lincoln and Durham and of Ralph Paynel as Goscelin de Mondeville.

2925 BINNALL, P.B.G., 'Descent of lands in East and West Barkwith, co. Lincoln', *RPLAAS*, ns, 3 (1945–7), 138–43. Brief biographies of some TRE landholders.

2926 HILL, J.W.F., *Medieval Lincoln* (Cambridge UP, 1948).

2927 DARBY, H.C., 'Domesday woodland in Lincolnshire', *Lincolnshire Historian*, 1, no.2 (1948), 55–9.

2928 MELLOWS, W.T., 'The estates of the monastery of Peterborough in the county of Lincoln', *Lincolnshire Historian*, 1, no.3 (1948), 100–14; no.4 (1949), 128–66. See **1026**.

2929 WILLIAMSON, D.M., 'Some notes on the medieval manors of Fulstow', *RPLAAS*, ns, 4 (1948–51), 1–56.

2930 OWEN, A.E.B., 'Early history of Saltfleethaven', *RPLAAS*, ns, 5 (1953), 87–100.

2931 WILLIAMSON, D. M., 'Kesteven villages in the middle ages', *Lincolnshire Historian*, 2, no. 2 (1955), 10–17.

2932 RUDKIN, E. H. & OWEN, D. M., 'The medieval salt industry in the Lindsey marshland', *RPLAAS*, ns, 8 (1959–60), 76–84. The DB evidence for salt-pans in the context of later evidence.

2933 HALLAM, H. E., 'Salt-making in the Lincolnshire fenland during the Middle Ages', *RPLAAS*, ns, 8 (1959–60), 85–112.

2934 HALLAM, H. E.; *Settlement and society: a study of the early agrarian history of south Lincolnshire* (Cambridge UP, 1965).

2935 JENSEN, G. F., *Scandinavian personal names in Lincolnshire and Yorkshire*, Navnestudier udgivet af Institut for navneforskning, nr 7 (Copenhagen: I kommission has Akademisk forlag, 1968).

2936 DOVER, P., *The early medieval history of Boston, A.D. 1086–1400*, History of Boston ser., no. 2 (Boston: Guardian Press, 1970). Tries to reconstruct the township, which is not directly mentioned in DB, from entries under Skirbeck hundred.

2937 EVERSON, P., 'An excavated Anglo-Saxon sunken-featured building and settlement site at Salmonby, Lincs. 1972', *Lincs. History and Archaeology*, 8 (1973), 61–9. See p. 66 for suggestion that a DB entry may conceal settlement.

2938 KING, E., 'The origins of the Wake family. The early history of the barony of Bourne in Lincolnshire', *Northants. P&P*, 5 (1973–7), 166–76. The DB estates of Oger the Breton, Godfrey de Cambrai and Baldwin the Fleming.

2939 BERESFORD, G., *The medieval clay-land village: excavations at Goltho and Barton Blount*, Soc. for Medieval Archaeology, monograph, no. 6 (London: printed for the Soc. for Medieval Archaeology, 1975). For settlement and for omissions from DB.

2940 CLAY, C. T., *Notes on the family of Clere* (Wakefield: privately printed by West Yorks. Printing Co. Ltd., 1975). For DB lands held as a sub-tenant in Lincs. and Yorks. by Roger de Clères.

2941 HEALEY, R. H., 'Medieval salt-making', *South Lincs. Archaeology*, 1 (1977), 4–5. Contains a map of DB salt pans.

2942 ROFFE, D. R., 'The distribution of sokeland in south Kesteven in 1086', *South Lincs. Archaeology*, 1 (1977), 30–1.

2943 HARDEN, G., 'Historical development', in *idem, Medieval Boston and its archaeological implications* (Sleaford: South Lincs. Archaeological Unit, 1978), 9–15.

2944 SHERMAN, R. M., 'The continental origins of the Ghent family of Lincolnshire', *Nottingham Medieval Studies*, 22 (1978), 23–35.

2945 ROFFE, D. R., 'Origins', in C. M. Mahany & D. R. Roffe (eds), *South Lincs. Archaeology*, 3 (1979), 11–16. Concerns Sleaford.

2946 ROFFE, D. R., 'The Lincolnshire hundred', *Landscape History*, 3 (1981), 27–36.

2947 OWEN, D., 'The beginnings of the port of Boston', in N. Field & A. White (eds), *A prospect of Lincolnshire* (Lincoln: Lincs. County Council, 1984), 42–5.

2948 OWEN, A. E. B., 'Salt, sea banks and medieval settlement on the Lindsey coast', in N. Field & A. White (eds), *A prospect of Lincolnshire* (Lincoln: Lincs. County Council, 1984), 46–9.

2949 WHITE, A. J., 'Medieval fisheries in the Witham and its tributaries', *Lincs. History and Archaeology*, 19 (1984), 29–35.

MIDDLESEX

There is an early translation of Middx. DB by Bawdwen, **1201**. Baring produced a major study of Middx. DB statistics, **237**, as also did Vinogradoff, **236**. For the relevant section of the *DB Geography*, **370**. On hidation, see **203**. For the Middx. holdings of Albert the Lotharingian, Robert d'Ouilly and Miles Crispin, the archbishopric of Canterbury and the abbey of Westminster, **1007, 1113, 1212, 1027**. Seebohm produced a study of the manor of Westminster, **131**, on which see other references below.

3001 SAUNDERS, G., 'Results of an inquiry concerning the situation and extent of Westminster, at various periods', *Archaeologia*, 26 (1836), 223–41.

3002 GRIFFITH, E., 'Middlesex in the time of the Domesday survey', *TLMAS*, 1 (1860), 175–82.

3003 JAMES, H. (director), *Domesday Book: or the great survey of England of William the Conqueror, A.D. MLXXXVI. Facsimile of the part relating to Middlesex* (Southampton: Ordnance Survey Office, 1861). Photozincographic edition.

3004 ANON, *A literal extension of the Latin text; and an English translation of Domesday Book in relation to the county of Middlesex to accompany the facsimile copy photo-zincographed under the direction of Col. Sir H. James, RE, FRS, at the Ordnance Survey Office, Southampton* (London: Vacher & Sons; Longman, Green, Longman & Roberts, 1862).

3005 COOTE, H.C., 'Notices on Deorman of London, a Domesday tenant in capite', *TLMAS*, 3 (1870), 153–6.

3006 PLANTAGENET-HARRISON, G.H. de S.N., *Facsimile of the original Domesday Book, or the Great Survey of England A.D. 1080, in the reign of William the Conqueror, pt 1, Middlesex, with translation* (London: Head & Meek, 1876). No further vols were published.

3007 FÈRET, C.J., *Fulham old and new*, 3 vols (London: Leadenhall Press, 1900). See 1, 6–13.

3008 DAVIES, A.M., 'The Domesday hidation of Middlesex', *The Home Counties Magazine*, 3 (1901), 232–8.

3009 'T.P., WALTHAMSTOW', 'Hidation of Middlesex: Stanestaple', *The Home Counties Magazine*, 3 (1901), 330–1.

3010 SHARPE, M., *Some antiquities of Middlesex in British, Roman and Saxon times* (Brentford: Brentford printing and publishing co., 1905). See chapter 11 for an analysis of DB estates.

3011 SHORE, T.W., 'The Anglo-Saxon settlement round London and glimpses of Anglo-Saxon life in and near it', *TLMAS*, ns, 1 (1905), 283–318, 366–91, 469–505. See for DB woodland.

3012 SHARPE, M., *Some antiquities of Middlesex, addenda (no. 2): the ancient forests of Middlesex* (London: Chiswick Press, 1907). Some discussion of DB woodland.

3013 SHARPE, M., 'The Domesday survey of Middlesex', *The Home Counties Magazine*, 10 (1908), 315–16.

3014 SHARPE, M., *The Roman measures in the Domesday survey of Middlesex* (Brentford: Brentford publishing & printing co., 1909).

3015 RUTTON, W.L., 'The manor of Eia, or Eye next Westminster', *Archaeologia*, 62 (1910), 31–53.

3016 ROBINSON, J.A., *Gilbert Crispin, abbot of Westminster* (Cambridge UP, 1911). See pp. 39–40 for the Westminster DB entry.

3017 SHARPE, M., *The antiquities of Middlesex: the Middlesex district in Roman times, pts I & II* (Brentford: Brentford publishing and printing co., 1913). More on Roman origins of DB assessments.

3018 SHARPE, M., *The antiquities of Middlesex: the accuracy of the Domesday land measures in Middlesex and their Roman origin* (Brentford: Brentford publishing & printing co., 1914). Revised in M. Sharpe, *Antiquities of Middlesex in British, Roman and Saxon times* (London: Bell, 1919), 149–72.

3019 SHARPE, M., 'The Domesday survey of Middlesex', *38th annual report of the Ealing Scientific and Microscopical Society* (Ealing, 1915), 3–6.

3020 SHARPE, M., *The antiquities of Middlesex: the Middlesex district in Saxon times* (Brentford: Brentford publishing & printing co., 1916). Revised in *Antiquities of Middlesex: Middlesex in British, Roman and Saxon times* (London: Bell, 1919), 131–48. Discussion of DB hundreds and ecclesiastical lands. Cf. **3029** on Ossulston hundred.

3021 ASHRIDGE, A., 'St Marylebone and its Anglo-Saxon manors', *TLMAS*, ns, 4 (1918–22), 56–74.

3022 GOVER, J. E. B., *The place-names of Middlesex* (London: Longman, 1922).

3023 SHARPE, M., 'The making of Middlesex: its villages, fields and roads', *TLMAS*, ns, 5 (1929), 237–55. Includes DB statistics of hundreds, people and livestock.

3024 BRETT-JAMES, N. G., 'Some extents and surveys of Hendon', *TLMAS*, ns, 6 (1929–32), 547–78.

3025 SHARPE, M., *Middlesex in British, Roman and Saxon times* (London: Methuen, 1932).

3026 SHARPE, M., 'Middlesex parishes and their antiquity', *TLMAS*, ns, 7 (1937), 91–8.

3027 SHARPE, M., 'Middlesex in Domesday Book', *TLMAS*, ns, 7 (1937), 509–27.

3028 BRAUN, H., 'The hundred of Gore and its moot-hedge', *TLMAS*, ns, 7 (1937), 218–28.

3029 MADGE, S. J., *The early records of Haringay, alias Hornsey, from prehistoric times to 1216 A.D.* (Hornsey: Public Libraries Committee, 1938). Full discussion of the DB manor of Hornsey.

3030 SHARPE, M., 'An address on Roman rural economy and its effect on Middlesex', *TLMAS*, ns, 8 (1940), 1–13. For a tabulation of DB material.

3031 SHARPE, M., *Middlesex in the eleventh century* (Brentford: Brentford printing & publishing co., 1941). A discussion of Middx. DB with tables and maps. Particular treatment is given to the manor of Westminster.

3032 GOVER, J. E. B., MAWER, A. & STENTON, F. M., with the collaboration of S. J. Madge, *The place-names of Middlesex apart from the city of London*, EPNS, 18 (Cambridge UP, 1942).

3033 BAYLIS, C.F., 'The omission of Edgware from Domesday Book', *TLMAS*, ns, 11 (1952–4), 62–6.

3034 ROBBINS, M., 'A note on early Finchley', *TLMAS*, 18 (1955), 65–7.

3035 URWIN, A.C.B., *Hampton and Teddington in 1086 – an analysis of the entry in the Domesday Book*, Borough of Twickenham Local History Soc., papers no. 2 (Twickenham, 1965). See especially for land use.

3036 PINDER, T.G., 'Introduction to the Domesday survey', *VCH Middx.*, 1, ed. J.S.Cockburn, H.P.F.King & K.G.T.McDonnell (OUP, for the Institute of Historical Research, 1969), 80–118.

3037 PINDER, T.G., 'Translation of the text', *VCH Middx.*, 1, 119–29, with appendices tabulating hides and teamlands and discussing the *Hidagium comitatus totius Middlesexe* of 1151–1153/4.

3038 *MORRIS, J. (ed., from a translation prepared by S. Wood), Domesday Book. 11. Middlesex* (Chichester: Phillimore, 1975). Has a brief appendix devoted to the holdings of villeins and others. For additions and corrections, see **1028, 2418**.

3039 URWIN, A.C.B., *Twickenham, Whitton, Isleworth, Hounslow and Heston in 1086. An analysis of the entry in the Domesday Book*, Borough of Twickenham Local History Soc., papers no. 34 (Twickenham, 1976).

3040 McDONNELL, K.G.T., *Medieval London suburbs* (London & Chichester: Phillimore, 1978). Concentrates on East London.

NORFOLK

All work on Norfolk DB must take account of studies of Little DB and of discussions of the social structure of East Anglia. See especially **271, 316, 331, 345, 397**.These should be taken alongside items listed below, notably the work of B.Dodwell. For the relevant sections of the *DB Geography*, **332**. For hundreds, leets and revenues therefrom, **270, 274**. For studies of the Fenland and salt-making, see **1317, 1328**. On IE and the holdings of the abbey of Ely, **1005, 331, 1321**. For a discussion of the destruction of woodland, **2055**, in contrast to **3127, 3128**. On the landholdings in Norfolk of Ramsey abbey and TRE of Turkil of Harringworth, **1006, 1023, 1323, 1327**. For an early and entirely superseded discussion of Norfolk place-names, **1303**. For discussions of the 'exchange of Lewes' mentioned in Norfolk DB, see **4122, 4134, 4140, 4159, 4161**. For Eudo *dapifer*'s succession to Lisois de Moustiers, **1005**.

3101 BLOMEFIELD, F., *An essay towards a topographical history of the county of Norfolk*, 11 vols (London: William Miller, 1805–10). An early attempt at DB identifications.

3102 HUNTER, J., 'The history and topography of Ketteringham', *NA*, 3 (1852), 245–314.

3103 MUNFORD, G., *An analysis of the Domesday Book of the county of Norfolk* (London: J. R. Smith, 1858). Mostly devoted to accounts of Norfolk tenants-in-chief, but also gives a brief analysis of population, animals, churches, etc.

3104 JAMES, H. (director), *Domesday Book: or the great survey of England of William the Conqueror, A.D. MLXXXVI. Facsimile of the part relating to Norfolk* (Southampton: Ordnance Survey Office, 1862). Photozincographic edition.

3105 CARTHEW, G. A., *The hundred of Launditch and deanery of Brisley in the county of Norfolk*, 3 vols (Norwich: Miller & Leavins, 1877–9). For much tabulated DB material.

3106 ROUND, J. H., 'The death of William Malet', *The Academy*, no. 625 (26 April 1884), 297. For the passage *quando ivit in marisco* (DB, 2, fo. 133b).

3107 COULTON, J. J., 'Names on the Nar', *NA*, 11 (1892), 208–27.

3108 COULTON, J. J., 'Names on the Wissey', *NA*, 12 (1895), 13–24.

3109 ROUND, J. H., 'Hainfridus de St-Omer dans le Domesday', *Bulletin historique trimestriel de la Société des Antiquaires de la Morinie*, 10 (1897–1901), 679–80.

3110 JOHNSON, C., 'Introduction to the Norfolk Domesday', in *VCH Norfolk*, 2, ed. W. Page (London: Constable, 1906), 1–38.

3111 JOHNSON, C. & SALISBURY, E., 'Translation of the Norfolk Domesday', *VCH Norfolk*, 2, 39–203.

3112 JOHNSON, C., 'The danegeld in Norfolk', *VCH Norfolk*, 2, 204–11.

3113 DAVENPORT, F. G., *The economic development of a Norfolk manor, 1086–1565* (Cambridge UP, 1906). Deals with Forncett.

3114 TENCH, E. J., 'Norwich castle mound', *NA*, 17 (1910), 42–5. An excavation report which showed that there was habitation not mentioned in DB under the motte site. See **3418**.

3115 HOWLETT, R., 'The ancient see of Elmham', *NA*, 18 (1914), 105–28. A confused discussion of the DB evidence for the bishopric.

3116 CAM, H.M., 'The English lands of the abbey of St Riquier', *EHR*, 31 (1916), 443–7. See also for the forfeited estates of earl Ralph.

3117 HOARE, C.M., *The history of an East Anglian soke* (Bedford: Beds. Times Publishing Co. Ltd., 1918). For Gimingham. See especially pp. 6–14.

3118 HUDSON, W., 'The Anglo-Danish village community of Martham, Norfolk: its pre-Domesday tenants and their conversion into the customary tenants of a feudal manor in 1101', *NA*, 20 (1921), 273–316.

3119 HUDSON, W., 'Status of "villani" and other tenants in Danish East Anglia in pre-Conquest times', *TRHS*, 4th ser., 4 (1921), 23–48. Deals mainly with Martham. Also with Hemsby, Caister, Ormesby, Happisburgh, East Ruston and Ludham.

3120 STENTON, F.M., 'St Benet of Holme and the Norman Conquest', *EHR*, 37 (1922), 225–35.

3121 TINGEY, J.C., 'Some notes on the Domesday assessment of Norfolk', *NA*, 21 (1923), 134–42.

3122 BEEVOR, H., 'Norfolk woodlands from the evidence of contemporary chronicles', *Trans. Norfolk & Norwich Naturalists' Soc.*, 11 (1924), 487–508. Reprinted in *Quarterly Jour. of Forestry*, 19 (1925), 87–110. Contains a map showing woodland for more than 100 swine.

3123 LANDON, L., 'The Bainard family in Norfolk', *NA*, 22 (1926), 209–20.

3124 SCHRAM, O.K., 'Some early East Anglian wills', *NA*, 22 (1926), 350–69. For the wills of two Norfolk DB tenants.

3125 LANDON, L., 'The sheriffs of Norfolk', *NA*, 23 (1929), 147–65. Short biographies of several DB tenants.

3126 WEST, J.R., *St Benet of Holme 1020–1210*, 2 vols (Norfolk Rec. Soc., 2–3, 1932). See especially vol. 3 for DB estates in Norfolk and Suffolk.

3127 DARBY, H.C., 'Domesday woodland in East Anglia', *Antiquity*, 8 (1934), 211–15. Cf. **2055**.

3128 DARBY, H.C., 'The Domesday geography of Norfolk and Suffolk', *Geog. Jour.*, 85 (1935), 435–52. An interesting concluding

3129 DODWELL, B., 'The free peasantry of East Anglia in Domesday', *NA*, 27 (1941), 145–57.

3130 JOPE, E.M., 'Excavations in the city of Norwich, 1948', *NA*, 30 (1952), 287–323. See especially pp. 288–90 and fig. 1.

3131 ALLISON, K.J., 'The lost villages of Norfolk', *NA*, 31 (1955), 116–62.

3132 YONEKAWA, S., 'A study of the social and economic structure of rural Norfolk in the eleventh century', *Shigaku-Zasshi*, 57, no. 4 (1958), 1–34. In Japanese.

3133 GREEN, C., 'East Anglian coast-line levels since Roman times', *Antiquity*, 35 (1961), 21–8. Includes a map of the DB coast-line.

3134 DODWELL, B., 'The honour of the bishop of Thetford/ Norwich in the late eleventh and early twelfth centuries', *NA*, 33 (1965), 185–99.

3135 GREEN, C., 'The lost vill of Ness', *NA*, 34 (1966–9), 2–8. Identifies *Nessa* as a berewick of Caister which formerly stood on a promontory of the Caister shore.

3136 DODWELL, B., 'The making of the Domesday survey in Norfolk: the hundred and a half of Clacklose', *EHR*, 84 (1969), 79–84. An important article which discusses the making of Norfolk DB and has general significance for the making of DB. See **364, 410**.

3137 PARKER, V., *The making of Kings Lynn* (London & Chichester: Phillimore, for the Kings Lynn Archaeological Survey, 1971). For N.W. Norfolk DB. See further **3144**.

3138 ROBERTS, J.P. *et al*, 'Excavations in Norwich – 1974. The Norwich survey – fourth interim report', *NA*, 36 (1974–7), 99–110. See p. 105 for identification of the church of All Saints in DB Norwich with All Saints' Westlegate. See also **3130**.

3139 CLARK, C., 'Women's names in post-Conquest England: observations and speculations', *Speculum*, 53 (1978), 223–51. For a clarification of the DB entry for South Pickenham at p. 223.

3140 DAVISON, A.J., 'West Harling: a village and its disappearance', *NA*, 37 (1979–80), 295–306.

3141 CAMPBELL, B.M.S., 'The extent and layout of commonfields in eastern Norfolk', *NA*, 38 (1981–3), 5–32. See pp. 18–20 for discussion of density of ploughteams in DB and later surveys.

3142 ADDINGTON, S., 'Landscape and settlements in south Norfolk', *NA*, 38 (1981–3), 97–139.

3143 BROWN, P. (ed., from a draft translation by M. Hepplestone, J. Mothersill & M. Newman), *Domesday Book. 33. Norfolk*, 2 vols (Chichester: Phillimore, 1984).

3144 OWEN, D. M., *The making of Kings Lynn: a documentary survey*, Records of social and economic history, ns, 9 (London: OUP, for the British Academy, 1984). For DB and NW Norfolk. Cf. **3137**.

NORTHAMPTONSHIRE

There has been extensive discussion of the hidation of Northants. through comparisons between DB, the 'Geld Roll' and the 12th-century Northants. survey. In addition to all the studies mentioned below, it is necessary to consult **3506**. For the relevant section of the *DB Geography*, **340**. For the *terra regis* of Northants. DB and the 'Geld Roll', see **323**, but cf. **3226**. For several insights into Northants. DB, see **256**, for a brief general treatment of DB which uses Northants. for local examples, **341**, and for Scandinavian place-names, **1624**. There are numerous studies of Northants. landholders. For Peterborough abbey, **1026, 2503**. For Ramsey abbey, **1006, 1023**. For Evesham abbey, **281, 2136, 2138**. For Crowland and Thorney abbeys, **1313, 1029**. For the Chocques ('de Cioches') family, **1024**. For the TRE holdings of Turkil of Harringworth, **1323, 1327**. For Westminster abbey, **1027**.

3201 MORTON, J., *The natural history of Northamptonshire: to which is annex'd a transcript of Doomsday Book, so far as it relates to that county* (London: Knaplock & Wilkin, 1712). The Latin text, with abbreviations extended. Not entirely accurate. For the author's notes on Northants. DB, see BL, ms. Sloane 3560.

3202 BRIDGES, J., *The history and antiquities of Northamptonshire*, 2 vols (Oxford: sold by T. Payne, D. Prince, J. Cooke & Mr Lacy, 1791). Made considerable use of DB. Contains a list of the DB hundreds.

3203 BAKER, G., *The history and antiquities of the county of Northampton*, 2 vols (London: Nichols & Son and J. Rodwell, 1822–41). Used DB extensively. Deals only with the southern part of the county.

3204 JAMES, H. (director), *Domesday Book: or the great survey of England of William the Conqueror, A.D. MLXXXVI. Facsimile of the part relating to Northamptonshire* (Southampton: Ordnance Survey Office, 1862). Photo-zincographic edition.

3205 MOORE, S. A., *Domesday Book: the portion relating to Northamptonshire* (Northampton: Mark Dorman; London: Longman, Green, Longman, Roberts & Green; Letts Son & Co.; Vader & Sons, 1863). Parallel Latin and English texts, with an introduction and notes.

3206 SHARP, S., 'On the Anglo-Saxon "Hamtune", the Norman "Northantone", Northampton castle, and the antiquities found on its site', *AASRP*, 16 (1881–2), 63–70. A mediocre discussion of the Northampton DB entry.

3207 MARKHAM, C. A., 'Domesday Book, Northamptonshire', *AASRP*, 19 (1887–8), 126–39. Valuable for bibliographical material.

3208 ROUND, J. H., 'The Northamptonshire Geld Roll', in J. H. Round, *Feudal England* (London: Swan Sonnenschein, 1895; 2nd edn, London: Allen & Unwin, 1964), 147–56 (1st edn) and 124–30 (2nd edn). For a discussion of the Geld Roll's date and some comment on its relationship to DB. See further **3223, 3226**.

3209 ROUND, J. H., 'The Northamptonshire survey (Hen. I – Hen. II)', in J. H. Round, *Feudal England* (London: Swan Sonnenschein, 1895; 2nd edn, London: Allen & Unwin, 1964), 215–24 (1st edn) and 175–81 (2nd edn). Mainly concerned with the survey's date. See **3213** for its relationship with DB.

3210 ROUND, J. H., 'The hidation of Northamptonshire', *EHR*, 15 (1900), 78–86.

3211 ROUND, J. H., 'Introduction to the Northamptonshire Domesday', in *VCH Northants.*, 1, ed. W. R. D. Atkins & R. M. Serjeantson (Westminster: Constable, 1902), 257–98. One of the best of Round's VCH introductions.

3212 ROUND, J. H., 'Text of the Northamptonshire Domesday', *VCH Northants.*, 1, 301–56.

3213 ROUND, J. H., 'The Northamptonshire survey', *VCH Northants.*, 1, 357–92. A translation with an introduction on its relationship with DB.

3214 BARING, F. H., 'The hidation of Northamptonshire in 1086', *EHR*, 17 (1902), 76–83.

3215 BARING, F. H., 'The pre-Domesday hidation of Northampton-shire', *EHR*, 17 (1902), 470–9.

3216 MAXWELL LYTE, H. C., 'Fitzurse', *SANHSP*, 68 (1922), 93–104. Identifies Urse who held ½ hide in Corby with the Urse who held the abbey of Glastonbury in Wilts.

3217 GOVER, J.E.B., MAWER, A. & STENTON, F.M., *The place-names of Northamptonshire*, EPNS, 10 (Cambridge UP, 1933).

3218 CAM, H.M., 'The hundreds of Northamptonshire', *Jour. Northants. Nat. Hist. Soc. & Field Club*, 27 (1934), 99–108.

3219 BAYLEY, C.P., 'The Domesday geography of Northampton-shire', *Jour. Northants. Nat. Hist. Soc. & Field Club*, 29 (1938), 1–22.

3220 BEAVER, S.H., *Northamptonshire*, pt 58 of L.D.Stamp (ed.), *The land of Britain: the report of the land utilisation survey of Britain* (London: Geographical Publications Ltd., 1943). See pp. 386–8.

3221 BALFOUR-MELVILLE, E.W.M., 'A Northamptonshire estate of Malcolm Canmore', *Scottish historical review*, 26 (1947), 101–2.

3222 LEE, F., 'A new theory of the origins and early growth of Northampton', *Arch. Jour.*, 110 (1953), 164–74.

3223 ROBERTSON, A.J., *Anglo-Saxon charters* (Cambridge UP, 1956). See pp. 230–7 for the most modern edition of the Geld Roll. See pp. 481–4 for notes which make several corrections to Round's analysis (**3208**).

3224 ALLISON, K.J., BERESFORD, M.W. & HURST, J.G., *The deserted villages of Northamptonshire*, Dept. of English Local History, occasional papers, no. 18 (Leicester UP, 1966).

3225 REEDY, W.T., 'The first two Bassets of Weldon', *Northampton-shire P&P*, 4 (1966–72), 241–5, 295–8.

3226 HART, C., *The hidation of Northamptonshire*, Dept. of English Local History, occasional papers, 2nd ser., no. 3 (Leicester UP, 1970). The most modern discussion.

3227 STEANE, J.M., 'The forests of Northamptonshire in the early middle ages', *Northamptonshire P&P*, 5 (1973–7), 7–17.

3228 BROWN, A.E. & TAYLOR, C.C., 'Four deserted settlements in Northamptonshire', *Northamptonshire P&P*, 5 (1973–7), 178–98. For DB Kingsthorpe, Knuston and Sywell.

3229 BROWN, G., 'Kelmarsh and its deserted village', *Northamptonshire Ant. Soc. reports & papers*, 67 (1975), 16–23.

3230 ROYAL COMMISSION ON HISTORICAL MONUMENTS, ENGLAND, *An inventory of the historical monuments in the county of Northampton*, 4 vols (London: HMSO, 1975–82). Essential for the history of settlement in Northants. Gives many identifications of estates included in a single DB entry.

3231 BROWN, A.E., KEY, T.R. & ORR, C., 'Some Anglo-Saxon estates and their boundaries in south-west Northamptonshire', *Northamptonshire Archaeology*, 12 (1977), 155–76. Deals with Badby, Newnham, Dodford and Everdon. Suggests that *Celverdescote* be identified with Great Everdon.

3232 SKELTON, P.N., 'Chelverdescote', *Northamptonshire P&P*, 6 (1978–82), 115–17.

3233 BROWN, A.E., 'Chelverdescote again', *Northamptonshire P&P*, 6 (1978–82), 185–6.

3234 THORN, F. & C. (ed., from a draft translation by M.Jones, P.Morgan & J.Plaister), *Domesday Book. 21. Northamptonshire* (Chichester: Phillimore, 1979). Text, translation, valuable notes and a useful summary of the discussions of Northants. hidation.

NOTTINGHAMSHIRE

There is an early translation of Notts. DB by Bawdwen, **1601**. The work of Stenton on the social structure of the Danelaw and of Cameron and Jensen on Scandinavian place-names is important for the study of Notts. DB, **241, 256, 1623, 1624**. For the relevant sections of the *DB Geography*, **369**. On the holdings of Robert d'Ouilly and Miles Crispin, **1113**, of the Lisours and Lacy families, **1618, 395**, and of Peterborough abbey, **1026**.

3301 JAMES, H. (director), *Domesday Book: or the great survey of England of William the Conqueror, A.D. MLXXXVI. Facsimile of the part relating to Nottinghamshire* (Southampton: Ordnance Survey Office, 1862). Photo-zincographic edition.

3302 'STONE MAN', 'Notts. churches in Domesday', *Notts. & Derbys. N&Q*, 1 (1893), 83–4. Lists the DB churches.

3303 STAYCE, J., 'Studies of the Nottinghamshire Domesday', in R.White (ed.), *The Dukery records* (Worksop: privately printed, 1904), 1–60. Contains lists of landholders TRE and TRW and their holdings, with some commentary.

3304 STENTON, F.M., 'Introduction to the Nottinghamshire Domesday', in *VCH Notts.*, 1, ed. W.Page (London: Constable, 1906), 207–46.

3305 STENTON, F.M., 'Text of the Nottinghamshire Domesday', *VCH Notts.*, 1, 247–88.

3306 PRYCE, T.D. & DOBSON, F.W., 'An ancient village site: Whimpton, Nottinghamshire', *TTS*, 11 (1907), 139–44. Identifies the site of *Wimentun*.

3307 MUTSCHMANN, H., *The place-names of Nottinghamshire: their origin and development* (Cambridge UP, 1913). Superseded by **3311**.

3308 GILL, H., 'Colwick hall and church', *TTS*, 19 (1915), 35–46. Suggests location of a DB mill at p. 39.

3309 GILL, H., 'Notes and references to mills on the Leen', *TTS*, 20 (1916), 5–9.

3310 COSSONS, A., 'East Chilwell and Keighton', *TTS*, 33 (1929), 1–9. Suggests location for DB *Estrecilleuelle*. See **3311**.

3311 GOVER, J.E.B., MAWER, A. & STENTON, F.M., *The place-names of Nottinghamshire*, EPNS, 17 (Cambridge UP, 1940).

3312 CARTER, W.F. & WILKINSON, R.F., 'The Fledborough family of Lisures', *TTS*, 44 (1940), 14–34.

3313 WILKINSON, R., 'The ruined and lost churches of Nottinghamshire', *TTS*, 46 (1942), 66–72. See p. 66 for a list of DB churches which have disappeared.

3314 OWEN, L.V.D., 'The borough of Nottingham, 1066 to 1284', *TTS*, 49 (1945), 12–27.

3315 BARLEY, M.W., 'Cistercian land clearances in Nottinghamshire: three deserted villages and their moated successor', *Nottingham medieval studies*, 1 (1957), 75–89. For the depopulated DB settlements of Grimston, Rufford and Inkersall Grange.

3316 ROGERS, A., 'Parish boundaries and urban history', *JBAA*, 3rd ser., 35 (1972), 46–64. For DB Nottingham and Stamford.

3317 CAMERON, A., 'The deserted medieval village of Sutton Passeys', *TTS*, 80 (1976), 47–59. Suggests a location for a lost DB site.

3318 MORRIS, J. (ed., from a draft translation by C. Parker & S. Wood), *Domesday Book. 28. Nottinghamshire* (Chichester: Phillimore, 1977).

3319 BISHOP, M.W., 'The origins of East Retford', *TTS*, 82 (1978), 26–8. For unidentified DB *Odesthorpe*.

3320 BISHOP, M.W., 'Multiple estates in late Anglo-Saxon Nottinghamshire', *TTS*, 85 (1981), 37–47. For the territorial structure of Notts. DB.

3321 CAMERON, A. & O'BRIEN, C., 'The deserted medieval village of Thorpe-in-the-Glebe, Nottinghamshire', *TTS*, 85 (1981), 56–67.

3322 CROOK, D., 'The community of Mansfield from Domesday Book to the reign of Edward III', *TTS*, 88 (1984), 14–38.

OXFORDSHIRE

There is an early translation of Oxfords. DB by Bawdwen, **1201**. Lennard devoted a valuable chapter to DB Oxfords. in **360**. For the relevant section of the *DB Geography*, **370**. For the possible movements of William I's army in Oxfords. in 1066, **201, 392, 393**. For a comparison of the Bucks. and Oxfords. hundreds, **1213**, and for a suggested identification of *Acham*, **1214** (see also **420, 3427**). For a tabulation of Oxfords. values, **236**. On the holdings of Robert d'Ouilly and Miles Crispin, **1113**. For those of the archbishopric of Canterbury, **1212**, and of the Lacy family, **395**.

3401 JAMES, H. (director), *Domesday Book: or the great survey of England of William the Conqueror, A.D. MLXXXVI. Facsimile of the part relating to Oxfordshire* (Southampton: Ordnance Survey Office, 1862). Photozincographic edition.

3402 PARKER, J., *The early history of Oxford, 727–1100* (Oxford: Clarendon Press, for the Oxford Hist. Soc., 1885). See chapter 11.

3403 MOWAT, J. L. G., *Notes on the Oxfordshire Domesday* (Oxford: 116 High Street, 1892). A useful work, but with some mistaken identifications.

3404 BARING, F. H., 'Oxfordshire traces of the northern insurgents of 1065', *EHR*, 13 (1898), 295–7. The evidence used is not conclusive.

3405 BALLARD, A., 'Three surveys of Bladon', *Oxfords. Arch. Soc. Report*, 56 (1910), 20–7.

3406 ALEXANDER, H., *The place-names of Oxfordshire* (Oxford: Clarendon Press, 1912). Superseded by **3419**.

3407 MAXWELL LYTE, H. C., 'Curci', *SANHSP*, 66 (1920), 98–126. The DB estates of Richard de Coucy.

3408 EVANS, E., 'The manor of Headington', *Oxfords. Arch. Soc. Report*, 73 (1928), 161–216.

3409 LOBEL, M. D., *The history of Dean and Chalford*, Oxfords. Rec. Soc. publications, 17 (Oxford: for the society, 1935).

3410 CAM, H. M., 'The hundred outside the North Gate of Oxford', *Oxoniensia*, 1 (1936), 113–28. Reprinted in H. M. Cam, *Liberties and communities in medieval England* (Cambridge UP, 1944), 107–23. A study of an individual hundred, which also deals with the DB hundreds of Oxfords.

3411 CHAMBERS, E., *Eynsham under the monks*, Oxfords. Rec. Soc. publications, 18 (Oxford: for the society, 1936). See pp. 4–7.

3412 SALTER, H. E., *Medieval Oxford* (Oxford: Clarendon Press, for the Oxford Hist. Soc., 1936). See especially chapters 1 and 2. For comment see **3413**.

3413 LOBEL, M. D., 'Notes on the history of mediaeval Oxford', *Oxoniensia*, 3 (1938), 83–99. A review of **3412** with specific comment on Oxford DB.

3414 STENTON, F. M., 'Domesday survey: introduction', in *VCH Oxfords.*, 1, ed. L. F. Salzman (OUP, for the Institute of Historical Research, 1939), 373–95.

3415 STENTON, F. M., 'Domesday survey: the text', *VCH Oxfords.*, 1, 396–428.

3416 ARKELL, W. J., 'Place-names and topography in the Upper Thames country: a regional essay', *Oxoniensia*, 7 (1942), 1–23.

3417 LAMBORN, E. A. G., 'A problem of the Oxfordshire Domesday', *N&Q*, 187 (1944), 203–5. Suggests that *Hunesworde* is in Chislehampton. See **3427, 420**.

3418 JOPE, E. M., 'Late Saxon pits under Oxford castle mound: excavations in 1952', *Oxoniensia*, 17–18 (1952–3), 77–111. Discusses evidence of occupation found beneath the mound despite DB's silence

3419 GELLING, M. & STENTON, D. M., *The place-names of Oxfordshire*, 2 vols, EPNS, 23–4 (Cambridge UP, 1953–4).

3420 HOSKINS, W. G. & JOPE, E. M., 'The medieval period', in A. F. Martin & R. W. Steel (eds), *The Oxford region* (OUP, 1954), 103–20. Includes maps of population, woodland, towns and markets.

3421 JOPE, E. M., 'Saxon Oxford and its region', in D. B. Harden (ed.), *Dark-Age Britain* (London: Methuen, 1956), 234–58.

3422 ARKELL, W. J., *Oxford stone* (London: Faber & Faber, 1957). See pp. 54–64 for the DB quarry at Taynton and its later history. See also **3420, 3421**.

3423 JOPE, E. M., 'The Clarendon Hotel, Oxford. Part I. The site', *Oxoniensia*, 23 (1958), 1–83. See p. 7 for the topography of DB Oxford.

3424 ROBERTS, E., 'The boundary and woodlands of Shotover Forest *c.* 1298', *Oxoniensia*, 18 (1963), 68–73. Identifies and locates woodland mentioned under DB Islip.

3425 ALLISON, K. J., BERESFORD, M. W. & HURST, J. G., *The deserted villages of Oxfordshire*, Dept. of English Local History, Occasional papers, no. 17 (Leicester UP, 1965).

3426 EMERY, F., *The Oxfordshire landscape* (London: Hodder & Stoughton, 1974). See especially chapter 3.

3427 MORRIS, J. (ed., from a draft translation by C. Caldwell), *Domesday Book. 14. Oxfordshire* (Chichester: Phillimore, 1978). For additions and corrections, see **4523**.

RUTLAND

The county of Rutland did not exist in 1086. *Roteland* is included in DB after Notts. and includes only two of the wapentakes which were part of the county from the later 12th century. The third wapentake was surveyed under Northants. Several studies in the Northants. section should be consulted to complete the bibliography of the pre-1974 county of Rutland. See especially, **3211, 3212, 3226, 3234**. For early translations of the 'Rutland' folios, **1601, 2902**. Aspects of Rutland DB are illuminated by studies devoted to the Danelaw counties, **241, 1623, 1624**. For the relevant section of the *DB Geography*, **340**. For a comparative study of DB Stamford and Nottingham, **3316**. For the holdings in Rutland of Albert the Lotharingian, **1007**, and of Peterborough abbey, **1026**.

3501 ANON, *A literal extension of the Latin text, and an English translation, of Domesday Book in relation to the county of Rutland*, bound with **2803**, for which see for full ref.

3502 STENTON, F. M., 'Introduction to the Rutland Domesday', in *VCH Rutland*, 1, ed. W. Page (London: Constable, 1908), 121–37.

3503 STENTON, F. M., 'Translation of the Rutland Domesday', *VCH Rutland*, 1, 138–42.

3504 LOYN, H. R., 'Anglo-Saxon Stamford', in A. Rogers (ed.), *The making of Stamford* (Leicester UP, 1965), 15–33.

3505 ROGERS, A., 'Medieval Stamford', in A. Rogers (ed.), *The making of Stamford* (Leicester UP, 1965), 34–57.

3506 PHYTHIAN-ADAMS, C., 'Rutland reconsidered', in A. Dornier (ed.), *Mercian Studies* (Leicester UP, 1977), 63–84. Cf. **3226, 3502**.

3507 ROFFE, D. R., 'Rural manors and Stamford', *South Lincs. Archaeology*, 1 (1977), 12–13. For the topography of Stamford and the identification of one of its DB churches.

3508 THORN, F. (ed., from a draft translation by C. Parker), *Domesday Book. 29. Rutland* (Chichester: Phillimore, 1980). Text, translation and valuable notes.

3509 MAHANY, C. & ROFFE, D., 'Stamford. The development of an Anglo-Scandinavian borough', in R. A. Brown (ed.), *Battle, 5 (1982)* (Woodbridge: Boydell & Brewer, 1983), 197–219.

SHROPSHIRE

There is as yet no Phillimore edition of Shrops. DB. For the relevant section of the *DB Geography*, **340**. On the Shrops. estates of Roger de Montgomery, **380**. For Welsh settlement around Oswestry, **2328**, and for an unsatisfactory study of the border counties and Wales, **2334**. On DB Onibury, see **2315**. For the suggestion that DB values reflect the Conqueror's devastation of the N.W. Midlands, **281**. For the Shrops. holdings of the Lacy family, **395**. For a general essay in historical geography which makes some use of DB material, **1442**.

3601 EYTON, R. W., 'Wenlock Priory', *Arch. Camb.*, ns, 4 (1853), 98–108. Reprinted in *TSAS*, 5 (1882), 167–82. For Wenlock's DB holdings.

3602 EYTON, R. W., *Antiquities of Shropshire*, 12 vols (London: J. R. Smith, 1854–60). An important work which includes a table and map of each DB hundred, and much valuable detail which assists the identification of places and people.

3603 EYTON, R. W., 'The castles of Shropshire and its borders', *Collectanea archaeologica*, 1 (1862), 34–49. Reprinted in *TSAS*, 10 (1887), 10–32.

3604 JAMES, H. (director), *Domesday Book: or the great survey of England of William the Conqueror, A.D. MLXXXVI. Facsimile of the part relating to Shropshire* (Southampton: Ordnance Survey Office, 1862). Photozincographic edition.

3605 ANDERSON, J.C., *Shropshire: its early history and antiquities* (London: Willis & Southeran, 1864). Contains tables of DB hundreds.

3606 WRIGHT, T., *Domesday Book for Shropshire* (Shrewsbury: J.O. Sandford, 1865). Gives an extended Latin text and an English translation on opposite pages.

3607 BLAKEWAY, J.B., 'History of Shrewsbury hundred or liberties', *TSAS*, 2nd ser., 1 (1889), 93–128, 311–406; 2 (1890), 319–58; 3 (1891), 329–62; 4 (1892), 339–74; 5 (1893), 363–94; 6 (1894), 373–414. Contains some DB identifications.

3608 PALMER, A.N., 'Welsh settlements, east of Offa's Dyke, during the eleventh century', *Y Cymmrodor*, 10 (1889), 29–45. For *Mersete* hundred in Shrops.

3609 DUIGNAN, W.H., 'On some Shropshire place-names', *TSAS*, 2nd ser., 6 (1894), 1–18.

3610 'JULIANA', 'Shropshire churches in 1086', *Shrops. N&Q*, ns, 4 (1895), 28–9.

3611 KENYON, R.L., 'The Domesday manors of Ruyton, Wikey and Felton', *TSAS*, 12 (1900), 64–83.

3612 TAIT, J., 'Introduction to the Shropshire Domesday', in *VCH Shrops.*, 1, ed. W. Page (London: Constable, 1908), 279–308.

3613 DRINKWATER, C.H., 'Translation of the Shropshire Domesday', *VCH Shrops.*, 1, 309–49.

3614 WIGMORE, J., 'Turstin de Wigmore: *Turstin Flandrensis*', *N&Q*, 10th ser., 10 (1908), 205–6. Cf. **3212**.

3615 ROUND, J.H., 'Turstin de Wigmore: *Turstin Flandrensis*', *N&Q*, 10th ser., 10 (1908), 250.

3616 MORRIS, J.E., 'Ludlow: a study in local history', *History*, ns, 1 (1916), 159–73. Argued that *Lude* in Herefords. DB was Ludlow. Cf. **3613, 420**.

3617 BOWCOCK, E.W., *Shropshire place-names* (Shrewsbury: Wilding & Son, 1923).

3618 SYLVESTER, D., 'Rural settlement in Domesday Shropshire', *Sociological Review*, 25 (1933), 244–57. Should be used with caution.

3619 SLACK, W.J., 'The Shropshire ploughmen of Domesday Book', *TSAS*, 50 (1939–40), 31–5. A statistical study of *bovarii* and *servi* in relation to demesne teams.

3620 HOWELL, E. J., 'Shropshire', pt 66 of *The land of Britain: the report of the land utilisation survey of Britain* (London: Geographical Publications Ltd., 1941. See pp. 278–82 for maps of DB woodland and arable.

3621 MASON, J. F. A., 'Edric of Bayston', *TSAS*, 55 (1954–6), 112–8. For an English DB tenant.

3622 MASON, J. F. A., 'The officers and clerks of the Norman earls of Shropshire', *TSAS*, 56 (1957–60), 244–57. For DB sub-tenants.

3623 HARMER, F. E., 'A Bromfield and a Coventry writ of king Edward the Confessor', in P. Clemoes (ed.), *The Anglo-Saxons: studies on some aspects of their history and culture presented to Bruce Dickins* (London: Bowes & Bowes, 1959), 89–103. For DB Bromfield.

3624 MASON, J. F. A. & BARKER, P. A., 'The Norman castle at Quatford', *TSAS*, 57 (1961–4), 37–62. A DB entry in the light of topographical and archaeological evidence.

3625 MASON, J. F. A., 'The Norman earls of Shrewsbury: three notes. II. South-east Shropshire in 1086', *TSAS*, 57 (1961–4), 157–60. For Shropshire manors entered in Staffs. and Warws. DB. Has general significance for the Midland DB circuit.

3626 KING, D. J. C. & SPURGEON, C. J., 'The mottes in the Vale of Montgomery', *Arch. Camb.*, 114 (1965), 69–86.

3627 ROWLEY, T., *The Shropshire landscape* (London: Hodder & Stoughton, 1972). See chapter 3.

3628 GWYNNE, T. A., 'Domesday society in Shropshire', *TSAS*, 59 (1971–2), 91–103.

3629 REES, U. (ed.), *The cartulary of Shrewsbury abbey*, 2 vols (Aberystwyth: National Library of Wales, 1975). For the abbey's DB estates.

3630 HILL, M. C., 'The demesne and the waste: a study of medieval inclosure on the manor of High Ercall, 1086–1399', *TSAS*, 62 (1979–80). Occupies the whole issue of the journal.

3631 MEISEL, J., *Barons of the Welsh frontier: the Corbet, Pantulf and fitz Warin families, 1066–1272* (Lincoln, Neb. & London: University of Nebraska Press, 1981). Discusses their DB holdings. Of little value.

SOMERSET

The study of Somerset DB requires reference to studies of Exon DB, of which see especially **383**, and also reference to the DB-related texts from Bath abbey, on which see **13, 306, 410**. For the relevant section of the *DB Geography*, **396**. For woodland, **289**. There has been an extensive discussion of the Glastonbury abbey estates, **334, 348, 353, 422, 423**. For the reference under Taunton to *denarii de hundret*, see **252, 263**. For plough-teams in Somerset DB, **311, 327**. For villeins on comital manors, **257**. For the holdings of the Gournay family, **2002**, and of William de Mohun **1906**.

3701 COLLINSON, J., *The history and antiquities of the county of Somerset*, 3 vols (Bath: R.Cruttwell, 1791). Prints Exch. DB text in vol.1 and seeks to identify DB place-names.

3702 JAMES, H. (director), *Domesday Book: or the great survey of England of William the Conqueror, A.D. MLXXXVI. Facsimile of the part relating to Somerset* (Southampton: Ordnance Survey Office, 1862). Photozincographic edition.

3703 BOND, T., 'The honor of Odcomb and barony of Brito', *SANHSP*, 21 (1875), 28–35. For the DB holdings of Ansger *Brito*.

3704 BENNETT, J.A., 'Vestiges of the Norman conquest of Somerset', *SANHSP*, 25 (1879), 21–8. Uses DB values to trace William's army's movements in Somerset and those of Harold's brothers' raids from Ireland.

3705 EYTON, R.W., *Domesday studies: an analysis and digest of the Somerset survey (according to the Exon codex), and of the Somerset Gheld Inquest of A.D. 1084* (London & Bristol: Reeves & Turner and T.Kerslake, 1880). A major study. For critical comment on Eyton's belief in DB's exactitude of mensuration, see **3717**.

3706 HOBHOUSE, Rt Revd Bishop E., 'Remarks on the Domesday map (with map included)' and 'Domesday estates', *SANHSP*, 35 (1889), ix–x, 22–3.

3707 BATTEN, J., 'The barony of Beauchamp of Somerset', *SANHSP*, 36 (1890), 20–59. For the DB holdings of Robert fitz Ivo.

3708 HOBHOUSE, Rt Revd Bishop E., 'On the devolution of Domesday estates in Somerset', *SANHSP*, 36 (1890), 32–5.

3709 ROUND, J.H., 'Regenbald, priest and chancellor', in J.H. Round, *Feudal England* (London: Swan Sonnenschein, 1895; 2nd edn,

London: Allen & Unwin, 1964), 421–30 (1st edn) and 323–9 (2nd edn). For the DB and Exon entries for Rode.

3710 BATES, E.H., 'Omission in Eyton's Domesday studies – Somerset', *Somerset & Dorset N&Q,* 5 (1897), 346–50. For Milton Clevedon.

3711 COLEMAN, Prebendary, 'The descent of the manor of Allerton', *SANHSP*, 45 (1899), 25–50. For the DB holdings of Ralph de Conteville.

3712 BATES, E.H., 'The five-hide-unit in the Somerset Domesday', *SANHSP*, 45 (1899), 51–107.

3713 HEALEY, C.E.H.C., *The history of the part of west Somerset comprising the parishes of Luccombe, Selworthy, Stoke Pero, Porlock, Culbone and Oare* (London: Henry Southern & Co., 1901). Translates and comments on the relevant section of Exch. and Exon DB.

3714 WHALE, T.W., *Analysis of Somerset Domesday, terrae occupatae and index, with a reprint from transactions of the Bath Field Club, containing principles of the Domesday and analysis in hundreds* (Bath: Simms, 1902). A work severely criticised by Round, **3717**.

3715 WHALE, T.W., 'Principles of Somerset Domesday', Proceedings of the Bath Natural History and Antiquarian Field Club, 10 (1905), 38–86.

3716 TAYLOR, C.S., 'Banwell', *SANHSP*, 51 (1905), 31–76. See pp. 54–62 for the DB entry.

3717 ROUND, J.H., 'Domesday survey', in *VCH Somerset*, 1, ed. W. Page (London: Constable, 1906), 383–432. Notable for the extensive critique of Eyton's work (**3705**).

3718 BATES, E.H., 'Text of the Somerset Domesday', *VCH Somerset*, 1, 434–526.

3719 BATES, E.H., 'Geld Inquest', *VCH Somerset*, 1, 527–37.

3720 GRESWELL, W.H.P., 'The *Cantoche* of Domesday (1086)', *SANHSP*, 56 (1910), 79–84. Identified with Quantock Farm in Spaxton.

3721 HILL, J.S., *The place-names of Somerset* (Bristol: St Stephen's printing works, 1914). Mostly descriptive. Discusses the DB place-names.

3722 HARBIN, E.H.B., 'Hescombe in Domesday and after', *Somerset & Dorset N&Q,* 15 (1917), 234–41.

3723 MAXWELL LYTE, H.C., 'Burci, Falaise and Martin', *SANHSP*, 65 (1919), 1–27. For the DB fee of Serlo de Burci.

3724 MAJOR, A.F., 'The geography of the Lower Parrett in early times and the position of Cruca', *SANHSP*, 66 (1921), 56–65. For differing opinions on this identification, **420, 3718, 3732, 3737**.

3725 MAXWELL LYTE, H.C., *Historical notes on some Somerset manors formerly connected with the honour of Dunster*, Somerset Rec. Soc., extra ser. (1931).

3726 LEIGHTON, W., 'The manor and parish of Burnett, Somerset', *TBGAS*, 59 (1937), 243–85.

3727 MORGAN, F.W., 'The Domesday geography of Somerset', *SANHSP*, 84 (1938), 139–55.

3728 HELM, P.J., 'The Somerset levels in the middle ages (1086–1539)', *JBAA*, 3rd ser., 12 (1949), 37–52.

3729 TURNER, A.G.C., 'Notes on some Somerset place-names', *SANHSP*, 95 (1950), 112–24. Sets a small number of DB place-names in the context of other early forms.

3730 TURNER, A.G.C., 'A selection of north Somerset place-names', *SANHSP*, 96 (1951), 152–9. As **3729**.

3731 FINN, R.W., 'The making of the Somerset Domesdays', *SANHSP*, 99–100 (1954–5), 21–37. Of general significance for the making of DB.

3732 MORLAND, S.C., 'Some Domesday manors', *SANHSP*, 99–100 (1954–5), 38–48. For place-name identifications. Cf. **3724**.

3733 MORLAND, S.C., 'Further notes on Somerset Domesday', *SANHSP*, 108 (1963–4), 94–8. As **3732**.

3734 EVERETT, S., 'The Domesday geography of three Exmoor parishes', *SANHSP*, 112 (1967–8), 54–60. For the DB manors of Bagley, Stoke Pero, Wilmersham, Culbone, Doverhay and Porlock.

3735 MORLAND, S.C., 'Hidation on the Glastonbury estates: a study in tax evasion', *SANHSP*, 114 (1970), 74–90.

3736 ASTON, M.A., 'Deserted settlements in Mudford parish, Yeovil', *SANHSP*, 121 (1977), 41–53.

3737 THORN, C. & F. (eds), *Domesday Book. 8. Somerset* (Chichester: Phillimore, 1980). Text, translation and valuable notes. The text used is Exch. DB, with the substance of discrepancies and additional material in Exon included. There are notes and tables on the extra information in Exon and notes on place-name identifications. Three appendices discuss the Somerset hundreds, the DB-related surveys in the cartulary of Bath abbey with a printed text of both (see **13, 306**), and *Pirtochesworda*. See the review by S.C.Morland in *SANHSP*, 125 (1981), 137–40. For additions and corrections, **4523**.

3738 OGGINS, V.D. & R.S., 'Some hawkers of Somerset', *SANHSP*, 124 (1980), 51–60. For Siward the hawker in Exon DB.

3739 HAVINDEN, M., *The Somerset landscape* (London: Hodder & Stoughton, 1981). See chapters 3 and 4. Suggests corrections to **396**.

3740 DUNNING, R.W., 'The origins of Nether Stowey', *SANHSP*, 125 (1981), 124–6.

STAFFORDSHIRE

The study of Staffs. DB requires reference to the numerous studies of the Burton abbey surveys, which are themselves central to discussions of the size of England's population at the time of DB. See **196, 225, 251, 405, 436**, as well as **3825** below. For the relevant section of the *DB Geography*, **340**. For the suggestion that Staffs. DB reflects the Conqueror's devastation of the N.E. Midlands, **281**. On the holdings of Westminster abbey in Staffs., **1027**.

3801 ERDESWICK, S., *A survey of Staffordshire, containing the antiquities of that county, with a description of Beeston-Castle in Cheshire* (London: E.Curll & Bible, 1717; 2nd edn., London: W.Mears & J.Hooke, 1723). Made great use of DB. See further **3803**.

3802 SHAW, S., *The history and antiquities of Staffordshire*, 2 vols (London: J.Nicholls, 1798–1801). Included a transcription of Staffs. DB.

3803 HARWOOD, T. (ed.), *A survey of Staffordshire containing the antiquities of that county by Sampson Erdeswick* (Westminster: Nichols, Cadell & Davies, 1820; 2nd edn, London: Nichols, 1844). For a discussion of DB holdings and suggested identifications.

3804 JAMES, H. (director), *Domesday Book: or the great survey of England of William the Conqueror, A.D. MLXXXVI. Facsimile of the part relating to Staffordshire* (Southampton: Ordnance Survey Office, 1862). Photozincographic edition.

3805 WROTTESLEY, G. & EYTON, R.W., 'The Liber niger scaccarii, Staffordscira, or feodary of A.D. 1166, with notes added.

Notes on the fitz Alan fees, and those of feudatories holding land in Staffordshire, A.D. 1166, who made no return', *CHS*, 1 (1880), 145–240. Much important material on the feudal society of Staffs. DB.

3806 EYTON, R. W., *Domesday studies: an analysis and digest of the Staffordshire survey* (London: Trubner & Co., 1881).

3807 EYTON, R. W., 'The Staffordshire chartulary, series I of ancient deeds', *CHS*, 2, pt 1 (1881), 178–276. Annotations contain much material on DB tenants.

3808 WROTTESLEY, G., 'The Staffordshire chartulary, series III of ancient deeds', *CHS*, 3, pt 1 (1882), 178–231. Some material on Staffs. DB tenants. See **3809** for the Croc family.

3809 WATERS, E. C., 'A note on the Staffordshire chartulary, volume III of Staffordshire collections', *CHS*, 4, pt 1 (1883), reverse of contents page. See **3808**.

3810 MADAN, F., 'The Gresleys of Drakelowe', *CHS*, ns, 1 (1899), 1–335. For the Tosny and Stafford DB fees.

3811 DUIGNAN, W. H., *Notes on Staffordshire place-names* (London: Henry Frowde, 1902). For an appreciation of Duignan's work, see *TLSSAHS*, 9 (1967–8), 31–6.

3812 DANIEL, A. T., 'Staffordshire Domesday Book', *TNSFC*, 37 (1902–3), 37–60.

3813 WROTTESLEY, G., 'The forest tenures of Staffordshire', *CHS*, ns, 10, pt 1 (1907), 189–243. For Cannock forest in DB. See **3828**.

3814 WROTTESLEY, G., 'History of the Bagot family', *CHS*, ns, 11 (1908), 3–224. See pp. 3–4 for a suggested identification of the unnamed royal holding in Bramshall.

3815 CARTER, W. F., 'On the identification of the Domesday Monetvile', *CHS*, ns, 11 (1908), 227–30. A new Norman formation in Castle Church.

3816 BURNE, S. A. H., 'A note on the Domesday *Niwetone*', *TNSFC*, 50 (1915–16), 90–1. Identifies as a hamlet in Draycott-in-the-Moors.

3817 WEDGWOOD, J. C., 'Early Staffordshire history (from the map and from Domesday)', *CHS* (1916), 138–208. Discusses hundreds, hidage, Norman tenants, churches and pre-Conquest personal names. See **3818**.

3818 BRIDGEMAN, C.G.O., 'Notes on the contents of the volume for 1916. 4. The five-hide unit in Staffordshire. 5. The carucate in Staffordshire', *CHS* (1919), 134–51. Cf. **3817**.

3819 BRIDGEMAN, C.G.O. & MANDER, G.P., 'The Staffordshire hidation', *CHS* (1919), 154–81.

3820 BRIDGEMAN, C.G.O., 'Some unidentified Domesday vills', *CHS* (1923), 23–44.

3821 FRASER, H.M., *The Staffordshire Domesday* (Stone: T.G.Adie, 1936). Gives parallel Latin and English texts.

3822 STYLES, D., 'The early history of Penkridge church', *CHS* (1950–1), 3–52. See p.4 note 4 for rubrication of DB, 1, fos 246r, 247v.

3823 THORPE, H., 'Lichfield: a study of its growth and function', *CHS* (1950–1), 139–211.

3824 MYERS, J., 'Staffordshire and the Domesday Book', *TNSFC*, 87 (1952–3), 31–57. An essay in DB geography with 9 maps.

3825 SLADE, C.F., 'Introduction to Staffordshire Domesday', in *VCH Staffs.*, 4, ed. L.M.Midgley (OUP, for the Institute of Historical Research, 1958), 1–36.

3826 SLADE, C.F., 'Translation of the text of the Staffordshire Domesday', *VCH Staffs.*, 4, 37–60.

3827 MEREDITH, W.D., 'Water mills in North Staffordshire', *NSJFS*, 4 (1964), 1–10.

3828 GOULD, J., 'Food, foresters, fines and felons. A history of Cannock forest (1086–1300)', *TLSSAHS*, 7 (1965–6), 21–39.

3829 CANTOR, L.M., 'The medieval forests and chases of Staffordshire', *NSJFS*, 8 (1968), 39–53.

3830 TAYLOR, C.C., 'The origins of Lichfield, Staffs.', *TLSSAHS*, 10 (1968–9), 43–52.

3831 BATE, P.V. & PALLISER, D.M., 'Suspected lost village sites in Staffordshire', *TLSSAHS*, 12 (1970–1), 31–6.

3832 GOULD, J., 'The medieval burgesses of Tamworth: their liberties, courts and markets', *TLSSAHS*, 13 (1971–2), 17–42.

3833 PALLISER, D.M., 'The boroughs of medieval Staffordshire', *NSJFS*, 12 (1972), 63–73.

3834 PALLISER, D.M., 'A thousand years of Staffordshire man and the landscape, 913–1973', *NSJFS*, 14 (1974), 21–33.

3835 PINNOCK, A.C., 'Staffordshire medieval population and prosperity: a study of available sources', *NSJFS*, 14 (1974), 34–45.

3836 CANTOR, L.M., 'The medieval landscape of Staffordshire', in A.D.M.Phillips & B.J.Turton (eds), *Environment, man and economic change. Essays presented to S.H.Beaver* (London: Longmans, 1975), 181–95.

3837 MORRIS, J. (ed., from a draft translation by A.Hawkins and A.Rumble), *Domesday Book. 24. Staffordshire* (Chichester: Phillimore, 1976).

3838 PALLISER, D.M., *The Staffordshire landscape* (London: Hodder & Stoughton, 1976).

SUFFOLK

A great deal of material relevant to DB Suffolk has been published under the general heading of East Anglia. For more than any other county therefore it is necessary to refer to other sections, notably the General Section and Norfolk. For general work on Little DB and the social structure of East Anglia, see **271, 316, 331, 345, 397, 3129**. For the relevant section of the *DB Geography*, **332**. For IE and the holdings of the abbey of Ely, **1005, 331, 1321**. For a discussion of the destruction of woodland, **2055**, in contrast to **3127, 3128**. For hundreds, leets and the revenues therefrom, **270, 274**. On the Suffolk coast-line in DB, **3133**. For an early and entirely superseded study of Suffolk place-names, **1303**. For a confused discussion of the lands of the bishopric of Elmham and a good one of its successor at Thetford/Norwich, **3115, 3134**. For the Suffolk holdings of Edith the Fair, **1204**; of Ramsey abbey, **1006, 1023**; of St Benet of Holme, **3126**; of the archbishopric of Canterbury, **1212**; of Hainfrid de St-Omer, **3109**; of Roger de Rames, **2053**; of Walter the Deacon, **2046**; and of Richard fitz Gilbert, **2067, 2070**. For the succession of Eudo *dapifer* to Lisois de Moustiers' estates, **1005**.

3901 JAMES, H. (director), *Domesday Book: or the great survey of England of William the Conqueror, A.D. MLXXXVI. Facsimile of the part relating to Suffolk* (Southampton: Ordnance Survey Office, 1863). Photozincographic edition.

3902 HERVEY, J., *Suffolk Domesday: the Latin text extended and translated*, 2 vols (Bury St Edmunds: 'Free Press', 1888–91). Text and translation, but with the material arranged by hundreds. See further, **3903**.

3903 BEDELL, A.J., GOWERS, W.R. *et al*, 'Suffolk Domesday', *The East Anglian*, ns, 3 (1889–90), 12, 25–6, 97–8, 146–7, 215, 225–6, 311–12. Place-name identifications supplementary to **3902**.

3904 PEARSON, W.C., 'Notes on the Suffolk Domesday. Hundreds of Blything, Bosmere, Claydon, Carlford, Colneis and Samford', *The East Anglian*, ns, 4 (1892), 233–8.

3905 CORBETT, W.J. & METHOLD, T.T., 'The rise and devolution of the manors in Hepworth, Suffolk', *PSIANH*, 10 (1900), 19–48.

3906 LEES, B.A., 'Introduction to the Suffolk Domesday', in *VCH Suffolk*, 1, ed. W.Page (London: Constable, 1911), 357–417.

3907 ANON ('adapted from the translation by the late Lord Hervey'), 'Translation of the Suffolk Domesday', *VCH Suffolk*, 1, 418–582.

3908 SKEAT, W.W., *The place-names of Suffolk*, Cambridge Ant. Soc., Octavo Pubs., no.46 (London: Bell, 1913). Dated but not yet superseded.

3909 MORLEY, C. & COOPER, E.R., 'The sea port of Frostenden', *PSIANH*, 18 (1924), 167–79. For the *i portus maris* (DB, 2, fo.414b).

3910 THORNTON, G.A., 'A study in the history of Clare, Suffolk; with special reference to its development as a borough', *TRHS*, 4th ser., 11 (1928), 83–115.

3911 LOBEL, M.D., *The borough of Bury St Edmunds* (Oxford: Clarendon Press, 1935).

3912 COOPER, E.R., 'Old time saltworks in Suffolk', *PSIANH*, 24 (1949), 25–9.

3913 PARR, R.T.L., 'Two townships in Blything hundred', *PSIANH*, 25 (1952), 297–303. Suggests identifications for *Hoppetuna/Oppituna* and *Warabetuna*.

3914 DAVIS, R.H.C. (ed.), *The kalendar of abbot Samson of Bury St Edmunds and related documents*, Camden, 3rd ser., 84 (London for the Royal Historical Soc., 1954). See the introduction for a discussion of Danegeld and socage.

3915 MUNDAY, J.T., 'The topography of mediaeval Eriswell', *PSIANH*, 30 (1967), 201–9. Suggests a location for DB Coclesworth (cf. **3907, 332**) and an omission of freemen.

3916 DYMOND, D.P., 'The Suffolk landscape', in L.M.Munby (ed.), *East Anglian studies* (Cambridge: Heffer, 1968), 17–47.

3917 SCARFE, N., *The Suffolk landscape* (London: Hodder & Stoughton, 1972). See pp. 134–48.

3918 SCARFE, N., 'Notes on Domesday Book's evidence touching Worlingham, North Cove and their early churches', *Lowestoft Arch. & Local Hist. Soc., annual report*, 13 (1980–1), 13–15.

SURREY

For an early translation of Surrey DB, **2606**, and an early discussion of Surrey DB churches, **2607**. Baring's statistical tables dealt with Surrey, **237**, and he also produced a study of the hidation, **203**, and suggested the possible movements of the Conqueror's army in Surrey in 1066 on the basis of DB values, **201**. He suggested that the army may have crossed the Thames at Hampton, **2218** For the relevant section of the *DB Geography*, **370**. For the holdings of Albert the Lotharingian in Surrey, **1007**; of Robert d'Ouilly and Miles Crispin, **1113**; of the archbishopric of Canterbury, **1212**; of the Lacy family, **395**; of Westminster abbey, **1027**; and of Richard fitz Gilbert, **2067, 2070**.

4001 MANNING, O. & BRAY, W., *The history and antiquities of the county of Surrey*, 3 vols (London: J. White, 1804–14). Vol. 1 contains a facsimile copy of the Surrey DB folios and an extended Latin text.

4002 JAMES, H. (director), *Domesday Book: or the great survey of England of William the Conqueror, A.D. MLXXXVI. Facsimile of the part relating to Surrey* (Southampton: Ordnance Survey Office, 1861). Photozincographic edition.

4003 ANON, *A literal extension of the Latin text, and an English translation, of Domesday Book in relation to the county of Surrey* (London: Vacher & Sons; Longmans, 1862).

4004 MALDEN, H.E., 'The Domesday survey of Surrey', in P.E. Dove (ed.), *Domesday studies: being the papers read at the meetings of the Domesday commemoration 1886*, 2 vols (London: Longmans, 1888–91), 2, 459–70.

4005 MALDEN, H.E., 'Blechingley castle and the De Clares', *SurreyAC*, 15 (1900), 17–26. For the Surrey DB estates of the Clares. See **2067**.

4006 ROUND, J.H., 'Introduction to the Surrey Domesday', in *VCH Surrey*, 1, ed. H.E. Malden (Westminster: Constable, 1902), 275–93.

4007 MALDEN, H.E., 'The text of the Surrey Domesday', *VCH Surrey*, 1, 295–328.

4008 MALDEN, H. E., 'Thunderfield castle', *SurreyAC*, 18 (1903), 1–8. Suggests an identification for an unnamed Chertsey abbey estate, cf. **4007, 4019**.

4009 MALDEN, H. E., 'Villeinage in the Weald of Surrey', *SurreyAC*, 20 (1907), 143–52.

4010 BONNER, A., 'A note on the name "Battersea" ', *TLMAS*, ns, 2 (1913), 434–7.

4011 BONNER, A., 'Surrey place-names', *SurreyAC*, 36 (1925), 85–101. Limited in content.

4012 MALDEN, H. E., 'The historical geography of the Wealden iron industry', *SurreyAC*, 36 (1925), 107–10. For DB settlement in the Weald.

4013 MALDEN, H. E., 'Kingsland in Newdigate and Newdigate in Copthorne hundred', *SurreyAC*, 39 (1931), 147–9. Identifies an unnamed settlement in Brixton hundred, Cf. **4019**.

4014 KENNEDY, E. H., 'The Domesday mill at Bletchworth', *SurreyAC*, 40 (1932), 120–2.

4015 GOVER, J. E. B., MAWER, A. & STENTON, F. M. (in collaboration with A. Bonner), *The place-names of Surrey*, EPNS, 11 (Cambridge UP, 1934).

4016 RUBY, A. T., 'The manor of Pachenesham, Leatherhead', *SurreyAC*, 55 (1958), 7–17.

4017 YATES, E. M., 'A study of settlement patterns', *Field studies*, 1, no. 3 (1961), 65–84. For the Reigate, Dorking and Guildford areas.

4018 NAIL, D., 'The meeting place of Copthorne hundred', *SurreyAC*, 62 (1965), 44–53.

4019 MORRIS, J. (ed., from a draft translation by S. Wood), *Domesday Book 3. Surrey* (Chichester: Phillimore, 1975). For additions and corrections, **1028, 2418**.

4020 BLAIR, J., 'The Surrey endowments of Lewes priory before 1200', *SurreyAC*, 72 (1980), 97–126.

4021 BLAIR, J., 'The early history of Horne: an addendum', *SurreyAC*, 73 (1982), 179–80. For the DB manor of Chivington.

4022 ALEXANDER, M., 'The mills of Guildford', *SurreyAC*, 74 (1983), 91–9.

4023 GERHOLD, D.J., 'In defence of Anglo-Saxon Putney and Roehampton', *The Wandsworth Historian*, no. 36 (1983), 6–16.

SUSSEX

The Sussex rapes have attracted much discussion and controversy over the years. For the main items, see **4112, 4113, 4114, 4139, 4140, 4159, 4161, 4166, 4170**. For an early translation of Sussex DB, **2606**, and for an early discussion of DB churches, **2607**. For the relevant section of the *DB Geography*, **370**. One of the papers delivered at the 1886 commemoration concentrated most of its attention on Sussex, **160**. For the suggestion that DB values reflect the movements of William I's army in 1066, **201**, and for DB values around Hastings, **3208**. For a comparison of settlement in N.W. Sussex with Berks. and Kent, **1117**. For the structure of Sussex DB estates, **430**. For the lands of Roger de Montgomery and the rape of Arundel, **380**. For a study of personal names which is far from satisfactory, **2224**. On the hides of DB and the Battle abbey surveys, see **148**, in addition to **4119, 4120, 4121, 4157**. On the holdings of Westminster abbey and the archbishopric of Canterbury, **1027, 1212**.

4101 HORSFIELD, T. W., *The history, antiquities and topography of the county of Sussex*, 2 vols (London: Nichols & Son, 1835). For an early attempt to identify DB place-names.

4102 LOWER, M. A., 'Observations on the landing of William the Conqueror and subsequent events', *SussexAC*, 2 (1849), 53–7. For DB values in the neighbourhood of Hastings. See **3208**.

4103 LOWER, M. A., 'Notes on the watermills and windmills in Sussex', *SussexAC*, 5 (1852), 267–76.

4104 ELLIS, W. S., 'Descent of the manor of Hurst-Pierpoint, and of its lords', *SussexAC*, 11 (1859), 50–72. Identifies DB tenant as Robert de Pierrepont.

4105 JAMES, H. (director), *Domesday Book: or the great survey of England of William the Conqueror, A.D. MLXXXVI. Facsimile of the part relating to Sussex* (Southampton: Ordnance Survey Office, 1862). Photozincographic edition.

4106 TURNER, E., 'Battel abbey', *SussexAC*, 17 (1865), 1–56. Some discussion of the abbey's DB holdings. See **4165**.

4107 ROBERTS, E., 'On Mayfield, in Sussex', *JBAA*, 23 (1867), 333–69. Transcribes and translates sections of DB for the archbishop of Canterbury's lands in Sussex.

4108 SAWYER, F.E., *Index of names of places in Domesday survey of Sussex* (no named publisher: nd, ?1880).

4109 SAWYER, F.E., *Land tenure and division in Brighton and the neighbour-hood* (London: Spottiswoode, 1881).

4110 PARISH, W.D., *Domesday Book in relation to the county of Sussex* (Lewes: Sussex Arch. Soc., 1886). Translation of DB, with a facsimile and extension of the Latin text. Contains an index of tenants, place-names, with notes and suggested identifications.

4111 SAWYER, F.E., 'Glossary of Sussex dialectal place-nomencla-ture', *SussexAC*, 35 (1887), 165–72. Of little value. A curiosity.

4112 SAWYER, F.E., 'Sussex Domesday studies. No.1. The rapes and their origin', *Arch. Rev.*, 1 (1888), 54–9. See **4113, 4114**.

4113 NAPPER, H.F., 'Notes on "Sussex Domesday studies". No.1. The rapes and their origin', *SussexAC*, 36 (1888), 239–40. See **4112**.

4114 ROUND, J.H. & HOWORTH, H.H., 'The Sussex rapes', *Arch. Rev.*, 1, (1888), 229–30. Critical of **4112**.

4115 ROUND, J.H., 'Some early grants to Lewes priory', *SussexAC*, 40 (1896), 58–78. For the identification of DB sub-tenants.

4116 HUDSON, W., 'The hundred of Eastbourne and its six "boroughs" ', *SussexAC*, 42 (1899), 180–208.

4117 HUDSON, W., 'The manor of Eastbourne, its early history; with some notes about the honours of Mortain and Aquila', *SussexAC*, 43 (1900), 166–200.

4118 ROUND, J.H., 'Note on the Sussex Domesday', *SussexAC*, 44 (1901), 140–3. On the DB holding of Ralph de Quesnay and the DB manor of Bosham.

4119 TAIT, J., 'Hides and virgates at Battle abbey', *EHR*, 18 (1903), 705–8. See further **4120, 4121, 4157**.

4120 SALZMANN, L.F., 'Hides and virgates in Sussex', *EHR*, 19 (1904), 92–6. See **4119, 4121, 4157**.

4121 TAIT, J., 'Hides and virgates in Sussex', *EHR*, 19 (1904), 503–6. See **4119, 4120, 4157**.

4122 ROUND, J.H. & SALZMANN, L.F., 'Introduction to the Sussex Domesday', in *VCH Sussex*, 1, ed. W.Page (London: Constable, 1905), 351–86.

4123 SALZMANN, L. F., 'Translation of the Sussex Domesday', *VCH Sussex*, 1, 387–451.

4124 SAYERS, E., 'The manor of *Dentune*', *SussexAC*, 50 (1907), 176. Identified with Dankton in Sompting.

4125 BALLARD, A., 'The Sussex coast line', *SussexAC*, 53 (1910), 5–21. For location of DB saltpans.

4126 ROBERTS, R. G., *The place-names of Sussex* (Cambridge UP, 1914). Superseded by **4138**.

4127 SALZMANN, L. F., 'Some Sussex Domesday tenants. I. Alvred pincerna and his descendants. II. The family of Dene. III. William de Cahagnes and the family of Keynes. IV. The family of Chesney or Cheyney', *SussexAC*, 57 (1915), 162–79; 58 (1916), 171–89; 63 (1922), 180–202; 65 (1924), 20–53.

4128 ROUND, J. H., 'The early history of North and South Stoke', *SussexAC*, 59 (1918), 1–24.

4129 ANSCOMBE, A., 'The Sussex place-names in Domesday Book which end in *-intun*', *SussexAC*, 59 (1918), 76–83.

4130 ANSCOMBE, A., 'The names of the Sussex hundreds in Domesday Book', *SussexAC*, 60 (1919), 92–125.

4131 THOMAS-STANFORD, C., 'The manor of Radynden: the De Radyndens and their successors', *SussexAC*, 62 (1921), 64–92. Discussion of the DB manor of Brightelmstone-Michelham.

4132 BUDGEN, W., 'The manor of Chollington in Eastbourne', *SussexAC*, 62 (1921), 111–32. Also deals with the DB holdings of the Dives family.

4133 SAYERS, E., 'The acre equivalent of the Domesday hide', *SussexAC*, 62 (1921), 201–3. Based on DB West Tarring.

4134 SALZMANN, L. F., 'The castle of Lewes', *SussexAC*, 63 (1922), 166–74; 64 (1923), 134–9. For the 'exchange of Lewes'. See **4122, 4140, 4159, 4161**.

4135 PECKHAM, W. D., 'Two Domesday Book freeholds', *Sussex N&Q*, 2 (1928–9), 17.

4136 ANSCOMBE, A., '*Segnescome*', *Sussex N&Q*, 2 (1929), 236–7.

4137 THOMAS-STANFORD, C., 'Hove in Domesday and after', *SussexAC*, 70 (1929), 86–92. Cf. **4142** at p. 70.

4138 MAWER, A. & STENTON, F. M., with the assistance of J. E. B. Gover, *The place-names of Sussex*, 2 vols, EPNS, 6–7 (Cambridge UP, 1929–30).

4139 JOLLIFFE, J. E. A., 'The Domesday hidation of Sussex and the rapes', *EHR*, 45 (1930), 427–35. See **4140, 4143**.

4140 SALZMAN, L. F., 'The rapes of Sussex', *SussexAC*, 72 (1931), 20–9. See **4139, 4159, 4161, 4166, 4170**.

4141 WARD, G., 'Some eleventh century references to Sussex', *Sussex N&Q*, 4 (1932–3), 238–40. Sussex material in Kent DB and DMon.

4142 PECKHAM, W. D., 'The parishes of the city of Chichester', *SussexAC*, 74 (1933), 65–97. See p. 70 for comment on **4137**.

4143 CLARK, D. K., 'The Saxon hundreds of Sussex', *SussexAC*, 74 (1933), 214–25. Cf. **4139**.

4144 WARD, G., 'Godfrey of Malling', *Sussex N&Q*, 5 (1934–5), 3–6.

4145 WARD, G., 'A suggested identification of Berts', *Sussex N&Q*, 5 (1934–5), 111–12.

4146 WARD, G., 'The Hoeselersc charter of 1018', *SussexAC*, 77 (1936), 119–29. For Hazelhurst in DB.

4147 BUDGEN, W., 'The manor of Radmeld-Beverington in Eastbourne', *Sussex N&Q*, 6 (1936–7), 15–18.

4148 HARRIS, E., 'Doomsday or Domesday Book', *Sussex County Magazine*, 19 (1945), 101–2. Of mediocre quality.

4149 BUDGEN, W., 'The acreage of the Sussex hide of land', *Sussex N&Q*, 11 (1946–7), 73–7.

4150 FLEMING, L., 'Pigs in Domesday Book', *Sussex N&Q*, 11 (1946–7), 32, 34.

4151 POOLE, H., 'The Domesday Book churches of Sussex', *SussexAC*, 87 (1948), 28–76.

4152 FLEMING, L., *History of Pagham in Sussex*, 3 vols (Ditchling: for the author, 1949–50).

4153 BUDGEN, W., 'The manor of Broughton in Jevington', *SussexAC*, 90 (1952), 13–26.

4154 YATES, E. M., 'Medieval assessments in north-west Sussex', *Institute of British Geographers Trans. & Pubs.*, 20 (1954), 75–92. Relates DB and later surveys to soil fertility and distribution.

4155 SALZMAN, L. F., 'Early taxation in Sussex', *SussexAC*, 98 (1960), 29–43. Assessments and geld.

4156 YATES, E. M., 'History in a map', *Geog. Jour.*, 126 (1960), 32–51. For South Harting and Rogate.

4157 SEARLE, E., 'Hides, virgates and tenant settlement at Battle abbey', *Econ.HR*, 2nd ser., 16 (1963–4), 290–300. See **4119, 4120, 4121**.

4158 MOORE, J. S., 'Two Domesday identifications', *Sussex N&Q*, 15 (1958–62), 263–5.

4159 MASON, J. F. A., 'The rapes of Sussex and the Norman Conquest', *SussexAC*, 102 (1964), 68–93.

4160 MOORE, J. S., *Laughton: a study in the evolution of the Wealden landscape*, Dept. of English Local History, Occasional papers, no. 19 (Leicester UP, 1965).

4161 MASON, J. F. A., *William I and the Sussex rapes* (Hastings & Bexhill Branch of the Historical Association, 1966. Reprinted, 1967).

4162 YATES, E. M., *A history of the landscapes of the parishes of South Harting and Rogate* (Chichester: Phillimore, for the Harting Society, 1972).

4163 BURLEIGH, G. R., 'An introduction to deserted medieval villages in East Sussex', *SussexAC*, 111 (1973), 45–83.

4164 BRANDON, P. F., *The Sussex landscape* (London: Hodder & Stoughton, 1974). See chapters 3 and 4.

4165 SEARLE, E., *Lordship and community: Battle abbey and its banlieu, 1066–1538* (Toronto: Pontifical Institute of Medieval Studies, 1974). Valuable for settlement in the Weald and for Battle abbey's *leuga*.

4166 MORRIS, J. (ed.), *Domesday Book. 2. Sussex* (Chichester: Phillimore, 1976). Contains notes on the rapes and on manorial outliers. Also an appendix containing a wide-ranging discussion on the hide.

4167 BURLEIGH, G. R., 'Further notes on deserted and shrunken medieval villages in Sussex', *SussexAC*, 114 (1976), 61–8.

4168 BELL, M., 'Excavations at Bishopstone', *SussexAC*, 115 (1977), 1–299. See pp. 243–8.

4169 HASELGROVE, D., 'The Domesday record of Sussex', in P. Brandon (ed.), *The South Saxons* (Chichester: Phillimore, 1978), 190–220, 245–8. A good survey. An appendix on the hundreds.

4170 HUDSON, T. P., 'The origins of Steyning and Bramber, Sussex', *Southern History*, 2 (1980), 11–29. See for the Sussex rapes.

4171 HOLDEN, E. W. & HUDSON, T. P., 'Salt-making in the Adur Valley, Sussex', *SussexAC*, 119 (1981), 117–48.

WALES

Entries relating to Wales occur in all four of the DB border counties of Glos., Herefords., Shrops. and Cheshire. For a full bibliography of Wales DB it is therefore necessary to consult the main editions of DB for these counties. See especially, **1424, 1446, 2141, 2309, 2310, 2341, 3612, 3613**. For a general treatment of the border counties in DB, see **432**, and for some comment on the DB evidence as part of a general essay in historical geography, **1442**. Other works dealing specifically with the border counties and Wales in DB are **1441, 2305, 2334, 3626, 3630**. For the lands of St Florent of Saumur, **231**. Several studies in the sections for the English border counties deal with the Welsh in those areas.

4201 JONES, M. C., 'The territorial divisions of Montgomeryshire: I. ancient civil divisions', *MC*, 2 (1869), 71–80. Heavily dependent on **3602**.

4202 PALMER, A. N., *A history of ancient tenures of land in North Wales and the Marches* (Wrexham: for the author, 1885; 2nd edn, with E. Owen, Wrexham: for the authors, 1910). See especially App. III.

4203 PALMER, A. N., 'Notes on the early history of Bangor Is Y Coed', *Y Cymmrodor*, 10 (1889), 12–28. Identifies the TRE DB holder of Erbistock (Denbigh).

4204 SHRUBSOLE, G. W., 'The Castreton of Atis-cross hundred in Domesday identified with the town of Flint', *Arch. Camb.*, 5th ser., 8 (1891), 17–22. *Castretone* is usually identified with Llys Edwin. See **420, 1446, 4217**. Cf. **4210**.

4205 LLOYD, J. E., 'Wales and the coming of the Normans (1039–1093)', *Trans. Hon. Soc. Cymmrodorion* (1901), 122–79.

4206 WOOD, J. G., 'Radnor as a place name', *TWNFC* (1905–7), 367–9.

4207 PALMER, A.N., 'Isycoed, county Denbigh', *Arch. Camb.*, 6th ser., 10 (1910), 229–70. Reprinted in A.N.Palmer, *The town of Holt, in county Denbigh: its castle, church, franchise, demesne fields, etc., together with the parish of Isycoed* (London: Bedford Press, 1910), 223–82. Argued that Isycoed appears under the name *Sutune* in DB.

4208 LLOYD, J.E., *A history of Wales from the earliest times to the Edwardian conquest* (London: Longmans, 1911; 2nd edn, 1912; 3rd edn, 1939).

4209 PATERSON, D.R., 'The pre-Norman settlement of Glamorgan', *Arch. Camb.*, 7th ser., 2 (1922), 37–60. For DB Gwent.

4210 TAIT, J., 'Flintshire in Domesday Book', *Flintshire Hist. Soc. Pubs.*, 11 (1925), 1–37. An important study, giving text and translation of the portion of Cheshire DB which was in the county of Flint before 1974.

4211 REES, W., 'Medieval Gwent', *JBAA*, ns, 35 (1929–30), 189–207.

4212 VENABLES-LLEWELYN, C., 'Domesday Book in Radnorshire and the border', *TRS*, 2 (1932), 14–17.

4213 MOSTYN, J., *'Haiae* in Domesday', *TRS*, 3 (1933), 26.

4214 DAVIES, J.C., 'Lordships and manors in the county of Montgomery', *MC*, 49 (1945), 74–150.

4215 HOWSE, W.H., 'Presteigne in Domesday', *TRS*, 21 (1951), 48–9.

4216 EDWARDS, J.G., 'The Normans and the Welsh March', *Proc. British Academy*, 42 (1956), 155–77. An important survey.

4217 DAVIES, E., *Flintshire place-names* (Cardiff: University of Wales Press, 1959). At least one correction to **4210**.

4218 JONES, G.R.J., 'The pattern of settlement on the Welsh border', *AgHR*, 8 (1960), 66–81. For DB, settlement and social stratification on the Welsh border.

4219 COLE, E.J.L., 'Barland: a Domesday manor?', *TRS*, 31 (1961), 20–2. Seeks to identify *Bernoldune* with Barland.

4220 JONES, G.R.J., 'The tribal system in Wales: a reassessment in the light of settlement studies', *Welsh History Review*, 1 (1961), 111–32. Some comment on DB and social structure.

4221 BARKER, P. & LAWSON, J., 'A pre-Norman field system at Hen Domen, Montgomery', *MA*, 15 (1971), 58–72.

4222 RICHARDS, M., 'The population of the Welsh border', *Trans. Hon. Soc. Cymmrodorion* (1971), 77–100.

4223 MORGAN, R., 'Trewern in Gorddwr: Domesday manor and knight's fief 1086–1311', *MC*, 64 (1976), 121–32. Identifies *Alretone* in Shrops. DB, previously thought to be Caus.

4224 WALKER, D., 'The Norman settlement in Wales', in R.A. Brown (ed.), *Battle 1 (1978)*, (Ipswich: Boydell, 1979), 131–43, 222–4.

WARWICKSHIRE

For the relevant section of the *DB Geography*, **340**, and for an essay in historical geography, **2134**. For a discussion of settlements on the Warws./Leics. border, **2837**. Since Burton abbey held a small amount of land in the north of the county, the discussions of the Burton abbey surveys have relevance to DB. Warws., **196, 225, 251, 405, 436, 3825**. For the lands of Evesham abbey, **281, 2136, 2138**; of the bishopric of Worcester, **2140**; of St Nicholas of Angers, **231**.

4301 DUGDALE, W., *Antiquities of Warwickshire* (London: Thomas Warren, 1656). 2nd edn, revised and augmented by W. Thomas (London: J. Osborn & T. Longman, 1730). A famous work, which made great use of DB and identified many place-names.

4302 READER, W., *Domesday Book for the county of Warwick* (Coventry: W. Reader, 1835). 2nd edn, with a brief introduction and notes by E. P. Shirley (Warwick: H. T. Cooke, 1879). Text and parallel translation.

4303 JAMES, H. (director), *Domesday Book: or the great survey of England of William the Conqueror, A.D. MLXXXVI. Facsimile of the part relating to Warwickshire* (Southampton: Ordnance Survey Office, 1862). Photozincographic edition.

4304 TWAMLEY, C., 'Notes on the Domesday of Warwickshire', *Arch. Jour.*, 21 (1864), 373–6. Deals mainly with the DB holding of William fitz Ansculf.

4305 JABET, G., 'The ethnology of Warwickshire, traced in the names of places', *TBAS*, 4 (1873), 1–26. Much enthusiastic comment on the DB place-names.

4306 LANGFORD, J. A., 'Birmingham, Aston, and Edgbaston as seen in Domesday Book', *TBAS*, 10 (1880–1), 43–53.

4307 ANON, 'Four-fold Domesday Book of Warwickshire', *The Midland Antiquary*, 3 (1884), 117. Announces the prospective publication by W. W. Wilson of an edition of Warws. DB. Apparently never published.

4308 CARTER, W. F., 'Notes on the Domesday of Warwickshire', *TBAS*, 18 (1892), 28–9.

4309 SKEAT, W. W., *'Batsueins'*, *N&Q*, 9th ser., 5 (1900), 384–5. For the DB account of Warwick.

4310 WALKER, B., 'Some notes on Domesday Book, especially that part of it which relates to the county of Warwick', *TBAS*, 26 (1900), 33–80. An attempt at a general survey.

4311 WALKER, B., 'The hundreds of Warwickshire at the time of the Domesday survey', *The Antiquary*, 39 (1903), 146–51, 179–84. See **4314** for an improved version.

4312 ROUND, J. H., 'Introduction to the Warwickshire Domesday', in *VCH Warws.*, 1, ed. W. Page (London: Constable, 1904), 269–98.

4313 CARTER, W. F., 'Text of the Warwickshire Domesday', *VCH Warws.*, 1, 299–344.

4314 WALKER, B., 'The hundreds of Warwickshire', *TBAS*, 31 (1905), 22–46.

4315 DUIGNAN, W. H., *Warwickshire place-names* (London: Henry Frowde, 1912). Superseded by **4318**.

4316 POWER, C. J., *The Domesday Book and Birmingham, Erdington, Edgbaston, Aston and Witton* (Birmingham: E. F. Hudson, 1929). A facsimile with text.

4317 NICKLIN, P. A., 'The early historical geography of the forest of Arden', *TBAS*, 56 (1932), 71–6. Includes a map of DB population.

4318 GOVER, J. E. B., MAWER, A. & STENTON, F. M., *The place-names of Warwickshire*, EPNS, 13 (Cambridge UP, 1936).

4319 BERESFORD, M. W., 'The deserted villages of Warwickshire', *TBAS*, 66 (1945–6), 49–106.

4320 THORPE, H., 'The growth of settlement before the Norman Conquest', in R. H. Kinvig, J. G. Smith & M. J. Wise (eds), *Birmingham and its regional setting* (Birmingham: British Association, 1950), 87–112.

4321 KINVIG, R. H., 'The Birmingham district in Domesday times', in R. H. Kinvig, J. G. Smith & M. J. Wise (eds), *Birmingham and its regional setting* (Birmingham: British Association, 1950), 113–34.

4322 CRONNE, H.A., *The borough of Warwick in the middle ages*, Dugdale Society occasional papers no. 10 (Oxford: C. Batey, for the Dugdale Society, 1951).

4323 LANCASTER, J.C., 'The Coventry forged charters: a reconsideration', *BIHR*, 27 (1954), 113–40. For DB Coventry and the estates of Coventry abbey. Cf. **4334**.

4324 HARLEY, J.B., 'Population trends and agricultural developments from the Warwickshire Hundred Rolls of 1279', *EcHR*, 2nd ser., 11 (1958–9), 8–18. For a statistical comparison of 1086 and 1279.

4325 THORPE, N., 'The lord and the landscape, illustrated through the changing fortunes of a Warwickshire parish, Wormleighton', *TBAS*, 80 (1962), 38–77.

4326 HARLEY, J.B., 'The settlement geography of early medieval Warwickshire', *Institute of British geographers. Publications*, no. 34 (1964), 115–30.

4327 CARUS-WILSON, E.M., 'The first half-century of the borough of Stratford-upon-Avon', *EcHR*, 2nd ser., 18 (1965), 46–63.

4328 PICKERING, J., 'Deserted medieval village site at Amington, Warwickshire', *TLSSAHS*, 8 (1966–7), 48. Locates DB *Ermendone*.

4329 DYER, C., 'Population and agriculture on a Warwickshire manor in the later middle ages', *University of Birmingham Historical Jour.*, 11 (1967–8), 113–27. Suggests that DB Hampton included the settlement of Hatton.

4330 BOND, C.J., 'The deserted village of Billesley Trussell', *Warwickshire History*, 1, no. 2 (1969), 15–24.

4331 GELLING, M., 'Some notes on Warwickshire place-names', *TBAS*, 86 (1974), 59–79.

4332 MAYNARD, H., 'The use of the place-name elements *mor* and *mersc* in the Avon valley', *TBAS*, 86 (1974), 80–4. A contribution to DB geography.

4333 BOND, C.J., 'Deserted medieval villages in Warwickshire: a review of the field evidence', *TBAS*, 86 (1974), 85–112.

4334 DAVIS, R.H.C., *The early history of Coventry*, Dugdale Society occasional papers, no. 24 (Oxford: V. Ridler, for the Dugdale Society, 1976).

4335 FORD, W.J., 'Some settlement patterns in the central region of the Warwickshire Avon', in P.H. Sawyer (ed.), *Medieval settlement:*

continuity and change (London: Edward Arnold, 1976), 274–94. Reprinted in P. H. Sawyer (ed.), *English medieval settlement* (London: Edward Arnold, 1979), 143–63. Suggests a modification to **340** on the treatment of DB woodland.

4336 MORRIS, J. (ed., from a translation by J. Plaister), *Domesday Book. 23. Warwickshire* (Chichester: Phillimore, 1976). Contains remarks on Warws. DB identifications and discusses places given the same name in DB. For additions and corrections, see **4523**.

4337 HOOKE, D., 'The Anglo-Saxon landscape', in T. R. Slater & P. J. Jarvis (eds.), *Field and forest: an historical geography of Warwickshire and Worcestershire* (Norwich: Geo Books, 1982), 79–103.

4338 ROBERTS, B. K., 'Village forms in Warwickshire: a preliminary discussion', in T. R. Slater & P. J. Jarvis (eds.), *Field and forest* (Norwich: Geo Books, 1982), 125–46.

4339 BOND, C. J., 'Deserted medieval villages in Warwickshire and Worcestershire', in T. R. Slater & P. J. Jarvis (eds.), *Field and forest* (Norwich: Geo Books, 1982), 147–71.

4340 SLATER, T. R., 'Urban genesis and medieval town plans in Warwickshire and Worcestershire', in T. R. Slater & P. J. Jarvis (eds.), *Field and forest* (Norwich: Geo Books, 1982), 173–202.

4341 SLATER, T. R., 'The origins of Warwick', *Midland History*, 8 (1983), 1–12.

WILTSHIRE

There is some Wilts. material in Exon DB and a study of the county must therefore take into account publications which deal with Exon. See especially **383**. For an article which discusses the hidation of Wilts. DB, **216**. For the relevant section of the *DB Geography*, **396**. On woodland, **289**, and for Malmesbury in DB, **230**. For villeins on comital manors, **257**. For the identification of a tenant of the abbot of Glastonbury, **3216**, and for the considerable discussion of the estates of the abbey of Glastonbury, **334, 348, 353, 422, 423, 3735**. For the holdings in Wilts. of Durand, sheriff of Glos., and his nephew Walter fitz Roger, **2131**. For those of Westminster abbey, **1027**.

4401 WYNDHAM, H. P., *Wiltshire extracted from Domesday Book: to which is added a translation of the original Latin into English* (Salisbury: E. Easton, 1788). Some attempt made to identify place-names.

4402 SCROPE, G.P., 'History of the Wiltshire manors subordinate to the barony of Castle Combe', *WANHM*, 2 (1855), 261–89. A little on the DB fee of Humphrey de L'Isle.

4403 JONES, W.H., 'Bradford-upon-Avon: general history of the parish', *WANHM*, 5 (1859), 1–88, 210–55, 342–90. See pp. 23–6 for the DB entry.

4404 WILKINSON, J., 'History of Broughton Gifford', *WANHM*, 5 (1859), 267–341; 6 (1860), 11–72. See 5, 267–80 for the DB entries.

4405 JAMES, H. (director), *Domesday Book: or the great survey of England of William the Conqueror, A.D. MLXXXVI. Facsimile of the part relating to Wiltshire* (Southampton: Ordnance Survey Office, 1862). Photozincographic edition.

4406 JONES, W.H., *Domesday for Wiltshire* (London & Bath: Longman etc. & R.E. Peach, 1865). An extended text, translation and notes, with a long introduction. Generally regarded as being of high quality.

4407 JONES, W.H., 'Gleanings from the Wiltshire Domesday', *WANHM*, 10 (1866–7), 165–73; 13 (1871–2), 42–58. For the boundaries of DB Wiltshire and DB personal names preserved in modern place-names.

4408 JONES, W.H., 'The history of the parish of All Cannings', *WANHM*, 11 (1867–9), 1–40, 175–203. See pp. 5–6, 176–8.

4409 JONES, W.H., 'The names of places in Wiltshire', *WANHM*, 14 (1873–4), 156–80, 253–79; 15 (1875), 71–98.

4410 JONES, W.H., 'Potterne', *WANHM*, 16 (1876), 245–86. See pp. 250–4.

4411 BEDDOE, J., 'A contribution to the anthropology of Wiltshire', *WANHM*, 34 (1906), 15–41. Includes a table of DB population and a discussion of Norman immigration into Wilts.

4412 JONES, W.H. & JACKSON, J.E. (annotated and brought up to date by J. Beddoe), *Bradford-on-Avon: a history and description* (Bradford-on-Avon: W. Dotesio, 1907).

4413 EKBLOM, E., *The place-names of Wiltshire: their origin and history* (Upsala: Appelbergs boktryckeri, 1917). Superseded by **4420**.

4414 GRUNDY, G.B., 'The place-names of Wiltshire', *WANHM*, 41 (1920–2), 335–53. Identifies some DB place-names. See **4420**.

4415 WALTERS, H.B., 'The Wiltshire hundreds', *WANHM*, 46 (1932–4), 301–11.

4416 KIDSTON, G., 'Notes on the early history of Box', *WANHM*, 46 (1932-4), 568-78.

4417 MORGAN, F.W., 'Woodland in Wiltshire at the time of Domesday Book', *WANHM*, 47 (1935-7), 25-33.

4418 MORGAN, F.W., 'The Domesday geography of Wiltshire', *WANHM*, 48 (1937-9), 68-81.

4419 GRUNDY, G.B., 'The ancient woodland of Wiltshire', *WANHM*, 48 (1937-9), 530-98. Some of his calculations are questionable.

4420 GOVER, J.E.B., MAWER, A. & STENTON, F.M., *The place-names of Wiltshire*, EPNS, 16 (Cambridge UP, 1939).

4421 ARKELL, W.J., 'Some topographical names in Wiltshire', *WANHM*, 49 (1940-2), 221-4.

4422 BRENTNALL, H.C., 'The hundreds of Wiltshire', *WANHM*, 50 (1942-4), 219-29.

4423 FINN, R.W., 'The assessment of Wiltshire in 1083 and 1086', *WANHM*, 50 (1942-4), 382-401.

4424 PUGH, R.B., 'The early history of the manors in Amesbury', *WANHM*, 52 (1947-8), 70-110.

4425 FINN, R.W., 'The making of the Wiltshire Domesday', *WANHM*, 52 (1947-8), 318-27. Of general significance for the making of DB.

4426 KIDSTON, G.J., 'Cumberwell near Bradford-on-Avon', *WANHM*, 53 (1949-50), 471-85. Identified *Cumbrewelle*.

4427 HUGHES, M.W., 'The Domesday boroughs of Wiltshire, with special reference to Marlborough', *WANHM*, 54 (1951-2), 257-78.

4428 DARLINGTON, R.R., 'Anglo-Saxon Wiltshire', in *VCH Wilts.*, 2, ed. R.B.Pugh & E.Crittall (OUP, for the Institute of Historical Research, 1955), 1-34.

4429 DARLINGTON, R.R., 'Introduction to Wiltshire Domesday', *VCH Wilts.*, 2, 42-112, 169-77. A good discussion of many matters of both general and local significance. For a correction, **357**.

4430 DARLINGTON, R.R., 'Translation of the text of the Wiltshire Domesday', *VCH Wilts.*, 2, 113-68.

4431 DARLINGTON, R.R., 'Text and translation of the Wiltshire Geld Rolls', *VCH Wilts.*, 2, 178-217.

4432 DARLINGTON, R. R., 'Summaries of fiefs in the Exon Domesday', *VCH Wilts.*, 2, 218–21.

4433 THOMSON, T. R., 'The bounds of Ellandune *c.* 956', *WANHM*, 56 (1955–6), 265–70. For the DB manors of Salthorpe, Elcumbe, Ellandun, Nether Wroughton, Over Wroughton and Westlecott.

4434 HODGETT, G. A. J., 'Feudal Wiltshire', in *VCH Wilts.*, 5, ed. R. B. Pugh & E. Crittall (OUP, for the Institute of Historical Research, 1957), 44–71.

4435 THOMSON, T. R. (ed.), *Materials for the history of Cricklade* (OUP, for Cricklade Hist. Soc., 1958–61).

4436 THOMSON, T. R., 'English Place Name Society, volume xvi (Wiltshire)', *WANHM*, 58 (1961–3), 228–9. Identifies *Sevamentone* with Sevington in Leigh Delamere.

4437 LOYN, H. R., 'The origin and early development of the Saxon borough with special reference to Cricklade', *WANHM*, 58 (1961–3), 7–15.

4438 TAYLOR, C. C., 'Whiteparish: a study of the development of a forest-edge parish', *WANHM*, 62 (1967), 79–102. For settlement pattern of DB entries for Cowesfield and Frustfield.

4439 TAYLOR, C. C., 'Three deserted medieval settlements in Whiteparish', *WANHM*, 63 (1968), 39–45. For deserted DB settlements in Cowesfield and Frustfield.

4440 MUSTY, J., 'A preliminary account of a medieval pottery industry at Minety, North Wiltshire', *WANHM*, 58 (1973), 79–88. An omission from DB (Minety).

4441 THORN, C. & F. (eds), *Domesday Book. 6. Wiltshire* (Phillimore: Chichester, 1979). Text, translation and valuable notes. Includes some new place-name identifications and notes on the hundreds and the county boundary. For additions and corrections, **4523**.

4442 WHITEHEAD, B. J., 'The topography and history of North Meadow, Cricklade', *WANHM*, 76 (1981), 129–40. For DB entries for Cricklade and surrounds.

WORCESTERSHIRE

The study of Worcs. DB needs to take account of the DB 'satellites' and DB-related texts preserved at Evesham and Worcester. For the especially important text known as Evesham 'A', see **20**. In general see **281, 398, 417**, and especially **4523** below. Freeman gave special attention to Worcs. DB in his *Norman Conquest*, **115**. For the relevant section of the *DB Geography*, **340**, and for other general essays on historical geography, **2134, 4337**. For deserted villages and towns, **4339, 4340**. For Droitwich and its salt-ways, **276, 1223**, in addition to the references given below. For the hidation of Worcs. demesne land, **2324**. For the estates of Evesham abbey, **281, 2136, 2137, 2138**. For the bishopric of Worcester's estates, **2140**. For Westminster abbey, **1027**. For the Worcs. evidence for William fitz Osbern's earldom, **2132**, and for the holdings of the Lacy family, **395**. For the identification of several place-names mentioned under Westbury-on-Severn, **2105, 2116**.

4501 NASH, T. R., *Collections for the history and antiquities of Worcestershire*, 2 vols + supplement (London: John White, 1799). Contains a facsimile copy of Worcs. DB.

4502 JAMES, H. (director), *Domesday Book: or the great survey of England of William the Conqueror, A.D. MLXXXVI. Facsimile of the part relating to Worcestershire* (Southampton: Ordnance Survey Office, 1862). Photo-zincographic edition.

4503 SANDERS, M. B., *A literal extension of the Latin text, and an English translation of Domesday Book in relation to the county of Worcester* (Worcester: Deighton & Sons, 1864).

4504 WILLIS-BUND, J. W., 'Doomsday Book so far as it relates to Worcestershire', *AASRP*, 21 (1891–2), 253–70. Devoted to the Norman landholders of Worcs. DB.

4505 WILLIS-BUND, J. W., 'Worcestershire Doomsday', *AASRP*, 22 (1893–4), 88–108. For ecclesiastical estates and their population, especially slaves.

4506 KINGSFORD, H., 'Worcestershire Doomsday place-names', *AASRP*, 22 (1893–4), 108–108f. Of little value.

4507 MERCIER, J.J., 'A history of Kemerton', *TBGAS*, 19 (1894–5), 24–40. Kemerton is in Glos. DB, but the place was transferred to Worcs. in 1931.

4508 ROUND, J.H., 'The Worcestershire survey (Hen.I)', in J.H. Round, *Feudal England* (London: Swan Sonnenschein, 1895; 2nd edn, London: Allen & Unwin, 1964), 169–80 (1st edn) and 140–8 (2nd edn). Gives a full comparison with DB.

4509 ROUND, J.H., 'Military tenure before the Conquest', *EHR*, 12 (1897), 492–4. For interpretation of the DB entry for Croome.

4510 ROUND, J.H., 'Introduction to the Worcestershire Domesday', in *VCH Worcs.*, 1, ed. J.W. Willis-Bund (Westminster: Constable, 1901), 235–80.

4511 ROUND, J.H., 'The text of the Worcestershire Domesday', *VCH Worcs.*, 1, 282–323.

4512 ROUND, J.H., 'Some early Worcestershire surveys', *VCH Worcs.*, 1, 324–31. Translates texts known as Evesham B and Evesham Q (see **4523**) and the survey of the Oswaldslow in Hemming's cartulary.

4513 DUIGNAN, W.H., *Worcestershire place-names* (London: Frowde, 1905). Superseded by **4516**.

4514 WILLIS-BUND, J.W., 'Worcestershire and Westminster', *AASRP*, 34 (1917–18), 329–62.

4515 WHITLEY, Revd Dr, 'Saltways of the Droitwich district', *TBAS*, 49 (1923), 1–15. Derivative from **4510**.

4516 MAWER, A. & STENTON, F.M., in collaboration with F.T.S. Houghton, *The place-names of Worcestershire*, EPNS, 4 (Cambridge UP, 1927). Note the discussion of salt-ways from Droitwich.

4517 GRUNDY, G.B., 'The Saxon settlement in Worcestershire', *TBAS*, 53 (1928), 1–17.

4518 GAUT, R.C., *A history of Worcestershire agriculture and rural evolution* (Worcester: Littlebury & Co., 1939). See chapter 3 for DB statistics.

4519 BERRY, E.K., 'The borough of Droitwich and its salt industry, 1215–1700', *University of Birmingham Historical Jour.*, 6 (1957–8), 39–61.

4520 CLARKE, H.B. & DYER, C.C., 'Anglo-Saxon and early Norman Worcester: the documentary evidence', *Trans. Worcs. Arch. Soc.*, 3rd ser., 2 (1968–9), 27–33.

4521 HAMSHERE, J.D., 'A computer-assisted study of Domesday Worcestershire', in T.R. Slater & P.J. Jarvis (eds.), *Field and forest: an historical geography of Warwickshire and Worcestershire* (Norwich: Geo Books, 1982), 105–24. Cf. **340**.

4522 HOOKE, D., 'The Droitwich salt industry', in D. Brown *et al* (eds.), *Anglo-Saxon studies in archaeology and history*, 2, British Archaeological Reports, no.92 (Oxford: British Archaeological Reports, 1981), 123–69.

4523 THORN, F. & C. (eds, from a translation by E. Whitelaw & S. Wood), *Domesday Book. 16. Worcestershire* (Chichester: Phillimore, 1982).

Contains text, translation and valuable notes. Also appendices on the county, the hundreds and the county boundary, a tabulation of the Worcester and Droitwich DB entries, and surveys of the DB-related material in the cartularies of the abbey of Evesham and Hemming's cartulary of Worcester cathedral. The last two appendices are extremely useful.

YORKSHIRE

For an early translation of Yorks. DB, **1601**. For an even earlier treatment of the honour of Richmond in DB, **103**. Of great importance for the landholders of Yorks. DB is **286**. For the relevant section of the *DB Geography*, **369**, which has an appendix which is important for the text of Yorks. DB. Stenton's work on the Danelaw is valuable, **241, 256**, as also is Kapelle's general treatment of northern England, **446**. For a general essay on geography and place-name identifications, **326**. Valuable for social structure is **430**. The significance of 'waste' in Yorks. DB has been much discussed, see especially **4638, 4645, 4673, 4676**. For the Lacy family and the honour of Pontefract, **395**. On the families of Lisours and Clères, **1618, 2940**. For the holdings of Edith the Fair in Yorks., **1204**. There is as yet no Phillimore edition of Yorks. DB.

4601 HUNTER, J., *South Yorkshire: the history and topography of the deanery of Doncaster, in the diocese and county of York*, 2 vols (London: J. B. Nichols, 1828–31). Made considerable use of DB. Vol. 2 contains a map of DB properties in the deanery of Doncaster.

4602 JAMES, H. (director), *Domesday Book: or the great survey of England of William the Conqueror, A.D. MLXXXVI. Facsimile of the part relating to Yorkshire* (Southampton: Ordnance Survey Office, 1862). Photozincographic edition.

4603 ELLIS, A. S., 'Biographical notes on the Yorkshire tenants named in Domesday Book', *YAJ*, 4 (1877), 114–57, 215–48, 384–415; 5 (1878), 289–330. Reprinted as *Some account of the landholders of Yorkshire named in Domesday* (no publisher named, 1878). Contains much valuable material on individual DB landholders.

4604 TAYLOR, I., 'Domesday survivals', in P. E. Dove (ed.), *Domesday studies: being the papers read at the meetings of the Domesday commemoration 1886*, 2 vols (London: Longmans, 1888–91), 1, 47–66. Examples are taken from Yorkshire, and mostly from the East Riding.

4605 TAYLOR, I., 'Domesday phonetics', *N&Q*, 7th ser., 8 (1889), 203. Examples are drawn from Yorks.

4606 ATKINSON, J.C., 'The site of the ancient vill of Danby' and 'Attempt to clear up the difficulties in the Domesday entries touching Danby', in J.C.Atkinson, *Forty years in a moorland parish* (London: Macmillan, 1891; repr., London: Macmillan, 1907), 429–43.

4607 ATKINSON, J.C., 'A further study of some archaic place names', *Reliquary*, ns, 6 (1892), 70–7. For *Camisedale* which is located in Greenhow.

4608 HOLMES, R., 'The manors of Osgoldcross, in Domesday', *YAJ*, 13 (1895), 287–311. Tabulates DB statistics and includes a map. See **4610**.

4609 SKAIFE, R.H., 'Domesday Book for Yorkshire', *YAJ*, 13 (1895), 321–52, 489–536; 14 (1898), 1–64, 249–312, 347–89. Printed separately as *Domesday Book for Yorkshire* (London: Bradley, Agnew & Co., 1896). A translation of Yorks. DB. For comments, criticisms and emendations, see **4611, 4617, 369**.

4610 TAYLOR, I., 'The manors of Osgoldcross, in Domesday', *YAJ*, 13 (1895), 486–8. See **4608**.

4611 TAYLOR, I., 'Note on the Domesday Book for Yorkshire', *YAJ*, 14 (1898), 242–3. Some amendments to identifications in **4609**.

4612 TURNER, J.H., *Yorkshire place-names as recorded in the Yorkshire Domesday Book* (Bingley: T.Harrison & Son, for the author, 1900). Unreliable.

4613 BEDDOE, J. & ROWE, J.H., 'The ethnology of West York-shire', *YAJ*, 19 (1907), 31–60. Includes a map of the West Riding showing DB vills.

4614 STEVENSON, W.H., 'Notes on the place-name "Filey" ', *Trans. East Riding Ant. Soc.*, 14 (1907), 10–12. Suggests an amendment to **1** where *Fucelac* (1, fo. 299r) should be *Fiuelac*.

4615 MOORMAN, F.W., *The place-names of the West Riding of Yorkshire*, Thoresby Soc. Pubs., 18 (Leeds, 1910). Superseded by **4652**.

4616 TRAVIS-COOK, J., 'Fiscal areas for geld', *Antiquary*, 47 (1911), 468–9. Concerns Myton amd Little Weighton.

4617 FARRER, W., 'Introduction to Yorkshire Domesday', in *VCH Yorks.*, 2, ed. W.Page (London: Constable, 1912), 133–89.

4618 FARRER, W., 'Translation of the Yorkshire Domesday', *VCH Yorks.*, 2, 191–327. See **369** for criticisms (p.82). Not necessarily superior work to that of Skaife (**4609**).

4619 ROWE, J. H., 'Cheldis: a Domesday manor in Craven, and its identification', *The Bradford Antiquary*, ns, 3 (1912), 246. For Keltus in Crosshills.

4620 SHEPPARD, T., *The lost towns of the Yorkshire coast* (London: A. Brown & Sons, 1912). For a valuable map showing the position of places lost to the sea. See **369** (p. 232) for criticisms.

4621 STEVENSON, W. H., 'Yorkshire surveys and other eleventh-century documents in the York Gospels', *EHR*, 27 (1912), 1–25. Comparisons with Yorks. DB.

4622 GOODALL, A., *Place-names of south-west Yorkshire* (Cambridge UP, 1914). Limited in scope. Superseded by **4652**.

4623 HORNSBY, W., 'A regrouping of the Domesday carucates in the Langbargh wapentake (N.R. Yorks.)', *YAJ*, 24 (1917), 286–96. See **369** (p. 163).

4624 HORNSBY, W., 'The Domesday valets of Langbargh wapentake', *YAJ*, 25 (1920), 334–40.

4625 WILSON-BARKWORTH, A., *The composition of the Saxon hundred in which Hull and neighbourhood were situate, as it was in its original condition* (Hull & London: A. Brown & Sons, 1920). For Hessle hundred.

4626 OWEN, L. V. D., 'Gilbert de Gant', *AASRP*, 37 (1923–5), 239–40. For a suggested correction to **4603**.

4627 EDWARDS, W., *The early history of the North Riding* (London: Brown, 1924). For some discussion of 'waste'.

4628 THOMPSON, A. H., 'The monastic settlement at Hackness', *YAJ*, 27 (1924), 388–405. For land in William de Percy's DB fee being 'of the land of St Hilda'.

4629 WILSON-BARKWORTH, A. B., *Domesday Book for the East Riding of Yorkshire excepting the lands in Holderness, arranged under places and not under tenants in capite* (Scarborough: W. H. Smith & Son, 1925). Translation and statistical tables.

4630 LINDKVIST, H., 'A study on early medieval York', *Anglia*, 50 (1926), 345–94.

4631 NICHOLSON, J., 'Place-names of the East Riding of Yorkshire', *Trans. East Riding Ant. Soc.*, 25 (1926), 1–136. Superseded by **4641**.

4632 SALTMARSHE, P., 'Ancient land tenures in Howdenshire', *Trans. East Riding Ant. Soc.*, 25 (1926), 137–48. For DB Howden.

4633 WILSON-BARKWORTH, A.B., *A brief account showing that the town of Kingston-upon-Hull as founded by king Edward comprised his estate in the Anglo-Saxon sheep farm of Wyke (Mortemer's Domesday Book estate of 120 acres in the district of Hase) and that to it was appended the ancient port of Hull (Mortain's Domesday book estate of 60 acres in the district of Ferriby) and the then newly created port of Kingston-upon-Hull* (Scarborough: W.H.Smith & Son, 1926).

4634 STENTON, F.M., *York in the eleventh century*, York minster historical tracts, no.8 (London: SPCK, 1927).

4635 SMITH, A.H., *The place-names of the North Riding of Yorkshire*, EPNS, 5 (Cambridge UP, 1928).

4636 COLLINGWOOD, W.G., *Angles, Danes and Norse in the district of Huddersfield* (Huddersfield: Tolson Memorial Museum, 1929).

4637 GOWLAND, T.S., 'Some Yorkshire field names', *YAJ*, 30 (1931), 225–30. Identifies four 'lost' DB vills in North Riding.

4638 BISHOP, T.A.M., 'The distribution of manorial demesne in the Vale of York', *EHR*, 49 (1934), 386–406. For waste vills in 1086 and their subsequent history. See **4638, 4645, 4673, 4676, 446**.

4639 KENDALL, H.P., 'Domesday Book and after', *Trans. Halifax Ant. Soc.*, (1935), 21–40. For the nine berewicks of Wakefield.

4640 BISHOP, T.A.M., 'Monastic granges in Yorkshire', *EHR*, 51 (1936), 193–214. For waste DB estates and later monastic granges.

4641 SMITH, A.H., *The place-names of the East Riding of Yorkshire and York*, EPNS, 14 (Cambridge UP, 1937).

4642 CLAPHAM, J.H., 'The Domesday survey of Yorkshire', in *VIIIe congrès international des sciences historiques, Zurich, 1938: communications présentées*, 1 (Paris: Presses universitaires de France, 1938), 355–7.

4643 GOWLAND, T.S., 'The honour of Kirkby Malzeard and the chase of Nidderdale', *YAJ*, 33 (1938), 349–96.

4644 HEBDITCH, W., 'The origin and early history of the Kilton fee', *YAJ*, 34 (1939), 296–309. Amendments suggested to **4609, 4618**.

4645 BISHOP, T.A.M., 'The Norman settlement of Yorkshire', in R.W.Hunt, W.A.Pantin & R.W.Southern (eds), *Studies in medieval history presented to Frederick Maurice Powicke* (Oxford: Clarendon Press, 1948), 1–14. Reprinted in E.M.Carus-Wilson (ed.), *Essays in economic history*, 2 (London: Edward Arnold, 1962), 1–11, with a postscript. See further **4673, 4676, 446**.

4646 ROBERTSHAW, W., 'The manor of Chellow', *The Bradford Antiquary*, ns, 7 (1952), 1–31. For a possible example of continuous possession from TRE by an English tenant.

4647 BERESFORD, M.W., 'The lost villages of Yorkshire', *YAJ*, 37 (1951), 474–91; 38 (1952–5), 44–70, 215–40, 280–309.

4648 DICKENS, A.G., 'The "shire" and privileges of the archbishop in eleventh century York', *YAJ*, 38 (1952–5), 131–47.

4649 LE PATOUREL, J., *Documents relating to the manor and borough of Leeds, 1066–1400*, Thoresby Society, 45 (Leeds, 1957).

4650 SHEPPARD, J.A., 'A Danish river-diversion', *YAJ*, 39 (1956–8), 58–66. For DB mills in and adjacent to Holderness.

4651 DONKIN, R.A., 'Settlement and depopulation on Cistercian estates during the twelfth and thirteenth centuries, especially in Yorkshire', *BIHR*, 33 (1960), 141–57. For DB estates subsequently depopulated.

4652 SMITH, A.H., *The place-names of the West Riding of Yorkshire*, 8 vols, EPNS, 30–7 (Cambridge UP, 1961–3).

4653 FRENCH, T.W., 'The advowson of St Martin's church in Micklegate, York', *YAJ*, 40 (1959–62), 496–505. For an identification of the church of St Martin in York DB with St Martin in Micklegate. Cf. **4609, 4618**.

4654 WAITES, B., 'The monastic grange as a factor in the settlement of north-east Yorkshire', *YAJ*, 40 (1959–62), 627–56. For DB settlement, see pp. 647–9.

4655 HARRISON, K., 'The pre-Conquest churches of York: with an appendix on eighth-century Northumbrian annals', *YAJ*, 40 (1959–62), 232–49.

4656 DICKENS, A.G., 'York before the Norman Conquest', in *VCH Yorkshire. City of York*, ed. P.M.Tillott (OUP, for the Institute of Historical Research, 1961), 2–24.

4657 JONES, G.R.J., 'Basic patterns of settlement distribution in northern England', *The Advancement of Science*, 18 (1961), 192–200.

4658 HARVEY, J.H., 'Bishophill and the church of York', *YAJ*, 41 (1963–6), 377–93. Cf. **4656**.

4659 SHEPPARD, J.A., *The draining of the marshlands of south Holderness and the Vale of York*, East Yorks. Local History ser., 20 (York: East Yorks. Local History Soc., 1966).

4660 BROOKS, F.W., *Domesday Book and the East Riding*, East Yorks. Local History ser., 21 (York: East Yorks. Local History Soc., 1966). A valuable study.

4661 UGAWA, K., 'Topography and early settlements in Holderness', in *Lay estates in medieval England* (Tokyo: Maraisha Co. Ltd., 1966), 54–73. In Japanese, with an English summary.

4662 WAITES, B., 'Aspects of medieval arable farming in the Vale of York and the Cleveland Plain', *Ryedale Historian*, 2 (1966), 5–11.

4663 SIDDLE, D.J., 'The rural economy of medieval Holderness', *AgHR*, 15 (1967), 40–5. For DB population and marshland. Cf. **369**.

4664 HIRD, H., 'Bradford in Domesday Book', in H. Hird, *Bradford in history* (Bradford: for the author, 1968), 5–18.

4665 HODGSON, R.I., 'Medieval colonization in northern Ryedale', *Geog. Jour.*, 135 (1969), 44–54. Reprinted with revisions, *Ryedale Historian*, 10 (1980), 47–62.

4666 JENSEN, G.F., 'The Domesday Book account of the Bruce fief', *The English Place-Name Soc. Jour.*, 2 (1969–70), 8–17.

4667 ALLERSTON, P., 'English village development: findings from the Pickering district of North Yorkshire', *Institute of British Geographers Trans.*, 51 (1970), 95–109.

4668 ALLISON, K.J., *East Riding water-mills*, East Yorks. Local History ser., 26 (York: East Yorks. Local History Soc., 1970). See especially pp. 5–6.

4669 RAISTRICK, A., *The making of the English landscape. West Riding of Yorkshire* (London: Hodder & Stoughton, 1970). Criticises **369** for treatment of population.

4670 LE PATOUREL, J., 'The Norman conquest of Yorkshire', *NH*, 6 (1971), 1–21. A mainly derivative survey of the landholders of Yorks. DB.

4671 FINN, R.W., *The making and limitations of the Yorkshire Domesday*, Borthwick papers, 41 (York: for the Borthwick Institute of Historical Research, 1972).

4672 JENSEN, G.F., *Scandinavian settlement names in Yorkshire* (Copenhagen: I kommission hos Akademisk forlag, 1972).

4673 RAISTRICK, A., *The Pennine dales* (London: Hodder & Stoughton, 1972). See pp. 83–4 for waste in Yorks, DB.

4674 CLAY, C.T. with GREENWAY, D.E., *Early Yorkshire families*, Yorks. Arch. Soc., record ser., 135 (Wakefield: West Yorks. Printing Co. Ltd., 1973).

4675 SHEPPARD, J.A., 'Pre-Conquest Yorkshire: fiscal carucates as an index of land exploitation', *Institute of British Geographers Trans.*, 65 (1975), 67–78. See **369**.

4676 WIGHTMAN, W.E., 'The significance of "waste" in the Yorkshire Domesday', *NH*, 10 (1975), 55–71. See **4638, 4645, 4673, 4676, 446**.

4677 ALLISON, K.J., *The East Riding of Yorkshire landscape* (London: Hodder & Stoughton, 1976).

4678 FAWCETT, R.H., 'The story of Wilsden', *The Bradford Antiquary*, ns, 9 (1976), 1–28. For a map of Wilsden and neighbouring DB manors.

4679 JENSEN, G.F., 'Place-names and settlement in the North Riding of Yorkshire', *NH*, 14 (1978), 19–46. Numerous comments on the topographical significance of DB place-names.

4680 ENGLISH, B., *The lords of Holderness 1086–1200: a study in feudal society* (OUP, for the University of Hull, 1979).

4681 POSTLES, D., 'Rural economy on the grits and sandstones of the south Yorkshire Pennines, 1086–1348', *NH*, 15 (1979), 1–23. For manorial organisation, population and waste.

4682 FAULL, M.L. & MOORHOUSE, S.A., *West Yorkshire: an archaeological survey to A.D. 1500*, 3 vols (Leeds: University of Leeds for the West Yorkshire Metropolitan County Council, 1981). For the identification of some DB vills and for DB and settlement.

4683 MORRIS, R.W., *Yorkshire through place-names* (Newton Abbot: David & Charles, 1982). See chapter 9.

4684 HARVEY, M., 'Planned field systems in eastern Yorkshire: some thoughts on their origin', *AgHR*, 31 (1983), 91–103.

INDEX OF NAMES

INDEX OF SUBJECTS

This subject index acts as an index to the Bibliography and, in a general way, indexes the chief works listed therein. As a result items such as **200** or **432** which are wide-ranging in their contents occur frequently in the index. The index includes, however, only those subjects which cannot be found via the arrangement of the Bibliography. Thus, there are no topographical references since these can be located simply by looking in the relevant county sections. Where an item deals with a specific landowner, his name appears in this index. An item which is or includes a general study of landholders and/or sub-tenants will be indexed only under those terms. The reader must then use the index of the work concerned to locate individual landholders.